SHINE A LIGHT

Tonkin Gulf Air War JFK
LBJ Pentagon Papers
DRV My Lai Hanoi
Winter Soldier CIA
AntiWar Movement
Hue Project Renew
Ky Geneva Accords
Nixon Ho Chi Minh
Haiphong Kissinger
Saigon Tiger Cages
Napalm Pacification
Christmas Bombing
Agent Orange Media
Best & Brightest VVAW
Draft Resist NLF My Khe
Madame Binh McNamara
Thieu Hugh Thompson Tet
Domino Theory Ngo Dinh Diem
Phoenix General Giap POW/MIA
Dan/Phil Berrigan Paris Peace Accords

Full Disclosure Full Disclosure

The American War In
VIETNAM

www.vietnamfulldisclosure.org

Veterans For Peace
Vietnam Full Disclosure

Letters to The Wall
Memorial Day Events
2015 & 2016

Edited by
John Buquoi, Julie Dobson
and Doug Rawlings

We owe John Buquoi our gratitude for his vision that began this book project, for his editorial and formatting skills that brought it to fruition, and for his persistent goodwill.

Photographs by Ellen Davidson
Layout and design by John Buquoi

ISBN: 978-1-365-27419-0

To those many souls on all sides lost and damaged
in the American War in Vietnam.

"Hold us America…"
- Peggy Akers
'A poem for Memorial Day… A poem for Peace'

Contents

Preface

When in mid-2014 we in Veterans For Peace (VFP) first heard of the Pentagon's Vietnam War history project, we were initially intrigued. Soon we were angry. Very angry. Their website revealed a game plan that appeared to be geared toward somehow justifying the American War in Vietnam. You know, revising history to fit present and future militaristic designs, while taking events out of context or providing a very superficial backdrop for major benchmarks of the war. Then and there we decided to mount a counter-offensive. We call this VFP project FULL DISCLOSURE.

The Full Disclosure campaign is a Veterans For Peace effort to speak truth to power and, among other efforts, to keep alive the anti-war perspective on the American war in Viet Nam — which is now approaching a series of 50th anniversary events. It represents a clear alternative to the Pentagon's current efforts to sanitize and mythologize the Vietnam war and to thereby legitimize further unnecessary and destructive wars. We quickly put up our own web page (vietnamfulldisclosure.org) to further contextualize the war and to provide a younger generation an alternative resource for studying its causes and consequences. Visiting our web site will provide the reader with a twelve year time-line to parallel the Pentagon's version, an in-depth historical analysis that includes anti-war resistance movement significant dates, a narrative that includes the voices of the Vietnamese people, and a rich and fascinating profile of the G.I. Resistance movement.

Well into our second year of work, the Full Disclosure committee decided to complement its series of regional teach-ins and speaking engagements with a national action. We sent word out that we would deliver "letters to The Wall" on each Memorial Day for the next decade. We feel that a very important voice in the discussion of the American War in Viet Nam was being muffled — we wanted to hear from anyone whose life was impacted by the war. That meant soldiers, family of soldiers and anti-war resistors. That meant children and grandchildren of soldiers whose names are on The Wall; that meant loved ones of nurses and the nurses themselves who participated in the war; that meant young men and women who gave up a good portion of their lives fighting against the war. And, if we are so fortunate, that means Vietnamese, Laotians, Cambodians, and Thai peoples who might want to engage in this dialogue.

Over the past two years we delivered 298 letters and 32 postcards. Many of them can be found in this book. They come from medics whose friends died in their arms, from granddaughters who never met their grandfathers, from United States citizens who sacrificed their careers and even their citizenship to stop the war. And so many others. Please take the time to listen to their voices.

Having read each one more than once, I can attest to their power. Anyone who has written for an audience beyond their immediate family and friends knows how tyrannical the blank page can be. Where to begin? What to say? Yet somehow these people represented here found the strength to plow forward. And what treasure they have given us. They are witnesses to this war, and their voices cannot be, should not be, ignored by anyone who takes history seriously.

Finally, I have to say that the tenor of many of these letters conveys a thought I have had over the last few years — the gap between those who fought in this war and those who fought against it is closing. Fifty years later most of us have come to realize what a tragic waste of life this war was. And as we wrote our letters to The Vietnam Veterans Memorial, we really did feel as if we were engaging in a dialogue with those who died so young. We told them they would never be forgotten. That our voices will carry within them their voices as well. That we will never stop working for a world without war.

Doug Rawlings
7/15th Artillery
Vietnam 1969-1970
Co-founder of Veterans For Peace
Father and Grandfather

Thanks to the many, many letter writers from inside and outside of VFP, be they veterans, family members of veterans, or dedicated anti-war activists, all of whom faced down the blank page and wrote from their hearts.

The editors

Letters to The Wall 2015

I am having a difficult time this Memorial Day

Letter to the Vietnam Veterans Memorial Wall

Memorial Day 2015

By Dan Shea

1968 Marine Veteran of the American War in Viet Nam

I am having a difficult time this Memorial Day – as an anti-war Veteran & survivor of Vietnam, I find all the well-meaning tributes to our fallen, raw and painful for me and the families of whom we should be respectful.

Yet it is their tears and ours that politicians with their pomp and circumstance and the retailers with Memorial Day sales shamefully exploit for votes and profits.

While those untouched by the wars are thankful for the holiday as an excuse for backyard barbecues and weekend vacations, the media, newspapers, radio & television news & every Tom, Dick & Jane speak with patriotic pride about the "Ultimate Sacrifice" these men and women laid down their lives for Country and Our Freedoms.

It is this hero glorification & martyrdom that perpetuates the lie and misdirects from view the truth that these young men & women were sacrificed on the Bloody Altar of War for the failures of Greedy Arrogant Men to learn how to share, compromise and make peace.

On this Memorial Day there is no mention of the millions of lives lost by those who felt our monstrous unmerciful killing rage. What of their families? Oceans are made of their tears.

This too must be told – I found this very profound post which put a chill up my spine as it tells a legacy of war that never ends.

Please read and share – this link:

http://www.mission22.com/battlefields#warathome6

3

Memorial Day Letter to Charles D. McCann

Dear Charlie,

It's Memorial Day, 2015, forty years after your return from Vietnam. Wow! You brought a Vietnamese wife, mother-in-law, brother-in-law, 2 sisters-in-law, a son and a daughter. You moved into the house Bernie and Linda vacated for you!

We graduated from Chofu High School on Kanto Mura Housing Annex in Tokyo, in '68, and '69, respectively. You joined the Army in '69; I joined the Air Force in '70. We volunteered for 'Nam, and planned to be 'lifers'. You went to Cam Ranh Bay; I received orders to Da Nang AB. Glad I didn't go there, where they were spraying Agent Orange like crazy!

Our paths diverged. My military time led me to oppose U.S. militarism. After thirty days in the stockade, I received an undesirable discharge for resisting. You returned to civilian life, but reenlisted a short time later. On your 2nd tour, you met Edrina in Italy, and remarried. Your three boys (Charlie, TJ, and

Nathan) joined son Tham and daughter Mary in the world.

You drank yourself to death (2005), though that mission took decades to accomplish. Tham lived with me on numerous occasions before he passed in Miami, a year after you. I was happy to be his uncle, and a source of support. He had called me from Texas, complaining. I invited him to live in Miami with me. Before his death at 33, he had finally gotten it together. He moved from my place to live in a place where he was paying his own rent for the first time, ha ha!

Tham inherited alcoholism, diabetes and being overweight. We Irish-Catholic males seem genetically predisposed to this condition, but it killed you and your son. I am crying now as I type this letter, and I'm so angry at our government and the war corporations who dominate and control it.

Nobody knew you better than I, except Mom and Dad. We grew up in the same room; the next 3 boys shared a room. I'm upset you and Tam lived so briefly; it's been a decade since you passed. Now your daughter Mary (named after our mother) suffers from terminal cancer (related to chemical pollution in Vietnam where she was born?). She is stoic as she seeks joy in life now. I cry for her, too.

I repeat the eulogy from Mummy's memorial ceremony, prior to her internment in Brockton, Massachusetts, where you were born. At the ceremony you laid down your fatigue jacket (which I now wear), thanking her for keeping you warm when you needed help most. I repeat these words now for you.

<<Lyric from Luciano's 'Just Like The Wind' deleted due to copyright restrictions. Ed.>>

Love, Patrick

To Terry & Allan,

On this Memorial Day in 2015, I respectfully pay homage to you, my fallen Brothers. To be truthful, as a Vietnam vet I think about both of you often — very often, not just on Memorial Day or Veterans Day. Thoughts of Vietnam are never very far below my level of consciousness & rarely does a day go by when I don't think of it. And when I think of it, I think of both of you specifically & the 58,000 other names on the wall, generally.

Terry, you were a couple of years older than I & became a mentor to me in high school. You were the "all-American" boy — smart, handsome, varsity letterman in 4 sports, class president, student council, newspaper staff, prom king, etc. Everyone liked you & knew you had a great future. After college, you enlisted in the Marine Corp & became an officer. You were the first to die in Vietnam from our home-town. I was in that cruel time warp between college graduation & my draft induction into the Army when I read about your death in our hometown newspaper. I had trouble comprehending it. I didn't realize until later how indiscriminate combat can be when men die. The felon who serves to avoid prison time and the "all-American" boy are indistinguishable to the enemy who's trying to kill them. I still grieve for you, my friend.

Allan, you were several years younger than I & we didn't know each other well. But I knew/know your older brother & you lived just three houses away. You were a teenaged SP4 when you were killed while walking point on a patrol just southwest of Da Nang in January 1971. I read about your death a short time after I returned from Vietnam. Seeing you in your dress uniform in your casket & seeing your grieving family had a profound impact on me. You see, while we were in Nam, we became conditioned not to think much about death — not to fear it too much, not to dwell on it when we saw it, not to respect it — even though it was all around us. But after trying to re-enter life as we knew it before Vietnam, the lives lost in Vietnam had an enormous impact on me. Especially when I found your & Terry's names on The Wall for the first time. Seeing all those names! Again, I had trouble comprehending it. When I first walked along The Wall more than 30 years ago, my first reaction was to take a deep breath & then tears started rolling down my face as I thought of all the men & women who died and I thought of their grieving families. My reaction hasn't changed. It's the same every time I visit The Wall.

While I was in Vietnam, I wrote a letter to my Congressman, protesting the expansion of the war into Cambodia. Much later I received a form letter in response, thanking me "for my interest & for taking the time to write." The response did not address the reason why I wrote. My letter could just as easily have been a birthday greeting to the Congressman. Since Vietnam, I've never trusted the Government nor any politicians.

When the U.S. involvement in Vietnam ended in 1975, war protesters felt they had won a great victory and the sense of relief by American people — both Hawks & Doves — was palpable. There was a general feeling that we'd never again get involved in a conflict where our security is not directly involved nor in a conflict we're not committed to "win." But I felt Americans had short memories and American politicians had the attention span & memory of gnats and I predicted to anyone who would listen, that the United States would be involved in another Vietnam somewhere else in the world in about 20 years. Sadly, it didn't take that long.

Unfortunately, the leaders in the U.S. learned nothing from the Vietnam experience, or they've chosen to forget it. Everyone in Congress should have to read Dalton Trumbo's Johnny Got His Gun, which was first published in 1939 (prior to WW2).

I'd like to believe there are men & women of good conscience leading our country. But the fact is, it's easier to send someone to war than it is to have to fight it yourself — or than it is to have to send your own kids to war. Politicians are not leaders. They are politicians. They will say & do anything to get elected. And they only do what is politically expedient for them to get re-elected. In the guilt over the treatment of Vietnam vets, the American people have not blamed the troops in more recent wars for the decisions made in Washington.

My struggle, Terry & Allan, is to find meaning in your deaths. I want to believe that you and all of the others have died for sometime of value, something meaningful. It's just too terrifying to think that so many had their lives taken from them, for nothing more than some false geo-political doctrine (i.e. the "domino theory"), or some vague words like defending freedom or democracy or liberty. But it's been 50 years since the start of America's part in Vietnam, and I'm still searching for the meaning — for the value — and still I can't find it. During & after Vietnam, mostly only our close relatives and other vets thought or cared about us. Most Americans, it seemed, were embarrassed by us and just wanted to forget about us. We weren't treated well.

Forty years after we came home, people in this country started acknowledging us — & differentiating between the soldiers and the war doctrine. Still not much is ever said about the rightness or wrongness of the Vietnam War — because there is no justification for it and the politicians had for years quit trying to put a positive spin on it. But in their guilt over the way they treated the returning veterans then and in their zeal to justify continued wars of no meaning in far off lands, the politicians are now trying to spin Vietnam as an honorable event in our past and the troops as heroes. As I said, Americans have short memories. My fear is, they'll probably start believing this crap. I lost a lot in Vietnam: a year of my life, my transition from student to adulthood, experiencing the birth of my son, my trust in my government & its leaders, & my generally positive outlook on life was transformed into a cynicism previously reserved for someone much older than I was when I returned home. You, my Brothers, lost everything. I'm sorry for that.

I still wake up thinking about Vietnam — 45 years after I was there. I keep coming to the same conclusion: that all of the deaths of the Vietnam War were a waste. I hate that thought. But I can't escape it. Is the United States or Vietnam any better or worse off, for having fought that war — other than having lost 58,000 dead Americans or the millions of dead Vietnamese.

In the 1960's our government put us in a position to make a decision to accept induction into the military to fight an unjust, immoral war & to possibly die — or to go to prison, or to leave the country with the prospect of never seeing our homeland nor our families & friends again. Years after the war, what was clear to our "leaders" during the war, became clear to the rest of the citizens: our country had only the vaguest of objectives and no clear strategy to win. Our leaders then, like our leaders today, believe the U.S. is the "city on the hill" and that everyone else in the world looks up to us and wants to be us. They were wrong in the 1960's and they're wrong now.

Terry & Allan, you did not die defending the United States. You did not die defending our freedom, our honor, our republic, our liberty. I hate it that you died for nothing of value & that your lives were wasted. I weep for you and the others on the wall. I weep that you weren't given the chance to live.

SP5 Don C. Evon, Jr.
"B" Battery, 7th/15th Arty
LZ Two Bits, Binh Dinh Provence
1969-1970

I realize that you are not in Da Nang

March 25, 1962

Sgt. Wayne E. Marchand
US Army Special Forces
Da Nang, Vietnam

Dear Wayne,

I realize that you are not in Da Nang but rather out in the hills somewhere, but I suppose the army has to give you an address where they can reach you, but that doesn't tell where you are.

How are you finding the country and the people? As individuals with individual goals and desires, as a good Special Forces man would, or are they "Gooks" to you as they are to most other American military people? I can't see how we can win the hearts and minds of the people so they see the military and political perspective as we do, if we cannot think of them as humans with dignity, purpose, human worth. How are we to make them see our goals as their goals if we continue to distain them as mud under our boots, mattering little whether they live or die?

We say we are there to help them with democracy and independence but there is nothing democratic or independent in our treatment of them, their families, their farms, their country. We are there for our purposes, our goals, and treat them, their ideas and actions with distain when they differ from ours. Will our appeal to a vague democratic future weigh anything beside the communist appeal of their own country, with shared wealth and well-being, one and all? We have seen how that turned out in Russia and China, but can they see that? And even in China and Russia they are mostly better off than they were before. Still, we can try to hope it will turn out well in the future.

I shouldn't be lecturing to you, who are on the ground and face difficulties and dangers I can barely imagine, much less understand. Are you making any progress; do you see any hope? Here, we are hoping you have both, and safety in the bargain. I'll finish this later, but for now take care of yourself. I'll tip a beer for you and hope you have the chance to do the same for me.

.   .   .

Oh God! Since setting this aside I just read in Time Magazine that you are the first American killed in combat in Vietnam, along with a buddy I didn't know, and SFC Quinn has been taken prisoner! DAMN! You were still in your early twenties, with 50 or 60 years ahead of you, and now, . . . nothing! I never told you how good a man I thought you were, how much I admired your skill or professionalism. There was always plenty of time for that . . . . I hope some of my attitude rubbed off on you, so you at least understood some of the respect I felt.

If this affects me so much, who only knew you a couple of years and haven't seen you since I was sent to Berlin, what must it be for your mother, father and family? Besides your family it must be a shock to everyone in Chadron. Probably most people there must have known you. I can picture the shock in my small town if it had been me or one of my high school buddies. For us all the world has changed and your bright future foreclosed.

I can only hope that something better will come of this and that our presence there will give Vietnam a brighter future that not too many people have to die for, and hard as it is to think of, that you will only be the first of a very few, not a long line of dead. When I reflect on our recent wars, the outlook is not good. A "Peace Action" in Korea became a bloody mess and we ended up about where we started.

This line of thought is too depressing. Rest in Peace, Wayne. I salute you, and miss you.

Very sadly, Daryl

May 19, 2015

Dear Wayne,

It has been 53 years since I started my undelivered letter to you, almost twice as long as you lived. What kind of future would you have had, what attainments would we celebrate if you had lived? We can never answer that, but unfortunately we can see that your life and that of 58,000 other Americans and one or two hundred thousands of Vietnamese were in vain. SFC Francis Quinn's name is not on the Vietnam Wall (You don't know what that is, do you? It is a wall of polished black granite that has the names of the 58,000 American dead in Vietnam inscribed. And I hoped you were the first of only a few!) Well, Quinn is not listed there, nor can I find any record of him among the returned POWs. Just another MIA, I suppose the Army would say.

Nothing came out of the war that was useful to anyone, and a great deal was destroyed. That includes the innocence of naïve young men like me, the destruction of much of the country with our bombing and defoliants, and hundreds of thousands Vietnamese, hoping for a better life like you or me. Well, like me, anyway. Strangely, the Vietnamese do not seem to hate us. I wonder if I could be so forgiving if the shoe had been on the other foot. Our greatest loss might be what the 58,000 of you might have achieved for the nation and mankind. The Vietnamese must have had their talents, too. What would they have done?

Now we are still engaged in wars undertaken for mistaken purposes. Due to our technology and weaponry our deaths are very low compared to Vietnam or WWII (we kill the enemy remotely), but many of the living are returning without limbs, or with scrambled brains, or with PTSD and other nightmares, and we do not have any clear idea why we went there, or are still there.

Our record makes one wonder if yours was not the better fate after all. Again, Rest in Peace, Wayne.

Very sadly, Daryl

Formerly SGT Daryl K. Sherman © 2015
10th Special Forces Group, Airborne
Detachment A, Berlin, Germany

Vietnam is just a country

Full Disclosure
(Partial)
to my compatriots on this wall
and the many I met
During the War and
After the War...

Oh, and you late comers to the death this wall does not
record; you know, the ones who offed
yourselves when your drug of choice stopped
working for you or turned on you and you committed
Suicide
(late casualties of war).

Vietnam is just a country. We made it into an American
Epoch. It consumed our news, movies, books, arguments,
parades, demonstrations, parties, preaching, art, dreams, night
mares, day mares, drinking, women, children, grandchildren,
parents and all the relational people in our lives; so, OK our
whole culture.

I am 71, now. I still think about it; too often. My fault; I
guess. I did acquiesce. I did go. I did help make some Oriental
people dead. I was a part of it all. If you were in Vietnam, you
helped make it all happen. If you were in the US military, you
helped make it happen. In fact, if you were in the US of A, you
helped make it happen.

For long periods of time after my part in the craziness, I
could not resist reading any bit of news about whatever latest
killing America was doing for whatever given reason, which I
expected would be less than useful or kind. My country never
failed me in this area.

I was assigned to the 2nd Battalion, 1st Marines south of
Marble Mountain. Our area of operations (AO) went from there
to the Korean Marines south of us and from the beach, inland to
Highway 1. More than half of the battalion casualties came from
booby traps each month I was there. I was the battalion press
information man [a journalist for the crotch (as the Marine Corps

13

is known to many)].

On that pre-Christmas operation in 1968 at the south end of our AO a name was added to this wall. He was a second lieutenant, platoon commander, who was new to the bush. His opportunity to become seasoned ended as he was shot skyward on top of an exploding 105 artillery round. The company command team wore your body fragments during the rest of that operation. Moments later when you landed your first lieutenant, company commander stepped over to your blast powdered torso, checked your neck for a pulse, finding none, he reverently put his hand over your heart and bowed his head for a long moment. One of the more profound acts of honesty in the insane situation that was our war in Vietnam. There is a back story to this particular booby trap.

To what extent would you have gone to end the violence, which took your lives too, too early?

Some read your names from casualty lists before the war ended. They read them on the steps of Congress, only to be arrested. The next day they were back reading your names again and were again arrested. But, there were some Congressmen, who having immunity, continued reading your names. Even read the names of you dead into the Congressional Record. The war didn't miss a beat.

A President was elected on an anti-war platform. He was elected not just once; but twice, on a "peace is at hand" platform. The war didn't slow. It even got expanded. He changed the focus and came up with a great, new concept... Vietnamization. In other words, now that we have done our part in creating havoc, we will turn it over to the Vietnamese, who would have voted to unite the country nearly twenty years before in the 1950's. The minority, non-Buddhist Vietnamese, who had converted to a European religion in order to be in charge under the French had no chance to succeed. Their experience was in administration, not governance

Another lieutenant who was blown-up was standing up when he rode an exploding 105 round so he was able to sire two daughters and to write a best selling book, before his drug of choice returned to his use and he offed himself. But he's not on this wall.

14

Then there was the lieutenant in my military occupational specialty, who was in charge of the office in Hue City when it was over run during the 1968 Tet Offensive. Eight of his men were executed behind their office and he was walked north through the whole 3rd Marine Division between Hue and the demilitarized zone (DMZ). He came home with the prisoners of war (POWs) long after I got out of the Marine Corps.

I have lately wondered about the depth of his shock when North Vietnam Regulars walked in and took them all into custody. What comes to mind is disbelief, a deep sinking feeling with fear.

I wonder how come their office was in the city of Hue rather than at 3rd Marine Division headquarters in Dong Ha? Our main office at 1st Division was just down the hill from the general's command bunker. I guess until that morning in 1968, the war was in our pocket and hubris was in command.

Last year I showed my wife around the 1st Marine Division's AO with Veterans For Peace. We took in the titanic, earthen, electric oven current US of A funds have constructed to attempt to dispose of the Agent Orange which didn't get sprayed on the crop and woodlands of Vietnam. It had leaked into the soil where it was carelessly stored at the Danang air base.

The oven is only marginally smaller than that huge, blocks-long scrap pile of war waste stacked along the Main Supply Route (MSR) back from the beach between Monkey and Marble Mountains back in the day. One wonders how that load of steel tank bodies, gun tubes, blown-up trucks and towers of unidentifiable iron finally got back into the human supply chain.

Speaking of waste, isn't that what we said about those who died, so we didn't have to say that the people who had been with us earlier were dead and that we might join them at any moment. So, perhaps this is not a memorial wall but a wall of waste. A black mark on our country, which wasted your lives to act out our national McCarthyism on the international stage, which most of the Vietnamese didn't understand or care about.

Some few Vietnamese souls had been led down the primrose path of divide and conquer and bought the "but he's a communist," bullshit about Ho, the actual father of their country, who aided our military in the "big one," but got lost in the peace.

Enough waste to go around and around kicking up dust to obscure clarity about the deep emptiness of our Vietnam War, their "American War."

Many of the Vietnam veteran stories I've heard echo those of other wars. They are not widely circulated. After all, it is hard to raise a group of heroes-to-be, if they are conscious of these kinds of outcomes resulting from their service and sacrifice.

When other veterans have told me their stories they often tell of their military service as just like what their fathers had done in World War II. Well, my father was one of those who were held back to keep the country running while the war was on.

He worked for the city of Virginia, Minnesota, Water and Light Department. They also provided steam to heat all the houses in town, a public utility company. His uncle had been in WWI.

Perhaps his uncle had a less than jingoistic attitude as a result of his service. My dad told a story that his uncle had asked him when he was fourteen if he could keep his mouth shut while listening to war stories. When dad said, "Yes," his uncle had him join a couple of his war buddies and himself in the wine cellar one night.

A story from that night which stood out for my father was that one man's unit became surrounded and driven back into a swamp. Then he said the German's set up water cooled machine guns to traverse the swamp. The man reported seeing soldiers losing their grip and standing up to assault, only to be cut in half by the bullets, the top part of their bodies going one way and the bottom another way. My father's conclusion to this story was that both of these men had drunk themselves to death within a few years of returning from WW I.

On another occasion, when our family was traveling from Bismarck to Minneapolis for a holiday, dad spent most of the trip in the smoking car where a chaplain from a veterans hospital some where related stories about the veterans who were getting care. Apparently, a few of the patients had been with "raider groups" in the war. They were perfectly free to come and go as they pleased during the day. But, at night, they always returned to be locked in their bed rooms for the night; so they wouldn't hurt anyone.

My father also asked inconvenient questions like, "How come there were no aircraft carriers at Pearl Harbor that day in December?" I haven't heard an answer to that question.

Just stories. And questions.

But, so informed and with all that I read on my own about war confirming its pointlessness, cruelty, deep inequity and massive waste; plus with nuclear arms on the table, there seems to be a relentless dance with the extinguishment of the whole human endeavor.

You, here named, have died. I am sorry.

I have attempted to "do" my part.

When I helped oppose the MX Rail Garrison System, we stopped that military waste. They didn't build the ten bunkers for each missile, but they did get the MX missile and the peace community could be blamed for preventing the construction community from getting more Department of Defense (DOD) funds. The fortuitous ending of my job with the Veterans Administration a couple of days later was unrelated.

I am sure.

But I keep pitching.

Back when I took the oath of enlistment in Minneapolis on my way to boot camp in San Diego, I swallowed hard saying my name and all the words before, "to uphold and defend the constitution," at which point I had a great sense of "Yes, that I will do." The Marine Corps motto steers this eternal democratic task.

Your down payment was exceeded by the Vietnamese in the numbers of lives lost. But you are all part of the terrible waste of unlived lives. Only a small divot in the whole human endeavor but you could possibly become the first check point to ending the whole insane war business. What a nice memorial that would be.

I salute your loss, with a heavy heart.

Semper Fi. Always faithful.

Sincerely,

Ronald Staff

October 21, 1967, my first visit to Washington DC

A Letter to the Vietnam Memorial

Dear Comrades,

October 21, 1967, my first visit to Washington DC, and my first organized protest of the American War in Vietnam. My friend Bill and I had driven all night from Ann Arbor, Michigan, and arrived at dawn to see a rosy sun rising above the monuments and monumental architecture of the Capitol. An estimated 100,000 people marched on the Pentagon that day. Bill and I, sleepless as we were, got pressed into service as marshals, walking alongside the mostly young college kids.

Later in the afternoon I found myself on the steps of the Lincoln Memorial in conversation with a pro-war Vietnam vet. I was a smart-ass, know-it-all college punk, with a monopoly on the truth. He finally tired of arguing with me. He turned his back, and left me with these words: "If you haven't been there, you don't know what you're talking about!"

His words haunted me. By March, 1968, I dropped out of college and found a ride to San Francisco in search of a berth on a merchant ship bound for Vietnam. By a stroke of luck, we stopped for gas somewhere in the middle of Indiana just in time to see President Lyndon Johnson's face on the screen of a small black and white TV in the gas station. It was March 31st, and Johnson declared that he would not seek reelection as president. The Vietnam War had scuttled his presidency, and it was widely anticipated that his vice president, Hubert Humphrey, would run for the presidency as a peace candidate. The four of us on that all night ride from Ann Arbor to Kansas City were euphoric at the prospect of ending the war.

We woke up in Las Vegas a few days later, to see the headlines that Martin Luther King Jr. had been shot down in Memphis. It was April 4th, exactly a year after his historic speech "Beyond Vietnam" delivered in New York City's Riverside Church. Two months later, on June 5th, Bobby Kennedy was gunned down after winning the California Democratic presidential primary. The two assassinations shattered the optimism that had followed President Johnson's speech, and we sank into a deep depression.

The SS Whittier Victory was a vintage WW II supply ship pulled out of mothballs and crewed by a motley assortment of seasoned sailors and inexperienced ordinary deck hands like myself. We made a coast-wise run to take on cargo, then sailed from San Francisco. We crossed the Pacific in 21 days. I stood the 4-8 watch, which meant relieving the bow lookout at 4:00 am, standing watch until dawn, then again from dusk to 20 bells (8:00 pm). One night the lookout was changed from the bow to the flying bridge, because the entire forward deck had been freshly oiled. Sometime around dusk the ship's engines cut out. In place of the low rumble and vibration of a ship under way, there was a quiet and a sense of wallowing, bobbing like a cork, without direction. Before long our engines started and we were again on our way.

We made Qui Nhon, a port city about half way between Saigon (now Ho Chi Minh City) and the demilitarized Zone (DMZ), and the crew was given shore leave.

I was struck by the manner of the US soldier at the gate, brandishing his automatic weapon with a stagger or swagger of someone stoned or drunk. His slurred speech was deep south, as was the pidgeon English of the Vietnamese prostitutes who populated the bars just outside the gates of the military base. The entire economy of Qui Nhon appeared to be in the service of the US military occupation. I'm reminded that of an estimated 4.5 million refugees created by the US invasion of Iraq in 2003, as many as 50,000 displaced Iraqi women and girls were forced into prostitution in order to feed their families.

One brothel nearest the post provided packs of machine rolled marijuana cigarettes.

The cruise back home was a grim and lonely affair for this 21 year old sailor. We were 28 days steaming from Vietnam to Panama. Twenty eight days contemplating the destruction my country was inflicting on a poor Asian nation, 2 days in the canal, and another 5 days to cross the Gulf of Mexico to New Orleans, the Whittier Victory's home port. After my flight back to

Michigan I resumed my anti-war protests with greater fervor.

In January 1970 I refused induction into the army of Richard Nixon and became a fugitive from justice until I surrendered to the US Attorney in Detroit in January 1975. After 2 years of Reconciliation Service in Michigan and North Carolina, I received a letter from the Director of Selective Service indicating that my commitment had been fulfilled and the federal indictment against me dismissed.

It has been 47 years since I set foot on Vietnamese soil, and 2015 finds me working on campaigns for an honest commemoration of the American War in Vietnam and ending the current cascade of wars launched by the US in this young century. Veterans For Peace are encouraging those affected by the Vietnam War to write a letter in memory of the names of the US KIA as well as those unnamed Vietnamese victims.

Sincerely,

John Heuer

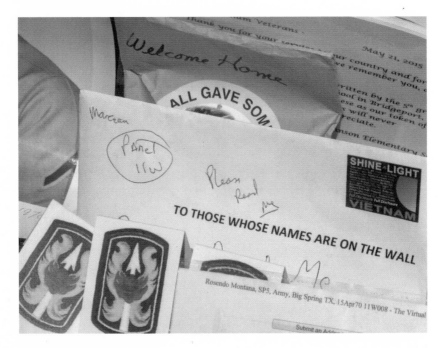

A poem for Memorial Day...

A poem for Memorial Day... A poem for Peace....

DEAR AMERICA

Remember me?
I was the girl next door.
Remember when I was 13, America, and rode on top of the fire engine in the Memorial Day parade? I'd won an essay contest on what it meant to be a proud American.

And it was always me, America, the cheerleader, the Girl Scout, who marched in front of the high school band . . . carrying our flag . . . the tallest . . . the proudest . . .

And remember, America, you gave me the Daughters of the American Revolution Good Citizen Award for patriotism, and I was only sixteen.

And then you sent me to war, America, along with thousands of other men and women who loved you.

It's Memorial Day, America. Do you hear the flags snapping in the wind? There's a big sale at Macy's, and there's a big parade in Washington for the veterans.

But it's not the American flag or the sound of drums I hear – I hear a helicopter coming in – I smell the burning of human flesh. It's Thomas, America, the young Black kid from Atlanta, my patient, burned by an exploding gas tank. I remember how his courage kept him alive that day, America, and I clung to his only finger and whispered over and over again how proud you were of him, America – and he died.

And Pham..... He was only eight, America, and you sprayed him with napalm and his skin fell off in my hands and he screamed as I tried to comfort him.

And America, what did you do with Robbie, the young kid I sat next to on the plane to Viet Nam? His friends told me a piece of shrapnel ripped through his young heart – he was only seventeen – it was his first time away from home. What did you tell his mother and father, America?

Hold us America...

Hold all your children America. Allen will never hold any one again. He left both his arms and legs back there. He left them for you, America.

America, you never told me that I'd have to put so many of your sons, the boys next door, in body bags. You never told me...

- Peggy Akers, who served as a nurse in Vietnam.

I've looked at photographs of "the Wall"

To All Those Named on The Wall (and the others who may not have died in country but also didn't survive Vietnam):

I've looked at photographs of "the Wall." I've never actually seen it. I can't bring myself to visit because whenever that monolithic black granite structure enters my dreams I see nothing but the horror of the unnamed: the thousands of children, their skin ablaze and oozing droplets of napalm; the untold number of women who were raped, then murdered by young American psychopaths dressed up in military attire; the staggering number of grandparents, their lungs burning from Agent Orange, who somehow managed to survive the onslaught of the colonial French only to die trying to protect their families. They took cover in ditches and rice paddies as B-52's out of Thailand dropped more tons of ordnance than were used during the entire Second World War. Then there's the "guerrillas," those who fought with the Provisional Revolutionary Government and those who traveled down the Ho Chi Minh Trail in their national struggle to rid their country of the invading imperial armies of Western democracies. Let's not forget the people of Laos, Cambodia, and Thailand who served as the backdrop for soldiers looking to spend a few bucks while on R & R, the bar girls, the hookers, the rickshaw drivers, pimps and the drug dealers whose lives were forever altered by the swaggering arrogant invaders.

58,286 names pale in comparison to the unnamed. This fact doesn't diminish your memory; rather it places your existence within its proper historical context, among millions of dead people who died at the hands of politicians without morals and corporations intent on profits. I remember the chants on the streets of Washington in October, 1967 — "Rich men lie, GIs die" — and it's the same today as it was then. We haven't learned a fucking thing. Today we know that women can pull the trigger as easily as men, that gays and lesbians can shoot straight, and that Latino, Native American, and Black soldiers can die as easily on the streets of Baghdad and Kabul as they can in South LA, or Pine Ridge and Ferguson.

Memorial Day has always been a difficult time for me, a weekend of fury watching endless news stories about graveside salutes wrapped in red, white, and blue. There aren't any memorial days for the unnamed. There aren't any memorial days for the thousands of deserters and draft resisters who refused to participate in the slaughter and yet are vilified as traitors and cowards. No one says "Thank you for your service," to those of us who spent years in prison or exile.

I'm sorry I won't be with you this weekend. I just can't do it. There are too many ghosts hidden behind each of your names and even after fifty years I just can't shake their memory.

Bruce Beyer

I am writing to you to express my sorrow

May 14, 2015
Dear Vietnam Memorial Wall,

I am writing to you to express my sorrow for the pain and agony inflicted 50 years ago on the Vietnamese people and on the American people by the elected leaders of the United States.

While you, The Wall, reflect the names of 58,000 United States military who died because of U.S. military action in Vietnam, you remind me also of those not named on The Wall–those six million residents of Southeast Asia who died during these military actions.

I served 29 years in the U.S. Army/Army Reserves and retired as a Colonel. I also was a U.S. diplomat for 16 years and was assigned to U.S. Embassies in Nicaragua, Grenada, Somalia, Uzbekistan, Kyrgyzstan, Sierra Leone, Micronesia, Afghanistan and Mongolia. I was on the small team that reopened the U.S. Embassy in Kabul, Afghanistan in 2001.

I was a part of the U.S. government for most of my adult life. However, in 2003, I resigned from the U.S. diplomatic corps in opposition to another war, the war on Iraq.

After I resigned, I joined Veterans for Peace to be with fellow veterans who believe that dialogue and diplomacy are the keys to conflict resolution instead of war.

I wish I could be at The Wall on May 25 for the Memorial Day observances, but instead I will be in North Korea with a group of 30 international women, including two women Nobel Peace Laureates, who will be speaking with North Korean women about peace and reconciliation on the Korean peninsula.

After our days in North Korea, we will cross the Demilitarized Zone (DMZ) by foot, only the third group in the 70-year history of the DMZ to walk across it. Once across the DMZ, we will be met by 2,000 South Korean women and then have several days with them discussing peace and reconciliation.

You have seen so much here at The Wall–families crying for their loved ones, buddies crying as they find the names of their friends, and persons who don't know anyone whose name is on

The Wall, but who wanted to come to the Vietnam Memorial to remind themselves of the folly of war.

We think of other countries as "conflict countries" and provide programs for these countries

We never stop to think that our own country is also a "conflict country" with a traumatized population whose younger generation knows nothing but war. I strongly believe that individually and as a country, we need assistance in stopping the propensity of our elected leaders to decide that war and occupation are the best ways to resolve their perceptions of threats to our country.

I will continue to work for peace around our world…and continue to challenge our own country to end the threat it poses to our planet in our politicians' thirst for war.

Peace ole Wall,

Ann Wright

You came from small towns and big cities

MEMORIAL DAY 2015

To Those Whose Names Are Here Memorialized:

You came from small towns and big cities; you came from different socio-economic backgrounds (though tilted, of course, toward the lower end of the income spectrum); you came from different ethnic and religious heritages. Some of you enlisted enthusiastically, believing you were saving "The Free World" from a communist menace; many of you, like myself, enlisted in order to "beat the draft"; but undoubtedly the majority of you were conscripted: "Take this rifle, son, or...meet your cellmates for the next few years in this Federal Penitentiary." A few of you were women, serving in a medical or perhaps clerical setting. Death, the Great Leveler, has here united you all.

But Death is not the only thing that binds you together. You were all victims of a national sickness, a belief that the United States of America has a God-given mandate to rule the entire globe, to its own economic benefit. You were all victims of a chain of monstrous lies which led to your deployment to a strange land that most Americans didn't know existed prior to the 1960s. The first of these was the fiction that there was a separate, sovereign nation called "The Republic of South Vietnam" that needed you to defend it against "aggression from the north." Democrat, Republican, it mattered not: our national leaders lied to us again and again and perpetuated one of the most criminal wars of modern times. Not a single one of you should have been deployed to Vietnam in the first place. Not a single one! And thus, as surely as the uncounted millions of inhabitants of the region killed by US weaponry, each and every one of you is a victim of US military aggression. And no one in the leadership of the war machinery, at any level, has ever been prosecuted for their roles in this criminal undertaking. Not a single solitary one.

If resurrected from the realm of the dead you could be, what would you make of the state of the world today? Sure, the advances in technology would wow you at first. Such wizardry!

Hey, what became of the USSR? And is that a black man in the White House?!? That would be a shocker, no doubt. But after examining what is recent history for us in this present era, I hope you would be alarmed and ultimately outraged that American troops are still deployed all over the world in the effort to maintain economic hegemony, and that they kill and occasionally get killed or maimed...for what, exactly? To "defend freedom"? While our own dwindling freedom here at home is in mortal peril of being extinguished, in the name of "our own protection"! While the streets of our cities and towns are patrolled by cops wearing full combat gear, generously donated by the Pentagon. And that very Pentagon is spending millions of taxpayer dollars on a campaign to persuade the generations following ours that the war that took your lives was far, far from the monstrous crime that it was. I hope you would be sufficiently appalled that the USA learned not a damned thing from its defeat in Vietnam and that you would be moved to actively resist current government policies. But that is a struggle we, the still living, will have to pursue. Continue to rest in peace, brothers and sisters. Your fighting days are over.

GREG LAXER
Spec. 4, Medic,
US Army
May 1967-July 1971

Dear comrades with whom I served

Dear comrades with whom I served and the Vietnamese people who suffered at our hands:

I went to fight in Vietnam to defend Freedom and Democracy. It took me too long to question what I was doing and if it really had anything to do with Freedom and Democracy.

On one mission, we were in a helicopter flying over a "free fire zone" near Cu Chi. I looked down and saw two Viet Cong. There were few times I could be sure who was and was not "the enemy," but these two guys were carrying AK47s and running for cover. I punched the pilot, but as we circled I lost them.

(Later I learned about all the tunnels in the area.) Where they had disappeared, I saw a destroyed hamlet... rubble house foundations pocked by bullet and shrapnel holes, ancestors graves blown apart by bombs, rice patties with cratered dikes and sprayed with defoliants, nothing but destruction as far as I could see. I thought, "You know, if I was a Vietnamese peasant I'd probably be out with the Viet Cong fighting the Americans." What the hell had I just thought?!

I started watching the war more closely, the dead women and children, young girls in a society that values chastity who had turned to prostitution to survive, street urchins who stole a watch from my arm for pennies, suffering and displaced people who had no idea what "capitalism" and "communism" meant.

Fellow soldiers were suddenly not there any more, not only the dead but also those who left us maimed and in one case a vegetable with shrapnel in his brain. It was not the threat of death that ate away at me, even when a bullet creased my ear and mortar shrapnel bounced off my helmet. It was seeing us decent but lonely and disoriented young American men finding the worse we can be as human beings, doing things that violated the very core values that our parents, churches, and schools instilled in us...things that can never be undone. I saw the phenomenal waste in military operations and "aid" to the Vietnamese... brand new equipment being shipped back to the U.S. to be rebuilt under military contracts, and once even being told to dismantle operational howitzers to meet the recoil mechanisms' quotas. I kept thinking, "This is stupid! Just stupid!"

I finally decided that this war had nothing to do with Freedom and Democracy. For decades now I've been trying to understand why we got into this war… and who really benefited (it certainly wasn't us soldiers or the Vietnamese or even the American people). As calls for new wars began, I started seeing the same rhetoric and lies, with "terrorism" taking the place of "communism." A few years ago, I went back to Vietnam. I met many gracious Vietnamese and saw a thriving society. I kept thinking if we had just left them alone they would have gotten here thirty years sooner. I also thought, "Oh my God…we're doing the same thing all over again in Iraq."

My fellow soldiers and Vietnamese whom we assaulted, how can I express my sorrow and pain? I really regret that we did not know enough to question what we were doing. But now it cannot be undone, and the dreams that ruin my sleep and disturb my soul are still here.

The only way I know how to deal with my experience in Vietnam is to learn the lessons of the past to use for the future, so we can find the positive and constructive alternatives to resolving conflicts. I haven't been very successful, but I will keep asking the critical questions, challenging the assumptions and myths, and trying to help others see what I did not see when I volunteered, thinking I would make a career of the Army. For your sakes and for those Americans and Vietnamese and other people around the world who have come after us, I will keep trying to search for and promote peaceful alternatives to resolving conflicts.

Ken Barger
Memorial Day 2015

I wrote book reports in middle school

April 25, 2015

I wrote book reports in middle school to learn about the "facts" of our arrival to the U.S. From family, I understood that we fled Cambodia as a matter of survival, not choice. We came here because of the Khmer Rouge, a radical arm of the Communist Party whose policies led to the deaths of millions of Cambodians.

I still didn't understand why. How could our people kill our own people? I then learned that even before the Khmer Rouge came to power that my mother had lived much of her life under war and uncertainty. The U.S. government had been bombing the countryside and destroyed her home. As a result, they were constantly fleeing in search of safety. These bombings created a political vacuum that the Khmer Rouge was able to fill. I remember feeling deep anger towards the U.S. government and at my classmates' ignorance surrounding this significant and devastating aspect of U.S. history.

It was in college that I began to learn about the role of the U.S. antiwar movement, the suffering experienced by young men drafted to fight this unjust war, the poor treatment they received by their government when they came back home. I also learned of the acts of resistance by veterans in protest of this imperialist war and its toll on them and Southeast Asian families.

As time has passed, I also learned from my family about acts of resistance waged by everyday Cambodians under the Khmer Rouge regime to maintain their humanity.

Our family has been here for 33 years, the larger Southeast Asian community close to 40. Let us acknowledge how our communities got here and commemorate the misguided rationale and collective human costs of this war as well as the acts of resistance demanding that humanity do better.

To a more just and peaceful future.

In solidarity,

Valerie Taing

My promise to you still stands

Dear Joe Brown,

My promise to you still stands that I will not forget you. This Memorial Day, Veterans for Peace has provided me an opportunity to put it in writing and hand deliver this letter to the Vietnam Memorial where your name is inscribed.

Two days ago my wife and I travelled through Jackson, Mississippi, your hometown. When I told her about whenever I see the name or hear about Jackson, I think of you and we both started to tear up. In the last few years I was twice given an opportunity to offer remarks on Memorial Day and on both occasions mentioned you by name and how I started measuring my life in multiples of yours and others who were killed in Vietnam. Currently it stands as $3 X + 2$. It sort of puts things into perspective and keeps me from falling into the trap of each successive day just like the day before it. When that happens there is no point in counting further when one day is just like another. Measuring my life in multiples of yours keeps me aware of the importance of each day. This is your gift to me for which I can never fully repay you. Thank you Joe Henry Brown. Rest In Peace.

John Jadryev

President, VFP Chapter #161

Iowa City, IA

Hello, 2 West,

I would have addressed this letter to The Wall, as requested by the Full Disclosure campaign, but, let's face it, this corner of Constitution Gardens has never meant more than Panel 2W to me. Since I first stood on the cobblestone near the vertex of the Vietnam Veterans Memorial, transfixed, late at night in 1984, my focus has always been 2 West. In fact only a millisecond of blind luck, much later at night, prevented my name from being one of the 685 exploited service members immortalized on this particular slab, chronologically arrayed behind my aging reflection.

Over the years, whenever I scanned row after row of Panel 2W's forever young, from apex to a reverent half-kneel, my line of sight always gravitated to Row 122 and the etching of best friend and childhood protagonist Richard C. Halpin's "special place in history."

And like so many Vietnam combat veterans I have always second-guessed my chance exclusion from such "prominence" with every visit. A row 121-123 inscription of my own should have resulted from another shoot down the same night forty-three years ago over the Gulf of Tonkin. The missile should not have missed my aircraft, but it did. I should not have been that lucky, but I was. And decades later, sheer terror has morphed into a reminiscent "Why me?" hybrid.

The Wall has never been a friend of mine, certainly never revered. Now more tourist attraction than sacred ground, and decades after its commemoration, it ranks high among the US military's most effective recruitment tools, right up there with the National World War II Memorial. Someday even surviving reluctant warriors will have their own Honor Flights, with top priority given to the frailest Vietnam vets, those most inflicted with Agent Orange maladies. Think of the endless marketing opportunities for the next fabricated fight for freedom.

Like all war tributes, though, the Wall and future walls will omit the victims – innocents caught in fields of fire; the millions of demonized "others" who will die to expel US invaders; and the countless casualties on both sides, living and dying for decades to come, like discounted detritus.

But 2 West, my friend, we'll always have our special bond, sharing it only with aging family members and acquaintances.

I'll see you soon, but again don't expect tears. Grieving never seems to help.

Peace,

Gene

This letter is just one of many

5/3/15 11:35 AM

This letter is just one of many letters to the Vietnam Veterans Memorial Wall being delivered by Doug Rawlings, a Vietnam Veteran and founding member of Veterans For Peace (VFP), who will deliver this letter and many others on Memorial Day, May 25th, 2015. I am an associate member of VFP and assist with volunteering my time to administer to www.vietnamfulldisclosure.org. This website was created so that those who died in vain in Vietnam, those that survived, and those who want to know the truth about that fucking war and what led up to it can read an honest FULL DISCLOSURE historical accounting of that war as opposed to the whitewashing website that the Pentagon has created to commemorate this war and its soldiers. I am thankful to speak truth to power any day but especially this Memorial Day, 2015. And this is why I'm just now writing my letter to an unknown soldier, my unknown cousin, Richard Seglem. I must say thank you, Doug Rawlings, and all the others in the Full Disclosure group for allowing me in, for taking me as I am, a 50 year old "green" gal who hardly knew much of the Truth about the American War in Vietnam. But I'm learning thanks to you and so are many others. And for that, I write and do what I do.

Dear Richard, millions of Vietnamese, and all the rest who died in Vietnam,

It's hardly fair that this is all I know of you.

I have your photo too.

You were a good-looking young man from a Christian family. And yet, even though I do not know your beliefs, I imagine you were the good Christian boy our family expected you to be. And, as you lay dying, I imagine you questioned God as you lost your young life. Perhaps like millions of others. And perhaps, that is an unfair assumption. Maybe I shouldn't think it, but I do.

I can imagine that if I were fighting in some fabricated war, (unbeknownst to you at the time I'm quite sure), that I would wonder why I would have signed up at all. I think ego had a lot to do with it and self-preservation. The irony kills. I think maybe pride and not looking like a pussy too. But I imagine your religiosity made you do it. I could be wrong but I know how it is stressed in our family. And I'm really sorry. I wonder if you thought that, like many others perhaps, God had told you to. I wish you knew then that you didn't have to, nor they, give your life for a fucking lie.

No, you didn't get to live your life. And, I'm sure since you were killed within three months of being there that you didn't know that innocent millions of Vietnamese perished too. That was the goal right: To kill the commies, to stop the dominoes from falling, to win. Unfortunately, you were just one of nearly 58,000 American soldiers who died in Viet Nam.

And all I can do is sit, think and stare at your photograph, my mother's cousin, my second cousin totally unknown to me who died at only 20 when I was just 6. I think of the sadness our family, like so many others, felt when they received the tragic news of your death; their beloved son had died in the war. And you, like so many, who died by friendly fire. Did you know? Did you see it coming? I know you saw plenty. I believe you did. You saw tragedies that your mind didn't want to see, or believe was happening. I hate you did. I hate that anyone did. I hate that American politics – the powers that be — did this to all those Vietnamese, to so many millions, to you and others just like you. We are still killing, Richard, but from afar with drones that drop bombs from computers manned by people at desks. It is quite incredible to think how far we've come and how much we've learned to destroy people to continue to spread American Democracy.

I've learned over the course of my life, amongst the many lies in our "great nation", that the average age of American men that died over there was 21. It's mind blowing. I can't even begin to relay the continued onslaught of what the American military killing machine has continued to do all around the world, but if you and I could talk, I'd want you to know that we've had more than just one Vietnam and that the US war machine is a fucking killer. It's sickening to say the least.

But Richard, (my mother and family called you Dick I've heard), I want you to know, the world to know, and the truth to be told and shared, that even though you died in vain, and you did, …you really did, just like all the rest who perished, to know that 50 years later after the beginning of that dreadful war that there are a group of Americans all over this nation that still care, that give a damn, that want the truth to continue to be told. We will do so by honoring you and all those who died and those that continue to be affected, impacted and killed by that war's legacies of Agent Orange and Unexploded Ordnances by sharing the historical Truth, so that you will not have perished without a noble and honest effort to commemorate you with the Truth.

In loving kindness,

Julie Dobson

[1] *The Full Disclosure campaign is a Veterans For Peace effort to speak truth to power and keep alive the antiwar perspective on the American war in Viet Nam - which is now approaching a series of 50th anniversary events. It represents a clear alternative to the Pentagon's current efforts to sanitize and mythologize the Vietnam war and to thereby legitimize further unnecessary and destructive wars.*
From www.vietnamfulldisclosure.org

Reflections Fifty Years after the Escalation

It's not easy to look into a mirror these days. The years and life have left baggage under my eyes, sculpted lines on my face and left grey ashes in my hair. But I can do it.

The Vietnam War Memorial is an unforgiving mirror that I turn to for self appraisal. Did I live a good life? Did I make the right decisions, especially the most difficult one of my young life? Walk the wall and you see in the polished surface those who died far from home, family and friends staring back through the flat reflection of your external form. Those names summon memories that command us to look at our real selves, the thinking, feeling self and command us to consider our actions. Did I do right? Did I make the right decision? Why am I alive and my peers are not? Am I a good man? Am I a coward?

I chose to oppose the war and avoid the draft. I chose to live. I chose to give peace a chance. I became a teacher. I was ready to go to Canada but a sympathetic doctor helped me avoid service and stay close to my family. Others were much braver than I'll ever be. I still don't know if my decision grew from roots of fear or conscience. History tells of a futile effort to preserve a government in the south of Vietnam — atrocities, obscene loss of life, calls to patriotism, a divided country, chemical warfare that still scars people and places, psychological damage, political awakenings and permanent damage to American world leadership. But the war did end. The protest movement speeded our withdrawal.

So I return to have those names judge me or help me judge myself and to be reminded of lessons learned. I am no longer naïve. My vision extends beyond the political boundaries that divide us. Calls to patriotic action do not move me. I know that war is not to be entered into lightly. Most of all I know that we must follow our convictions with actions. Did I do enough? Not nearly. But I still have the chance to do some good. There is meaning to our lives because we can make a difference.

B. Abrams

40 Years Later, Remembering the Legacy

By Dik Cool

The PBS documentary, "Last Days in Viet Nam" is an excellent piece of cold war propaganda. What could be better than to show two hours of Vietnamese fleeing the (gasp!) advancing "communist hordes." The map drips red, the people flee and the talking heads intone that Saigon is "falling to the communists." But wait, aren't the communists also Vietnamese and isn't this their country? So Viet Nam has fallen to the Vietnamese? Isn't the US the invader, the occupier, the imperial force that has tried to subjugate a nationalist movement? In 1776, didn't we fight to expel the occupying British? A more accurate description would be that the capitalist invaders had finally been driven out by Vietnamese forces committed to freedom and independence for their country. Their only sin was that they believed in a different economic system, communism, for their country.

Perhaps a brief history will bring perspective to all this.

During WWII, U.S. fliers shot down by the Japanese were frequently rescued by Ho Chi Minh's guerrilla force, the Viet Minh, the only reliable ally that the US had in the area. After the war ended, at a million-person rally, Ho declared Viet Nam's independence from France, using language from the U.S. Declaration of Independence, a document he revered. The United States, led by anti-communist zealots, chose to betray Ho Chi Minh and support France's re-colonization of Viet Nam.

In 1954, at Dien Bien Phu, the Vietnamese defeated the French, by then 80% financed by the United States. The Geneva Accords temporarily divided Viet Nam into north and south, with elections to be held in 1956. The United States refused to support the elections because, as President Eisenhower admitted in his memoirs, "Ho Chi Minh would win." Washington proceeded to install a series of puppet dictators in the south, claiming it was defending democracy and freedom.

By 1967, the United States had 500,000 troops in the south, was regularly bombing the north and using the carcinogenic herbicide Agent Orange over vast areas. The anti-war movement – military and nonmilitary – grew rapidly. Immolations, the ultimate protest, occurred in the south and in the United States.

The Pentagon does not want you to know any of the following information: The G.I. movement against the Viet Nam war was perhaps more important to ending the war than the civilian peace movement. By 1971, with 500,000 troops in Viet Nam, the US military was on the verge of collapse and the brass were panicked. Officers were being fragged, whole units were refusing to fight, drug use was rampant, black GIs had coined the phrase "no Vietnamese ever called me n ——," and antiwar GI coffeehouses and newspapers had sprung up at most US bases around the world. In April, 1971, several thousand Viet Nam vets, in a powerful, moving demonstration, threw their medals on the steps of the US Congress. Vets symbolically occupied the Statue of Liberty. US soldiers realized they had been lied to by a country they trusted. They came to understand that the people they were killing had done nothing to the US; they simply wanted to control their own destiny. The veterans then and now had to bear a double burden. They had fought a war and then had to fight to stop a war they realized was unjust. The toll this took on our soldiers is staggering. Over 150,000 have committed suicide, far more than died in the war, and the suicides continue to this day. Veterans also have had to fight to get the VA to acknowledge the effects of toxic Agent Orange and PTSD. They deserve better. Much better.

Mass demonstrations, draft resistance, civil disobedience, tax protests and lobbying involved millions in the United States and millions more internationally. In 1970, students were killed at Kent and Jackson State while protesting the US invasion of Cambodia. Most campuses went on strike. The United States signed the Paris Peace Agreement in January, 1973. US forces withdrew and prisoners of war were returned. The agreement guaranteed US aid to rebuild a devastated country. The United States violated the agreement, instead imposing a trade embargo. The war's horrific toll: Viet Nam – 2 million dead, 3 million wounded, 13 million refugees, 200,000 missing in action; the United States – 58,000 dead, 304,000 wounded, 1,900 MIAs.

Frequently the war is described as a "tragic mistake," an aberration in US foreign policy. As the Pentagon Papers showed, it was not a mistake, but a calculated attempt to suppress a popular movement that was unfriendly to capitalism and western domination. Similar actions against Guatemala, Chile, Nicaragua, the Zapatistas in Chipas, Mexico, Iraq and Afghanistan, show US foreign policy is not guided by democratic ideals. But if they said it was guided by corporate profits who would support it?

As with US veterans, the war's legacy continues to exact a horrible toll on the Vietnamese. Since the war's end, 40,000 people have been killed by unexploded ordnances (bombs, grenades, mines, artillery shells) and another 65,000 maimed. There are millions of these killers still in the ground. In areas heavily sprayed by Agent Orange (produced by Monsanto), birth defects are an epidemic as are neurological diseases. From 1961-1971 about 20,000,000 gallons of toxic herbicides were sprayed on southern Viet Nam (The Nation, 3/16/15). Many US veterans have returned to Vet Nam to help repair this devastation. They have also helped push the US to do the right thing, and finally the Obama administration has begun to do so.

What are the lessons of Viet Nam? The Pentagon and its PR firms learned to never again televise a war – it breeds opposition. Witness the almost total censorship of the Gulf War, Kosovo, Iraq and Afghanistan. We the people learned a painful lesson – that our government lies to us, and that its agenda is almost always aligned with the rich and powerful, in spite of assertions to the contrary.

We also learned that all authority must be challenged and held accountable to the needs of the people – and that this process never ends. Whether it is the US government, multinational corporations, the Pentagon or state governments, the need for vigilance, resistance and community-building is essential.

In late 2014 retired general Nguyen Van Rinh was asked how the US could make amends for the war. He said, "Admit the truth and acknowledge that a great crime was committed here."

Bio — Dik Cool first opposed the US war on Viet Nam in 1964. He was imprisoned in 1967-68 for draft and war resistance. In 1970 he joined the staff of the Syracuse Peace

Council and spoke against the war at colleges, schools and community groups. He is the founder and publisher of SyracuseCulturalWorkers.com, a national publisher which, in honor of the 40th anniversary of the war's end, has just republished an iconic Ho Chi Minh poster. Ho, like George Washington, is considered the father of his country.

Naming the Dead

Greetings,

Here is a letter for the full-disclosure-project and your plans for this May 25 in Washington DC. I wrote this letter and published it as a letter-to-the-editor in a local newspaper in 2005 as we were blasting Iraq into oblivion.

Naming the Dead

I felt a welcoming warmth at the sound of Mair's voice on the phone. Though we don't talk often, we've been through a few chapters together in the nearly 20 years that we've known each other. I was eager to hear her latest call to action.

Last year Mair had felt the need to walk from the Canadian border to Kittery for peace, which she did despite her 50+ years and creaky knees. "Listen, I have this idea, and I was wondering if you could help me with it," she began. I knew I would say yes to whatever, since I trusted her sense of adventure, and recognized her to be a fellow truth seeker. Her plan was to read the names of the American soldiers killed in the Iraqi war once a week on the Camden Village Green.

It was a two person job, with one reading and one offering a solemn drum beat after each name.

As I considered the reading it began to take on a much more personal meaning for me. As so many aspects of this current political climate have, this one brought me flashing back to the Vietnam years. I am 40 years older than I was when my family was torn asunder by that war, but the memories are still fresh.

When I was 12, my oldest brother Pancho really rocked the boat when he quit school shortly after his 18th birthday and joined the army. We were not a military family, per se, but my father had done the same thing at the same age during World War II, and perhaps Pancho was unconsciously honoring that rite of passage passed on from father to son. My parents were not opposed to the war, though they were worried for Pancho's safety. Dad was proud. His wartime experience had been profound and disturbing. It had felt so much Bigger than anything he had previously felt in his life, and he was still talking about it.

Unlike many of his fellow infantrymen, Pancho survived the combat zone and returned home. As he told my father in one long drunken night of sharing, he had worked very hard at staying alive. Pancho seemed to have a resilient soul. He had a great imagination, and was fond of writing stories as a kid that featured bizarre characters of his own making.

He had names for himself in his different personas; one of my favorites was Kelpy Whamo. It seemed like a part of him was always looking on from outside the game, and from there he usually found life pretty humorous.

Pancho was passionate about his interests. He was a natural scientist, and at 6 possessed a collection of butterflies that was the envy of much older boys. After we moved to California from the mid-west he switched to collecting snakes. There was one road trip to the mid-west where we traveled through an area where dozens of snakes were sunning in the roads and getting run over. Pancho was 12 at the time, and beside himself with grief and helplessness. Soon we were stopping for him to remove every dead snake from the road amidst angry tears.

When he came home from Nam he was sick at heart, and lost in a country that seemed to blame him and his fellow soldiers for an unjust war. I arrived home from school one day and there he was — a tense, well muscled young man.

We had moved to the East coast from our old neighborhood in California while he was in the army, and now he found himself surrounded by strangers, in a family that didn't know how to bring him back to wholeness. After casting about in Connecticut with us for a few months, he set off for California on his own, looking for a way to re-start a life of possibility. Before long he had a girlfriend and had enrolled in college. If you didn't look too hard, you could assume he was doing OK, and considering everything on my family's plate, we weren't looking too hard.

My middle brother had recently been drafted, and was evading the draft by traveling back and forth across the country and waiting for Selective Service to catch up with him. It was becoming increasingly evident that this war was a mistake, and Danny was not interested in dying for it.

At the same time our family was caught in the economic reality of moving every couple of years following Dad's jobs. We were back in the suburbs of Washington, when we got the news of Pancho's motorcycle accident and death. Danny was living with us again at that time.

My parents received the news while they were in New York exploring our next move. I had taken the call at home from the California State Police who told me nothing and asked for my parents' contact info. My parents were located in the city, and told the painful news.

We had no family in the area, and no time-tested friendships. Pancho had never visited us there. There was no one to share our loss with.

My parents decided we could only afford to send one of us, my father, to California to see my brother's body and to spread his ashes off the Huntington Pier, where my brother had spent many youthful days fishing.

It was a painful, lonely time for all of us, and a time when none of us could hide from the ways that our family felt broken.

It was many years later that I heard the statistics on how many Vietnam vets died of either accidental death or suicide within a year of coming home. Pancho's motorcycle accident had been unexplainable, nobody's fault but his own as he breezed through a stop sign and slammed into a car. Like many other vets he had come home with a fondness for certain drugs, and I've always suspected that there were drugs involved in the incident.

Recognizing my oldest brother as a war casualty was a radicalizing moment. It shook me awake and I was filled with pain and loss. It was so painful that I forgot, and lived in that place of forgetting for many years, until our invasions of Afghanistan and Iraq shook me awake again.

How do we honor our war dead? I honor my brother by doing whatever I can to discourage more young people from losing their lives and souls in yet another U.S. instigated, unjust war.

It's interesting that those of us who openly oppose this current war are accused of being unpatriotic. I oppose this war as an American, committed to America being the just and democratic country that it claims to be.

46

Reading the names has brought me full circle. Recently we were approached by a concerned mom and her teenage son after a reading. She asked, "Is this a memorial, or are you protesters?" And I answered, "We are both."

SUPPORT OUR TROOPS. BRING THEM HOME NOW.

N. Button

To You Who Lost Your Lives

Fellow Americans, I, too, am a casualty of the War in/on Vietnam. Although I registered for the Selective Service Draft when I turned 18 in October 1968, having already received an educational deferment for beginning to attend college that Fall, fear of being drafted affected some of my friends. I also got to know some Vietnamese and realized that our politicians consistently lied to us about the whys, the hows, and the wherefores of that war. The war stole my innocence, my patriotism, and my sense of honor in being an "American."

Granted, the costs to me (and others like me) pale in comparison to your willing or unwilling sacrifice. My nonviolent protests against the war (beginning in 1969) were, in part, an attempt to bring you home – safe and sound rather than in a body bag or coffin. I became a Draft Counselor in order to try to help other young men find legal ways to not contribute their bodies or monies to the war effort. Ultimately, I risked my freedom by participating in civil disobedience against that war one month before Saigon "fell" to the military forces opposing the South Vietnam regime. That arrest was a beginning for me to take seriously my responsibility to act nonviolently in trying to be a responsible citizen in what I now recognize as an imperial actor around the globe.

I am dismayed, yes, and outraged, – but not surprised – that the Pentagon and some politicians see this anniversary time as a venue to scrub the moral filth of this war, its lies, and shame it has brought our nation in an attempt to "whitewash" it as a noble attempt to bring democracy to others. Hearing the first-hand stories of friends who served as nonviolent aid workers among the people of Vietnam has convinced me that this war was a tragedy for peoples on all sides. I have come to the belief that all wars are immoral and counterproductive. It was the televised pictures from Vietnam that helped me face the reality of war rather than the propaganda from our government and its self-serving lies.

I grieve for the loss of your life. I grieve for your families. I grieve for our nation. But I also grieve for the millions of

Vietnamese on all sides who lost lives, limbs, livelihoods, lands, and loved ones. I fear we really need another "wall" to list not only the Vietnamese dead, disfigured, and displaced but also for all the US military who've committed suicide and/or suffer from PTSD from the moral injuries they both received and committed. We all need to heal and to join voices like my friends in Veterans For Peace in calling for an end to war.

Sincerely and in Solidarity,

Steve Clemens, Minneapolis, MN

Conscientious Objector, Associate Member, Veterans for Peace

We were all fooled

To All My Relations whose names are on this wall:

We faithfully fulfilled our government's calling to train for war and go to Vietnam to stop a communist takeover of the government by their native inhabitants. This "calling" was a fabricated lie designed to enrich the merchants and corporations who would then exploit the resources of Vietnam leaving little for the people who live there. It was a serious and compelling lie that nearly ruined the fabric of American cultures, political and otherwise.

We were all fooled, overruled, and coerced to do, and in your cases to die for this atrocious injustice. In the process of prosecuting this war we caused the deaths of millions of Vietnamese citizens, destroyed their livelihoods, poisoned their lands, and failed at our given mission. I am so sorry. Sorry I didn't know it was wrong, Sorry I didn't take a stand against my/our forced participation. And most of all, sorry it took your lives causing great grief among our families.

The only thing I don't regret now is that because of the American War, I took up study of all the American wars and found nothing justifiable about any of them.

I learned that war is always based on lies, deceit, coercion, and greed. I learned that what "good" that does come of war is only incidental to its true purposes. I learned that war is but a tool in the hands of imperial nations used to further their colonial exploits. I learned that armies, navies, and air forces are primarily developed and put in place to protect the colonial exploits of forceful nations ruled by the greed of merchants and corporate organizations. And I learned I could stand up to these abominable forces and do my best to educate my fellow citizens of the utter futility of war.

I promise you all, living and dead, that I will endeavor to continue my efforts, along with others of like mind, 'til breath leaves my body, to end the use of war for any purpose on the Earth.

Tomas Heikkala

You are so dark and so mute

Letter to the Vietnam Wall,
4.27.15

You are so dark and so mute. Won't you tell us how deep your cold stone wings are buried? How far East? How far West? Do they go to the bedrock? To the core of the earth? To hell, or the other side?

Where do the names begin and where do they stop? Are more being added where we cannot see?

The names of dead young men on your surface are being slowly eroded by acid rains. If the earth too were washed away would we see more? Would we see details of their unlived lives? Could we read the name of other lives touched, with ripples of despair, by the violence that took them?

Or perhaps would we find the names of millions of Vietnamese and their loved ones whose lives and land were laid to waste? The mothers and fathers and other survivors? The wounded in body, heart and soul? Those who went and came back? Those who wished they didn't and committed suicide? Those who could not, would not, felt they should not? The guilt-ridden and tormented?

Yet we only see the Americans, and we only see the soldiers who served and died in combat, and can no longer say what they thought about the war. And we also see the simple beauty of the monument being eroded with platitudes of politicians, and plans for a new gash in the earth for a 'Vietnam Education Center' (or 'Re-Education' Center?) which will likely tell us it all was 'The Price of Freedom.'

And who am I, to question the meaning of these losses? I, who was too young to worry much about being drafted, or whether I should enlist, or resist. The worst I suffered was war nightmares, in black and white, from watching coverage on the family Zenith TV. And, of course, the ongoing cycle of violence and waste that has followed. But most veterans and survivors suffer similar sentiments – that they suffered less than someone else. Are only those who 'paid the ultimate price' entitled to question comforting myths about war? Those who did, of course, can't speak. In a matter of decades all the survivors too, will have passed. You are a wall that both heals and conceals.

And the propaganda of those who profited and continue to profit from war, suggests the main crime was that soldiers were not given more support when they came back. And while they should have received more support from beginning to end, who is at fault and what sort of support should have been provided? What sort of support should be provided now?

One form of support, especially for those who still suffer from moral injuries – where survivors often suffer feelings of anger, guilt and betrayal – is to create more opportunities for healing and reconciliation. Instead of repressing dialogue with 'patriotic' platitudes, to provide veterans and other survivors– when and if they are ready – a chance to bear witness to the fullness of their experience. Some believe the war was good and necessary, and are proud of their role. For others only one or neither of these things is true, and they don't want to pretend otherwise. Most, I believe, are seeking peace in their hearts, and deeply wish to do something to prevent others from suffering war's trauma.

So Wall, one day I suppose the part of you we now see rising above the earth, will also be buried. But perhaps, if we are willing to listen more deeply, and if we are able to imagine what lies beneath your surface – which surely includes the unnamed dead and wounded soldiers and civilians on all sides of war – you may reach your full potential as "The Wall That Heals."

Roger Ehrlich,

Cary, NC

I was studying in the Columbia College library

I was studying in the Columbia College library in October of 1963 when I heard screaming outside. Madame Nhu, the outspoken sister of Ngo Dinh Diem America's hand-picked leader of the newly created Republic of South Vietnam, was speaking in a nearby hall and protesters were making noise. This was my first hint of the decade to come. But I remained mostly an interested spectator until 1966 when I moved to Chicago for graduate school.

There I joined SDS, eventually becoming quite active. In the fall of 1967, I met, along with other SDSers, with representatives of the 'enemy' — the National liberation Front of South Vietnam, (NLF) — at the Montreal Expo. They maintained, much to my surprise, that they would eventually defeat the US military. Later that fall, I attended the Bertrand Russell War crimes Tribunal in Copenhagen where I heard testimony about brutal US interrogation techniques, as well as the use of napalm, fragmentation bombs, and Agent Orange.

From then on, for better or worse, I became a staunch militant against this terrible war. In recent years I have become more and more concerned that the war be accurately remembered in all its horror.

Howie Machtinger

I met Walt in 1966

10 Days Difference — In Memory of SSgt. Walter J. Dart, Jr.
USAF.

I met Walt in 1966 at Webb Air Force Base in Big Spring, Texas. Webb was a pilot training base, and neither Walt nor I were pilots. We were support, and we both worked in the personnel office, keeping the records straight for the young lieutenants who would fly off to fight the air war in Vietnam. Truth be told, many of us had joined the Air Force to avoid being drafted into the Army or Marines for the ground war in the jungles. I certainly did. We thought we'd be safer.

We were a couple of fish far out of water in barren West Texas. I was from Chicago, Walt from New York and we both could not wait to get out of there. We were bored, but we were safe. During our free time, we traveled the Southwest and made several trips to Mexico, where as 20 year olds we could carouse legally with no interference from our military masters.

One of our other diversions was to take classes at the local college. One night, Walt and I were in the library together and we met two local girls. One would become my wife and the mother of my two daughters. But in 1968 before my love could blossom, Walt and I had both volunteered for Vietnam. We were the same rank, same job description, but one point was critically important; time in service. Walt had come into the Air Force 10 days before I did. He went to Southeast Asia, and I stayed in Texas, marrying the woman I met at the library that night.

Walt was off to a place called Phan Rang on the South China Sea, an old airfield used by the Japanese in WWII and by the French during their attempt to reestablish their colonies. Now the Americans held it, and it wasn't a safe place. But Walt persevered and did his time. The tour in Vietnam was a year. On June 7, 1969 Walt had been there 11 months, and was a short timer, with less than 30 days to go. As one of his fellow airmen recalled, it was the classic case of being in the wrong place at the wrong time. Daytime rocket attacks were usually random events

54

meant to harass rather than do any significant damage. Just a couple of rockets, which Walt, working at the office, would have had no idea were coming. His life ended that day.

Walt's little brother Frank later told a particularly horrific detail of when the family was notified. "When a Chaplin from Stewart AFB came to the house to inform us of Sonny's (Walt's) death, my mother saw the dress blue uniform on the front porch and thought it was Sonny coming home a month early to surprise us."

I left the service, got my college degree and life went on. In 1988 I was honored to have an AIDS education film I produced premier at the Kennedy Center in Washington. It was my first visit to the city, and I knew I had to see the Wall.

I found Walt at Panel 23W Row 098, and, seeing his name, started crying. But as those who've been to the Wall know, I was not crying alone. Others were also there decades after the fighting had stopped, and were crying for other young men and women whose lives would be cut so tragically short. And the question I could not answer was why me? Why did I get an additional half century of life, have two successful daughters, and a marvelous granddaughter. I got to do work which I enjoyed, and traveled the world telling stories on television and in films. But seeing Walt's name on the Wall changed something inside me, and made me forever skeptical of politicians promising that something good can come of war. I don't believe them.

Back in Vietnam, a building was named in Walt's honor. As one of his friends from Phan Rang, Chief Master Sgt. John Reeves told me, there is no question that Walt was a hero. I could not agree more, and think the same of the other 58 thousand plus on the Wall with him. As John Reeves said, we all gave some. Walt and the others gave their all. And so did their families.

One final note. Today, the Socialist Republic of Vietnam controls Phan Rang.

Jim Ryerson

It is with sadness

My Letter to the Soldiers Who Died in Vietnam

It is with sadness that I write this letter to those soldiers who died tragically in Vietnam during the Vietnam/Indochina War. I say "with sadness" and "died tragically" because most of you died young and were overwhelmingly from working class and economically disadvantaged backgrounds and disproportionately from racial minorities. Your lives were cut short by a tragic war, in a place of which few of you had any awareness, and in an unnecessary and immoral conflict not of your voluntary choosing.

I am also thinking not only of almost 60,000 of you who are officially recorded as dying in Vietnam, but also of the many times that number who later died from suicide and war-related physical and psychological devastation and should also be listed as our Vietnam War deaths. Finally, during the actually "official" fighting until 1975 and in the past 50 years, I think frequently of approximately 3,000,000 Vietnamese deaths and perhaps 4,000,000 total Indochinese deaths and the countless others who continue to suffer and die to this day. For me, they are the main innocent victims of our U.S. war on Vietnam.

My personal relation to the Vietnam/Indochina War was as a non-violent antiwar resister. This dominated my life for over ten years and was the key formative influence that has shaped my values and peace and justice commitments to this day. Working with so many others, I dedicated my life to lessening the suffering of the war, bringing our troops home, changing the militaristic and imperialist priorities of our nation, and working for the self-determination of Vietnamese abroad and our own citizens at home.

The specific key antiwar commitment for me occurred during my first full-time faculty position at Southern Illinois University in Carbondale from 1967 to 1972. The Center for Vietnamese Studies and Programs at SIU, funded through a US Agency for International Development grant in 1969, was in many ways a continuation of the infamous Michigan State University CIA project, exposed by Ramparts magazine and others. SIU had received two big US contracts to do work in Vietnam during the 1960s intended to restructure Saigon's educational and security programs.

The ambitious Vietnam Center funding in 1969 was part of Nixon's policy of Vietnamization. The purpose of the funding for the Vietnam Center was to assist the war effort and especially, assuming that the US would win the war, for postwar reconstruction. Wesley Fishel and other key individuals from the Michigan State project joined the SIU program. As outlined in the AID grant and other documents, SIU would perform services for Washington, the military, and others involved in US imperialist policies and would then be rewarded with massive postwar funds to restructure Vietnam's educational, legal, economic, agricultural, technological, police and security systems.

This became one of the most intense and one of the most successful antiwar struggles at any university in the United States. This "Off AID," antiwar, anti-Vietnam Center movement functioned on a range of levels: doing research, uncovering documents and working with insider whistle blowers, and then publicizing the findings through talks, teach-ins, articles, and books; working with the Committee of Concerned Asian Scholars to organize a very effective international scholarly boycott of the Vietnam Center; organizing a dramatic "Vietnamese invasion of Carbondale" with courageous antiwar Vietnamese coming from throughout the US; organizing major conferences at which Gabriel Kolko, Noam Chomsky, and other antiwar scholars and activists came in solidarity; and organizing ongoing protest activism through rallies, marches, sit-ins, and other actions.

There was a price to pay. In May 1970, about 400 of the antiwar protesters were arrested, and another 100 were arrested one night in May 1972. In May 1970, we lived under an armed occupation, with about 1,000 National Guard and several hundred state police as occupiers, with huge military vehicles and people with guns surrounding classrooms and other campus facilities. And yet militant antiwar and anti-Vietnam Center protests continued every day until the authorities lost control, and SIU was permanently shut down one month before the end of the semester. With guns fired, beatings, and mass chaos, we could have easily had an incident like the killings at Kent State or Jackson State.

I was alerted by an SIU administrator that my classes were being infiltrated with fake students who were informers and that I should tape-record every class. Subsequently I was fired twice on blatantly political grounds, and I was then blacklisted. I was very fortunate that I always received widespread support and solidarity from the overwhelming majority of students and faculty, all of the professional associations, the American Association of University Professors, which investigated and placed SIU on its National Censure List with major consequences, and the American Civil Liberties Union, which filed a successful suit in Federal Court on my behalf.

When I communicate with former students, faculty, and antiwar comrades from those years, they often assume that this was a terrible time for me and others, since there was so much local repression and suffering. (Of course, some of us were fully aware every day that the real suffering and death was being inflicted on the Vietnamese.) I often give the opposite response: I look back fondly to a time when every day seemed so intense with so much at stake, in which you had a deep sense of community and solidarity, and in which you could act on your antiwar, peace, and justice values and make a difference. And, most importantly in terms of the antiwar anti-Vietnam Center struggle, the Center, for all of its money and power relations, was totally unsuccessful and never achieved any of its objectives.

In 2015, we find renewed efforts by the disgraced Vietnam War planners, the Pentagon, the aggressive "patriotic" militarists and military contractors, what Fulbright called the military-industrial-academic complex, and the corporate media to rewrite "official" history and undo the real lessons of the Vietnam War. We, who learned the painful and tragic lessons of the Vietnam War must resist this mythic false rewriting of history, set the record straight, and work for a world of greater nonviolence, compassion, peace, and justice.

Douglas Allen
Professor of Philosophy
The University of Maine
Orono, Maine 04469 U.S.A.

To Don MacLaughlin

Panel 4E Row 51

Hey Mac,

It's now nearly 52 years since we threw our hats into the air in jubilation at our 1963 USNA graduation. The war was just then barely on the horizon, the U.S. Marines having arrived there in April of 1962. You were off for Navy flight school, I to become a weapons officer in the Air Force. It was not surprising that you graduated high in your flight class and won your wings as a Navy fighter pilot. You were unquestionably among the best and the brightest — Don MacLaughlin, All-American lacrosse and soccer player, recipient of the Naval Academy sword presented to the top athlete in our class, and always on the Superintendent's list for academic excellence. I was proud to call you teammate and best friend.

Two years later the Vietnam War was on its way to becoming an intractable mess. In late 1965, you were assigned to an A4C Skyhawk Squadron on board the carrier, USS Enterprise off the coast of Vietnam. I was fat-catting as the commander of an Explosive Ordnance Disposal Detachment at March AFB in Southern California. By then I doubt either of us or, for that matter, any of our 876 Naval Academy classmates harbored the least suspicion that the endeavor in Southeast Asia was anything less than necessary, righteous, and honorable; not if we were going to stop Communism by preventing a domino from falling. I know I didn't. As the war heated up the commonly held sentiment in E.O.D. was that, "Vietnam was a small war, but our only war and it was the only place where real E.O.D. work was being done." Several of my men found the siren call of glorious war seductive and volunteered.

In a letter you sent in mid-December of 1965, you wrote of the challenge of carrier-landings, and the Adrenalin-charge of your missions over suspected Viet Cong strongholds.

On the evening of January 4, 1966, I received the call from my parents. On a January 2nd bombing run over Quang Ngai

59

province your plane had gone down. The wreckage of your aircraft had been found and your body spotted. Due to ground fire your "remains" were never recovered and were left to enrich Vietnam's soil.

The following week I submitted my request for reassignment to Vietnam. Your death was the singular most motivating factor, but the preceding 21+ years had determined my course. Typical of those of our class, my opinions had been shaped by cultural forces that encouraged, in fact, nearly demanded unquestioning faith in the goodness of our country and the infallibility of American leadership.

In that letter written in your last month you had also said, "I only hope that what we are doing here will bring a better life to the people of Vietnam." Close observation of the conduct of the war would have exposed that to be an improbable outcome, but it was a fantasy I shared and, though secondary to my grief, was part of the rationale that prompted my volunteering. I recall my internal dialogue. "I need to test my manhood. How would I measure up? Who am I to question America's leaders? They have the intelligence? I need to see for myself."

Since then, Don, many truths have led me down a path distinctly divergent from that which the vast majority of our classmates, if not most Americans, have taken. I now see how the rationale that led me to war was embarrassingly specious. I'd like to think your perspectives from the hereafter, should there be such, would place you on my side of the divide.

I came home from 'Nam troubled by what I'd been a part of, but it was three decades later before I "found my way" — as I like to characterize the journey. Closer study of the war and of American foreign policy in those intervening years launched the transition, but a pivotal event occurred in 1998, when I returned to Vietnam to participate in a transformative bike ride from Hanoi to Ho Chi Minh City — the "Vietnam Challenge" was organized by World T.E.A.M. Sports, an NGO dedicated to bringing together disabled and able-bodied athletes to participate in extraordinary athletic events. My fellow-travelers were veterans from both sides of the war, former mortal enemies, most of whom had suffered terrible injury during the war — amputees, para and quadriplegics on hand-cycles, blind on the backs of tandem bikes. Each day's ride was punctuated with tearful admissions and heart-wrenching recognition of our shared humanity. The pain for at least a few of us Americans on the ride was compounded by awareness that as "soldiers" under misguided and duplicitous leaders we had forsaken our humanity. My personal disgraceful failure had occurred within my first few months in-country when needing to prove my manhood and out of boredom (E.O.D. work, like flying, could be described as hours/days of monotonous training, interrupted by seconds/ moments of terror) I volunteered to fly back-seat as an observer in an F-100 Super Sabre. For what was little more than a lark, I went 'along for the ride' as we dropped napalm on remote jungle villages along the Cambodian border. I have concluded that not seeing, and thus not knowing with certainty that there were victims beneath those bombs, is infinitely better than knowing, but guilt persists. I now know that U.S. napalm and other ordnance destroyed 70-80% of the Vietnamese homes in Quang Ngai province! And my cavalier joy-ride seems more to me to have been an unforgivable, reprehensible lack of humanity.

Mac, it may be clear to you in the hereafter, revelations since the war verify the abandoned humanity and criminality of Americans and our leaders in Vietnam. Truths ignored and, in some cases denied in the face of mountains of irrefutable evidence, would include:

The Gulf of Tonkin resolution that gave Congressional approval to the escalation of the war was based on an alleged incident never proven and most certainly fiction.

The deaths of over 500 mostly elderly men, women and children at My Lai was not an isolated case of a few GIs gone berserk, but was a sanctioned way of doing business.

The U.S. sprayed 20 million gallons of Agent Orange over an area of Vietnam equal to the state of Massachusetts, essentially seeding the countryside with a toxic contamination and leaving a legacy that includes 2-3 million Vietnamese institutionalized, incapable of taking care of themselves. Today the contaminated soils and waters of Vietnam assure the defoliant's continuing legacy just as does the genetic code carried by first and second generation victims, Vietnamese and American alike.

Fifty-eight thousand Americans were offered up to the alter of "spreading democracy." Among them were 130 Naval Academy grads, 12 of our classmates, and two other teammates.

Our way of war, bombing from the heavens, in particular, took 2-3 million Vietnamese, Laotian, and Cambodian lives, many of which were civilians.

From 1965-1973, 8 million tons of bombs were dropped — 300 tons for every Vietnamese man, woman, and child. South Vietnam, our ally, was struck by nearly twice the number of bombs dropped by the U.S. in WWII.

Over 20,000 Vietnamese prisoners died in the Tiger Cages of Con Son, victims of torture by Vietnamese police, trained by and operating under the influence if not direction of the U.S. military.

The implementation of a "body count" metric to "prove" American success led to the murder of thousands of innocents — losses of epidemic proportions as proven by author Nick Turse's search in the National Archives.

By the end over 5 million of our South Vietnamese allies, nearly 1/3 the population, had been made refugees, driven from their land.

This is merely a sampling of the criminal behavior of our country — a record that ought to convince Americans that we had gone horribly off course. In fact, even by 1971, 58% of the public believed the nation was fighting an immoral war. More than half of all draft-age men took steps to avoid the draft, 500,000 deserted the military. Many rejected the idea that military service was always honorable and heroic. In 1972, the noted historian, Henry Steele Commager, perhaps perplexed that even more weren't rising up against the war rhetorically wrote, "Why do we find it so hard to accept this elementary lesson of history, that some wars are so deeply immoral that they must be lost, that the war in Vietnam is one of these wars, and that those who resist it are the truest patriots?"

The really discouraging reality is that the record since, in spite of the stench of Vietnam, is equally criminal, equally devoid of humanity, makes a mockery of American convictions, and speaks of lessons unlearned.

Why do I say this? Very briefly:

A recent report asserts that up to 1.3 million people have been killed in Iraq, Afghanistan and Pakistan in the first 10 years of the so-called war on terror.

This included an estimate by the University Collaborative Iraq Mortality Study of 405,000 Iraqi dead due to the war thru 2011.

Targeted assassinations by drone.

Guantanamo

Abu Ghraib

The noted author-activist, Brian Willson, documents 390 overt U.S. military interventions between WWII and 2008, with at least 20 million killed. Note: That's exclusive of the toll of covert operations! Knowing this record it is not at all surprising that a 2013 WIN/ Gallup poll found that in the eyes of the world the U.S. is the greatest threat to world peace.

Beginning on Memorial Day of 2012 the Department of Defense launched a Vietnam War Commemoration Campaign. The campaign will terminate on Veterans Day of 2025. Its seemingly reasonable and innocuous objectives, in abridged form, are:

To thank and honor veterans of the Vietnam War

To highlight the service of the Armed Forces during the war

To pay tribute to the contributions made on the home front

To highlight the advances in technology, science, and medicine related to military research during the war

To recognize contributions by allies

Seems all fine and good. What's not to like? Well, Mac, Veterans for Peace, of which I'm a member, sees the campaign as a perpetuation of the failure of our government to acknowledge the costs of the war as suffered by the Vietnamese and will serve to continue to, "sanitize and mythologize the Vietnam War and thereby legitimize further unnecessary and destructive wars."

Veterans for Peace has launched its own counter-campaign at Vietnamfulldisclosure.org. It represents a clear alternative to the Pentagon's current efforts to legitimize further unnecessary and destructive wars.

There are direct lines that run from My Lai thru Nerkh in Afghanistan (where innocents were again slaughtered), from Agent Orange victims thru the deformed babies of Fallujah, from the Tiger Cages thru Abu Ghraib and Guantanamo, from the bombing of Hanoi thru the drone bombings of wedding parties in Pakistan and Yemen. Inhumanity is a common denominator.

While I have written that your death, Mac, prompted my "service" in Vietnam, it has been just as responsible for who I have become. At every vigil, every protest, every Congressional visitation, you, along with the 58, 000 other Americans and 2-3 million Vietnamese are with me.

No other nation on earth has intervened with armed force as America has. Though we know the fault lies with our leaders and a complicit media, we, the public, are not blameless. Our silence makes us morally complicit and assures a future of American violence and inevitable blowback.

Knowing the truths and committed to speak out, I will visit you again soon at Panel 4E Row 51.

In lasting gratitude,

Dud (Hendrick)

P.S. Written at a time when the Congressional leaders are calling for bombing Iran.

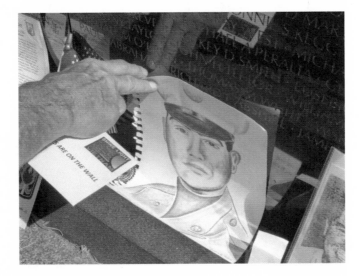

My father and my uncle both served

"Mourn the dead, but fight like hell for the living" said Mother Jones.

My father and my uncle both served in World War II and received their decorations, though neither ever spoke of the war, nor did I ask. As a boy, I played war with my older cousin who went off to Vietnam. Our idol was Audie Murphy; we both had his 3rd Infantry Division patch painted on our helmet liners.

So I was primed at a young age, ready to serve my country, a willing but unknowing patriot, dedicated to protecting and serving with honor my country 'tis of the flying red, white and blue. I had a feeling of pride and glory, thinking I was doing the right thing to stop the spread of communism. The domino-theory prevailed, and I knew so little…. "Be a good citizen… trust your government."

So, as the sabers rattled and the flags unfurled for the almighty USA, I was one of those young men going off to war. I was 17 and, like so many others coming from low-income families, the military held promise… a hopeful opportunity to gain knowledge, experience for future jobs, and the prospect of the GI Bill. High on my list was a chance to step away, exit from the insanity of my family. Sign me up, Uncle Sam!

I was stationed on the USS Duluth LPD 6 (landing platform dock), the last ship ever to be commissioned in the Brooklyn Navy Yard. The ship joined Amphibious Ready Group Alpha, US Seventh Fleet off Vietnam South China Sea in May 1967, and departed in November back to Subic Bay. With three companies of Marines, helos, and landing craft assault vehicles, we participated in seven Amphibious Assault Operations. And according to Rear Admiral W.W. Behrens, USN, we "made a major contribution to our ever growing success in the war… Congratulations on a job well done."

Well, get your rubber boots on and roll up your pants, for this is more of the BS we continually get from those who spin the truth into propaganda, more disingenuous lies. Let us not forget that the "The first casualty when war comes is truth" (US Senator Hiram Warren Johnson)

Do I remember the napalm strikes, the Medevac flights out, the 16-hour-day workloads, the smells, the heat, the prison-like confinement of being on a ship in close quarters day in and day out? Of course. Yet there is no one glaring event, rather a montage of images, a confluence of memories that flow down the river, all weaving that tapestry I call Vietnam.

What I remember most are the stories of those I have encountered. Here are but a mere few:

My colleague Ron, a psychologist, full colonel Army Reserve, who died of Agent Orange complications, leaving behind two young boys from his second marriage, now without a loving dad...

Tommy, served on ship with me, unable to manage, loses his home, living now in a small trailer provided by the church, his wife sobbing to me on the phone that disability benefits continue to be denied, yet our ship is listed on the Agent Orange: Mobile Riverine Force Alphabetized Ships List...

Russ, after a heavy firefight entering the village, picks up a small infant who dies in his arms, wondering what madness this is... Now he is a tireless witness for peace, working to stop the drones, to stop the killing of innocents...

My loving friend, Bill the iron-worker, two-tour 'Nam Vet. We spent 15 years in men's group together, did Bamboo Bridge... I cried a lot of tears with you, Brother. Haunted by the continual memories of the war, caught in the cycle of addiction unable to break free, gradually losing his mind, and living with his sister, unable to care of himself.... I haven't spoken to you in three years. You may be dead by now, dear friend, I don't really want to know... My heart aches...

Jim B., you fearless fighter for 9/11 Truth and Depleted Uranium, I miss your passion, your conviction for speaking the truth... locks himself in the bathroom and with shotgun unloads his troubles...

The funerals of veterans that I have attended, the stories heard from veterans and families, many offering the countless stories of suffering, carnage, suicide, addiction, homelessness, soulful injury... and the list goes on and on....

So I still carry some survivor guilt, for the message I received was that if you were wounded, that was a partial sacrifice, but the only ultimate way to truly fully serve, was to not come back at all. That level of insanity leaves little room for forgiveness and self-acceptance for the service that one was able to give. Of course, the participation in war needs to be reconciled with the cultural betrayal, the misdirected choice in submitting to such a misleading enterprise. "WAR is a racket. It always has been. It is possibly the oldest, easily the most profitable, surely the most vicious. It is the only one international in scope. It is the only one in which the profits are reckoned in dollars and the losses in lives" (Smedley Darlington Butler).

So what I walk away with is opening my heart to carry the sorrow of all the stories that I've heard... the suffering of humanity. I don't always feel that sadness but it is there, a low moaning wail of grief that never quiets itself, a manifestation of what we have done to grandmother earth and all our relations, not just the two-legged.

I go to the top of the hill, leave tobacco, and say prayers for my helpers, the spirits of the land. I use the sweet grass to clear my mind, with Chanupa in hand, the sacred prayer pipe; I say my prayers to the great mystery, to grandmother, the four directions. I ask that my mind, body, spirit be strengthened in all ways, to serve, Mitakuye Oyasin, all my relations in a good way. Let it be so.

I keep my boots on the ground, I keep my head high, and I stand shoulder to shoulder with others who want to see peace and justice prevail in a world filled with darkness. I will continue toward this end with the hope that the seven generations, those yet to come down the road of life, will have a better way.

For all of you who have come down the road or rest in the fields, I will burn some extra sweet grass, sage, cedar and perhaps copal. Gently smell the sweetness, shake your weariness. May you take a breath of sweet mercy. I am On Belay,

Douglas H. Ryder

President, VFP Eisenhower Chapter 157

Lying Is The Most Powerful Weapon In War

When I face the Wall alone in the dead of the night,
I bear witness out loud that the entire Vietnam War
was one of the greatest lies in American history.
I hear 58,000 citizens come alive with profound approval.
As an infant child reaches out to touch its mother's breast,
I just want to touch the names on the Wall.
For a chosen few the Wall will become flesh.

"If the thing they were fighting for was important enough to die for then it was also important enough for them to be thinking about it in the last minutes of their lives. That stood to reason. Life is awfully important so if you've given it away you'd ought to think with all your mind in the last moments of your life about the thing you traded if for. So, did all those kids die thinking of democracy and freedom and liberty and honor and the safety of the home and the stars and stripes forever? You're goddamn right they didn't." — Dalton Trumbo, *Johnny Got His Gun*, World War I

One of the greatest anti-war novels ever written

Mike Hastie

Army Medic Vietnam, Memorial Day 2015

Another Truth

By Jack Gray,
Seaman Apprentice, deserter, detained and released, 1966-68

To your name on the Wall and in your memory: I didn't go to Viet Nam. But I have as much sadness when I see your image, as when I first went to visit you shortly after your construction. I almost went to war, because like so many times of war, including now, we are told that it is the right thing to do, and for a while I believed them. And of course when we dared to question, our government, for greed and for power, would lead or drag us down this destructive path in its draft. Those in power would determine the only exceptions. I enlisted.

I enlisted in the Navy-USNR in 1966, so that I could finish college, perhaps become an officer, and eventually be able to choose a non-combatant service. This I so glibly swallowed at age 20, from my local recruiter. My folks were pleased and threw a party........ complete with cake. My picture went into the local paper. Shortly thereafter I was off to Officer Candidate School in Newport, Rhode Island, a long way from my small town in Washington State.

It was at OCS where I began to discover, under the sparkle of surrounding military and civilian "pomp and glitz," that few could explain why we were killing ourselves and multiples of others in the land of Viet Nam and its neighbors. And yet, so many around were saying that it was the right thing to do, and of course how important it is to "win" this war. It seemed important. We are the USA.

I was lucky. As I talked with others who, like me, enlisted, and to others who were drafted, I could only learn that this war was not making sense, in so many ways. Amidst the lies, deceptive propaganda, and oppression by military and government, questions were popping all around me. Answers and choices seemed all bad. For each answer would talk of death, by them or by us, or perhaps to prison. I chose to desert and to think. It was just one of those bad choices among all the other bad choices.

And so I went from Officer Candidate to Seaman Apprentice, to deserter, to Courts Martials, to detention, to awaiting handcuffs for transporting..... to what I was told would be a brig in Viet Nam. But then by some fortuitous trail of gossip and spreading of the word, a lawyer volunteered his service, as did War Resisters League. And after months as a detainee, I was released. Government lawyers were preparing their request for seven years at Leavenworth. But a Federal District Court Judge believed what I was saying and accepted my beliefs despite my lack of religion, as a conscientious objector. I actually had no hope and then my world changed. I didn't feel a lot of honor and, given a different day and no support, I easily may have chosen to cooperate. I was lucky in the midst of giving up hope.

And now when I remember The Wall, and your names, and your innocence, I honor you and I cry for you, and every part of your lives and the lives of those maimed and dying around you, before you and after you.

I'm still sad this war happens, and that it happens for all the bad reasons as proclaimed by other vets having experienced harm and real truths around Viet Nam. These truths are glaring, even though many in our government still wish to bury them in their proclamation of "support our troops," and yet vote against legislation that would ease the pain and suffering of those who survive. But know that we are many who now insist on full disclosure vs. a patriotic gloss-over in telling your truths and shouting your questions. We will keep talking about what happened to you, and about what happened in Viet Nam, because we know what happened. Most importantly your names and souls live with us.

With humility,

Jack Gray, veteran and deserter from Washington State

The Wall

The Wall

I set out with pen and paper
to write something poetic
about this black monument and
its neatly chiseled list of names,
only to be confronted with the
dead silence of so many voices
(plus millions in Southeast Asia)
and the unspeakable crime
of the American war in Viet Nam.

~B. L.

My prayers

Doug,

My prayers are that those on the Wall have found a peace you and I still seek. For those who bring their wars home, I offer the video below. Feel free to share/post/use it wherever you feel it would do the most good.

The video's been used by the VA's nationwide suicide prevention program, a leading mental health journal, the US Senate Committee on Veterans Affairs, a West Point faculty department head, Colin Powell's former chief of staff, and 20 other national and local entities serving vets & GIs.

The message encourages troubled vets (PTSD, etc.) to seek help, and is a tool for their families, friends, and counselors. Let me know how you like it.

…Roland

https://youtube/nNV-hEsidXY

My last conversation with my neighbor

My last conversation with my neighbor Kenny was out in front of his house. We were both standing there in the driveway and he says, "I heard from the Draft Board. I'm classified 1 – A." I said, "What's that mean?" He explained, "It means I'm ripe for pickin', gonna get drafted for sure. Probably go to Vietnam." I didn't know enough about Vietnam to ask a simple question about it. He didn't know enough about Vietnam to answer even if I did ask. Neither one of us could find Vietnam on an unmarked map, so we started talking about his car. Growing up he was a few years older than me and he worked his father's dairy farm and ranch in Willits, California. My house was across the road from his and our mothers knew each other well, exchanging gossip from time to time.

Kenneth Allan Butler, Jr. is inscribed on Panel 51 – Line 38 on the Vietnam Veterans Memorial Wall in our Nation's Capital. He was killed in Vietnam in 1968 while driving an Armored Personnel Carrier when it hit a land mine. He was in the US Army for less than a year. He was 20 years old.

Against the advice of all my friends I went in to see an Army Recruiter in December 1970 to enlist. I said, "I want to be a gunner on a helicopter." The Sergeant said, "We aren't recruiting for that MOS this month." I asked, "What's a MOS?" He explained, "It's your job. Everyone has a Military Occupational Specialty, or MOS. It's a specific job that you are trained to do." All along I thought everyone did what they thought they were good at in the Army. In the movies you just got into a jeep and took off. When the shooting started everyone just picked up their rifles and pitched in and did their best to shoot back. It wasn't like a job with a title. So I said, "What about tanks?" He suggested a MOS in electronics so I could learn a skill and after the Army I could get a good job. I said, "Nope. I want Tanks." He agreed to that, but I would serve "based on the needs of the Army, most likely Germany, because we don't have many tanks in Vietnam." So I said Okay.

I came home on Leave after Armor Advanced Individual Training in Fort Knox, Kentucky and my mother said Kenny's mom wanted to talk to me. I didn't have the courage. Talk to Kenny's mom, about what? About being in the Army? I liked it. I had been promoted to Private First Class upon graduation from AIT, I was selected Super-numerary in Guard Duty and received a letter commending me from the Executive Officer of the Training Brigade; a Major signed it. I liked the Army and I liked driving tanks and knocking down trees, driving through mud. It was a good move for me to enlist. How could I tell her that? I was 19 and I did not have the knowledge or the words for that kind of responsibility. I would say the wrong thing and make her feel bad. I didn't go.

I went on to make Sergeant, then after college and ROTC, I became an Officer in the Signal Corps and retired as an Army Major. If Kenny's mother were still alive today I think I now know what I would try to say to her. It would be something like this:

I am sincerely sorry for your loss. Kenny died so young and he missed so much. He missed not having children, birthdays, weddings, and reunions. He missed growing old with his wife and friends. Other classmates of his have died way too soon as well; a motorcycle accident by following too close, untreated cancer, drinking and driving, a drug addiction, etc. While those losses are tragic, they are without Honor. Kenny died while serving his country, doing what he thought was the right thing to do, like so many who have gone on before him, answering the Nation's call. He bravely served doing his duty and his name will always be associated with honorable and selfless service in time of war. His name is etched in stone for future generations to see on The Wall and pay tribute. He is with good company. So Mrs. Helen Butler, you are the mother of a very special man whose memory and place in history will go on after the rest of us are long gone and forgotten. Take comfort.

DENNIS W. MINER
Major, Retired
U.S. Army

Dear Joe — or Bob or John or maybe Susan

April 18, 2015

Dear Joe — or Bob or John or maybe Susan (...how many, many names...they seem to stretch forever on this wall).

I was probably just learning to write my own name when you died. Born in 1964, it was a confusing time to be a little girl. I am sure it was far more confusing — and frightening — for you to be in Vietnam.

I wondered about you back then. Who were you, this young man on my TV, running through tall grass and jungles, carrying a gun? Or perhaps you were a nurse treating the wounded. But why were they wounded? Why were they there? Someone must know, I thought.

I tried to ask my mom these questions but if she gave an explanation at all, I still could not understand it. The one thing I was sure of was that some of these men were killed. My oldest brother was of draft age and I was terrified to think he might have to go. I cried one day, asking Mom if he would be killed. Again, there was no sufficient answer, no reassurance.

That brother did not get the call. He is sixty-two now, alive and well.

But you had to go — and you died. You were somebody's brother or son or sweetheart.

As much as I tried to figure out "war" back then, no one — not even Walter Cronkite — could make it seem right. It was simply a nightmare no one could wake from. "That's the way it was," as Walter would say.

I am fifty now. You might think in all these years that I would have made sense of it, that I could finally believe it was more than just senseless death and destruction. Wasn't I taught that we were always "the good guys"? The powerful, the wealthy and elite, many in the halls of Washington, are still trying to spin it, to put it in some sort of good light. But if I bought that, if (even worse) I repeated that lie, I fear it would be one more betrayal of you.

Here is the ultimate haunting question, I think: Did you die in vain?

Never mind if it was heroic. Forget if you should have been there or not.

The fact is that you were there — and you died there. So, did it serve any greater purpose? When they folded up that flag and handed it to your loved one, was there anything they could take comfort in?

I cannot answer that.

All I know with certainty is this: Beginning with that war — maybe even on the day you fell — I knew there was something terrible about this whole business, no matter what Walter Cronkite or any Senators or the President had to say.

War should never be glorified, or worse, glamorized. It cheapens life, I think, to try to convince anyone that killing and being killed is anything but horrific.

So if you did die for a cause, let it go down in history as this — a lesson in the sanctity of every life and the horror of every war. For that lesson, I thank you.

May you now rest in peace.

Gail Coleman

I remember the day

Dear Paul,

I remember the day during our home leave when you took me into the bedroom to quietly tell me your "surprise"…

You had bought your girlfriend an engagement ring, and simultaneously announced that you had enlisted in the Army.

Without a moment's hesitation I mindlessly blurted out:

"O NO! What have you done! You'll be killed."

I lived in Germany…knew the kids from DOD schools. Saw them vacuumed up post-graduation and dead within a year or so…Ed from Frankfurt, Dave McKee, Ken Rogers, John Bennett…gone.

Phantoms. The rest of us, left behind to become phantoms too. When you are 15 it's hard to fathom the reality of death. Harder to watch the steady creep of a plague of death. And harder then have it all become a taboo…It was not OK to talk about that "war" in my small world overseas. It was even more bizarre to come back to the States and see the relative absence of ANY geopolitical awareness among most Americans about Viet Nam (as it used to be written then) or anywhere else either. Isolated by comforts and geography.

So I apologized to you instantly and sincerely and we talked. But I knew. And in some part of me, I realized you knew too.

All over America, the post WWII generation of our parents, could not see what we saw. Even then, I understood that. Their frame of reference and context was all about "Duty and

Country."

It was impossible for them to equate "malice aforethought" with their nation. They couldn't even do it when our president was assassinated. The initial gash in our moral fabric.

But their children, we were young and saw things with fresh eyes. Eyes that perceived something was out of control and growing worse. It steamrolled ahead unchecked for many reasons, but the first thing I saw was the disproportionate vehemence and rage directed towards anyone who spoke up or asked that anyone consider an examination of policy about that war.

Maybe no one could fathom "malice aforethought" as a national policy, or a hidden hand or a for-profit engagement.

We'd rather relegate all that stuff to the Nazis and the Communists.

Never dreaming that all those 'Paperclip imports' would mean we'd already adapted to a new playbook. Man.

If we thought it was screwed up then…You should see it now! Who knew we would ever consider that era to be the good old days… back when we still had a free press!

But you had died long before Daniel Ellsberg sent the Pentagon Papers to the press. And the NY Times and the Washington Post used to champion the rule of law and encourage vigorous debate….

That war ripped our guts out. Dismantled our souls. Divided families and friends. Created lasting scars. Our parents, in the end, were devastated. I think it was by grief and betrayal. A betrayal that created a schism so deep, they never recovered. It was like by the time we got to Iran-Contra they all just became more sullen and angry. And the rest of us gave up too.

And the Vets. God help us. They were abandoned. They were the only visible emblems of a war that made us all crazy. The whole nation was in shell shock…millions then and now, all with PTSD. There will never be a wall big enough to hold the names of all the casualties of that war.

When you look back, you can see that after JFK, MLK, RFK and about 60 thousand KIA we had a huge blanket episodic Amnesia from which we never recovered.

But maybe that too was by design. Brain damage — soul

damage by MK Ultra.

I can't tell you how many times I've said: "Thank God my father is dead because This would have killed him."

You know how Uncle Dave loved his country...

But you were already gone by the time all that happened in that decade and the next. And the next...Died long before then. Only 19.

Never married or a father or any of the million other experiences that were taken from you.

I am so sorry. And I thank you.

I understand — as I understood then — that you believed in the course you chose to take.

I see, all the time, the resounding impact of your death, and that war, on my life.

But until the Moving Wall came to my town, I had no place to mourn.

I took my grandson to The Wall in Washington. Brought him to see your name and hear me say "my cousin Paul" and tell him about you.

These days, I believe you, and your brothers in arms, will save the world. You will win the battles for our hearts and minds.

You will remind this nation to recall our own Humanity. To remember what it is to be human...to care, to feel.

To see Life as sacred. To remember all we have forgotten in fifty years. Peace, Truth, Justice and Freedom.

To understand that these are interdependent. As are we all... on this beautiful small planet, designed to thrive and live in beauty and peace.

I will look forward to that day with you.

Your loving cousin,

maggie

So many of you

To the Vietnam Veterans Memorial Wall

So many of you whose names are on this Wall were young, so very young when you went off to war. My friend, Ron Phillips, was a combat Marine in Vietnam (2nd Bat., 3rd Marines). He didn't die there, but came home wounded in body and spirit. After Ron returned, he applied for a position in the Waco, Texas Police Department and was told he was too young to be a policeman because he was too young to carry a gun. Too young to carry a gun in Texas, but not in Vietnam.

Ron died of heart disease 20 years ago, at age 45. He had finally been granted his PTSD claim, after seven years of appeals to the V.A. Before he died, he used years of his life and the pain of his experiences in Vietnam to reach young people, to tell them that service in the military is not the grand adventure portrayed by military recruiters.

It wasn't easy. Talking to students required Ron to remember the pain he had buried while he was in Vietnam. Once he told me about retrieving the weapon and going through the belongings of a dead Vietnamese soldier. He may have been the one who killed the man. He wasn't sure. He hadn't been the only one firing. In the dead man's clothing, he found his wallet and in it a picture of the man's wife and child. For a moment, Ron felt the full humanity of the man, the horror of his death, the sorrow his family would know. But only for a moment. Then he had to shut those feelings down, deep down. Marines are not supposed to cry. And he would have to fight again.

It would be years and many hours of therapy before Ron could confront his experiences. And it took writing a lot of poetry. When Ron went into high school classes, he read his poetry and the poetry of other veterans, and he talked about the war. One teacher always asked her students to write their responses when the class met next, and she shared those with Ron. A young man wrote, "Thank you for helping me understand my father. He fought in Vietnam but he doesn't talk about the war. He doesn't talk much at all."

Ron also coordinated the Alternatives to Militarism project. He wrote, designed and distributed leaflets, showed films, and organized anti-war events. He had a chance to make a difference, and he used that chance – even though it meant reliving the dehumanization and horror of his own experiences as a Marine.

You whose names are on this Wall died in Indochina, and so you never got a chance to mature and to make a difference as adult members of society. Our country has never been enriched by all the talents you might have brought to us. Our society has never benefited from all the work you might have done. We have been deprived of your stories, your music, your smiles, laughter, tears, and perhaps wisdom. Your loved ones never had the chance to watch as you tossed a ball back and forth with your children. Your children – those you left behind or those you never had – didn't have the chance to see you bounce your grandchildren on your knee. You likely would have had grandchildren by now.

There is simply no way to measure the loss to your comrades in arms, to your friends, your family and to all your fellow citizens. I wish I could believe that you died in a righteous cause. I do not. The only way we can bring meaning to your deaths is to remember you and to strengthen our resolve to work against war as an instrument of foreign policy.

And truth to tell, there ought to be another wall, a wall bearing the names of those who came home from Vietnam, but ultimately didn't survive the war. That wall would need to contain an even greater number of names, to include all those who committed suicide or who, because of drugs or alcohol, or depression or reckless driving, died as a result of self-destruction.

The name of my former brother-in-law, William Douglas Barnes, belongs on such a wall. A light-hearted young man before he went to war, he loved life and he loved good food. Billy would come in the front door of the family home in Connecticut and head directly to the kitchen to examine the contents of the refrigerator.

After the war, Bill moved to Oregon with his second wife. He earned a Masters degree at the University of Oregon, fathered a daughter, held a socially-useful job, worked on his house. He coped. He was still genial and quick to laugh.

Bill didn't talk about Vietnam when we were together. Except once. He was stoned. Then he talked about being blown out of his bunker. He talked about being abandoned in the jungle, Vietcong nearby, how very near he did not know, when the helicopter that came to evacuate them after a fire fight couldn't lift off without leaving someone behind.

In a way, he and so many other Vietnam veterans were abandoned again when a government that had sent them to war learned all the wrong lessons from that war. America launched another war in another country which we did not understand, and in which the U.S. utterly lacked the potential to bring its people a decent future. The Iraq War put Billy and so many other veterans over the edge. He couldn't continue to cope. He couldn't keep it together. They said he died as a consequence of alcoholism. His family knows he died as a result of his military service. His sister speaks of the heartbreak of watching a loved one slowly suffering and dying from carrying the weight of the war daily.

The only way we can bring meaning to 60,000 or more delayed deaths is to remember those who perished after the war because they did not come home from Vietnam whole in body or spirit, and sooner or later could no longer cope. They, too, should strengthen our resolve to work against war as an instrument of foreign policy.

And finally, there are the people of Vietnam, of Laos and Cambodia, who died in the millions in what they know as the "American War." It took twenty years after the war ended on April 30, 1975 for the U.S. to stop punishing Vietnam, to lift the embargo, to normalize relations. Now we wear clothes with labels that say, "Made in Vietnam," and Vietnam is a tourist destination. But people in Southeast Asia are still dying from Agent Orange and from the mines and bombs the U.S. left behind. Some Americans have accepted responsibility for that and they work to help clean up the mess our country left behind. Most of them are Vietnam vets. I honor them.

Marion Malcom

I knew two of the men

The Wall

I knew two of the men whose names are engraved on the Vietnam Veteran Memorial. The first, Artie Klippen, I saw a lot of that season in '63 when we both played Lacrosse at Georgetown. We had one of those anarchic undergraduate arrangements where we briefly shared a car, a beat-up old Chevy with the gear shift on the steering column.

Compared to so many guys at that age who are callow and two-faced, Artie was a straight-up, warm and friendly guy, qualities that make him continue to stand out in my memory, even though we never got to know each other well. After that year, I seldom saw Artie again. I had been in Brazil all of '64, but came back with too few credits to graduate with my class in '65, the year Artie did. Having completed ROTC, Artie got his lieutenant's butter bar along with his sheepskin. I was still at Georgetown, having stuck around an extra year in ROTC myself to avoid the draft, when I heard Artie had bought it in Nam as a platoon leader with a leg unit.

I read somewhere that the odds to survive a tour in Nam were a thousand to one. On average. The life expectancy for a grunt LT like Artie was averaged against that of a chaplain's assistant in the rear, a two-star general well behind the wire in his air conditioned trailer, a spoon in the mess hall who hugged an M-16 at night in a bunker to guard the perimeter, or a spook like me patrolling in harm's way by day, but generally secure overnight in a base camp. So Artie already faced poorer odds compared to most of us. But a soldier's superstition held that, no matter where you found yourself in Nam, if there was a bullet in Hanoi with your name on it, you weren't coming home. We called that blind luck, and Artie didn't have it.

I don't recall how Artie died exactly. It might have been a bullet; more likely a booby trap. Out on patrol where you stepped, and where you didn't, made all the difference. But given the routinely barbarous acts American GIs perpetrated on innocent Vietnamese civilians, I feel confident that Artie made his unit play by the rules of engagement to whatever the degree that was even possible in a peoples' war. He would not have been gung ho or reckless. Artie would have put a premium on the welfare of his men, even as he had the moxie to lead them in a deadly encounter. And if I were to learn Artie died bravely to ensure someone else might live, that would be consistent with the character of the man I knew. Even in an evil war like Vietnam, I want to believe a man like Artie Klippen could be a hero.

The other young man I knew whose name is on the Wall, wasn't even close to being a hero. But he was a tragic loss, and just as chosen by misfortune as anyone else whose name is inscribed there. I believe that Stanley Reed was not yet twenty when he died, right in line with the 'nineteen year, ten month average age of all American soldiers who served in Vietnam. Stanley was average in other ways too, I guess. An average smart ass, authority-allergic American teenage white boy, likely from a blue collar background in which a college deferment was not an option, and who enlisted for four years to avoid being drafted into the infantry for two. The Army trained Stanley to be an interrogator.

When I took command of the 1st Military Intelligence Team of the 11th Infantry Brigade, Stanley was already there in the interrogation unit. I had been trained as an infantry officer at Ft. Benning, then in a school for spooks in a compound near the Baltimore harbor. In the MI team, I ran the counter-intelligence unit, while interrogation was under the supervision of another lieutenant junior to me. The interrogation center was off site from our compound, so I seldom dealt directly with the interrogators, except after hours when all the team members filled our little club to drink beer over cards or ping pong.

I recall getting a whiff of Stanley's attitude a couple of times when he attempted to bait me in some childish test over authority. It was irritating, and I probably put him in his place. But I didn't spend a lot of time defending my military dignity. I detested the Army. Moreover I did not relish being officer-in-charge of anything, much less a team of fourteen American intelligence agents and as many South Vietnamese Army interpreters. In my mind I wasn't supposed to end up anywhere near the Infantry. It was a fluke. Like Stanley I had joined something bad to avoid something worse. But here we both were anyway on LZ Bronco with the 11th Infantry.

My section, CI, was out in the bush a lot, working the fringes of the Phoenix Program. But the interrogators had no business going on patrol. Stanley got restless I suppose. Said he didn't want to go home without having some small taste of the field. When the squad came back at dusk, I got the news. They'd made contact. In the fray, Stanley had been wounded, maybe a rocket from one of our own gunships, friendly fire. After a few days a couple of us flew down from Duc Pho to Qui Nhon to visit him at the evacuation hospital. The damage to some internal organs was serious, but he was expected to recover. Stanley was in good spirits, and he and I actually made real contact. I look back on that moment as redemptive. Two weeks later, the land line buzzed in my office tent when my colossal asshole boss up at Division called to tell me Stanley was dead.

That night Charlie pounded us relentlessly with mortars and rockets. The team huddled in the bunker to escape the shrapnel. Otherwise we were well protected from anything but a stray round, since the enemy's main target was the landing strip to our front. The news of Stanley's death had cast a spell of fatalism over all of us. No one felt safe that night. No one talked. No one played cards. Each individual was preoccupied with his private grief, his private thoughts. Who next among us might be disgraced by fortune? If Stanley could buy it, then why not me?

We who served in Vietnam and came home, stand before our Wall as survivors, and we are drawn inescapably into the world of our comrade spirits. Entering the aura of the dead, our faces melt in tears. It is not strange or exceptional to witness two aging men hugging each other, sobbing, shamelessly, inconsolably. They are still grieving the fate of a fallen brother, reliving the horrors of their war, crushed by the heaviness of the wound of survival they will carry to their graves. Me too. I have seldom wept as powerfully, as involuntarily, as profoundly intimately, exposing my most deeply buried existential sadness, as when I have stood before the Wall. In one sense, that's what it means to have beaten the odds.

Michael Uhl

I was born in 1944

I was born in 1944 and was of draft age during the Vietnam War. I opposed the war at its earliest stages based upon my religious beliefs. However, being a Catholic did not qualify me as a conscientious objector to the war. Since I was a top science student in college I instead was able to defer my induction through a series of student and marital deferments which lasted until the war's end. Not so fortunate were the mostly low income, minority boys who made up the draft pool in Bergen County, New Jersey.

This war profoundly affected me and the way in which I view my country. It opened my eyes to the warning President Eisenhower left office with about the threat posed by the military-industrial complex. It became the foundation upon which I judged the many military interventions that have occurred over my lifetime. What has followed this tragic war has been a never-ending series of equally tragic military blunders that have enriched the few: Halliburton, General Dynamics, Raytheon, Lockeed-Martin, Dow Chemical, etc.

I have worked since then to promote peace rather than war because it was the right thing to do. I no longer believe that peace has a chance. I have witnessed the unstoppable war machine that has become our principal method of foreign policy. What sickens me is the trail of the broken lives of some of our finest young men and women that have served as "ambassadors" of that foreign policy. If that were not terrible enough, I live with the dread of the millions of nameless civilians who have perished at our hands.

While I am convinced that our fragile democracy has been another casualty of letting corporations control our political process, I cannot stay silent about this latest attempt to whitewash the Vietnam War. The veterans of this war have my deepest appreciation for their efforts to keep this story from being manipulated. I hope that my statement can add to the many other voices for peace.

Sincerely,

Tom Mikulka

Dear: So many:

There are more than 58,000 of you on this Wall, "so many." I remember the first thoughts of building a memorial to Vietnam Vets and I am so grateful for Jan Scruggs and the many others who made it possible. I contributed cash but they made it happen, so that future generations could see the names of "so many."

It has been nearly 44 years since I first saw the hills around DaNang, since I saw the jungle at Chu Lai and the mud of the Mekong Delta. I was in the Navy, on the Westchester County LST 1167. To my knowledge I was a replacement for one of the crew who was killed by a sapper's mine the previous November 1, 1968. I didn't want to be there. I never wanted to be there, but I was so grateful to my Mother for making sure I was wearing Navy blue versus Army green, like so many of you.

My service was not yours. I was rarely in harm's way, sitting at the mouth of the Mekong River Delta providing support for huey gun ships and PBRs. I was close enough to hear the roar of the fighter jets, the endless rhythm of those damn helicopters and the gut wrenching thud of some far away bombing run. I was close enough to see the tracers, the sparkling trail of VC rockets, and the eerie motionlessness of flares. I was close enough to be a spectator but you all were there. "So many" of you were there. And yet it haunts me everyday.

I left the Navy after three years, nine months and eleven days, a number I will never forget. I went to college, got a job, got married and had children. I had a good life working in offices in and around Washington DC. Every Veteran's Day after The Wall was built, I would visit you all, look at the names of "so many" who I did not personally know but who I would cry out for and ask why. Why were you now just a name etched on a stone black wall, while I lived on? "So many," 58,000 etchings that seemed to go on and on and on. Why was I the lucky one to be left off the wall. Why was I the one who would continue to go to ball games, enjoy a beer, drive a little too fast with the radio turned way up, make love, be a dad and a husband and now a grand father. You the "so many" would never hear the call of GPA.

I tried in my own way to honor your life. When the second Bush administration chose to go to war with Iraq, I marched, I wore "no war" buttons. After years of war I helped organize a vigil in Asheville to remember those young people who were now joining you, the "so many." When I became a teacher, I would show the students my picture of the Wall with "so many" names. I would try to bring it home to them by showing them the list of you from North Carolina. I would bring it down to two of you, Ricky Propst and Ricky Lowder, who had learned in classrooms where they now learned, walked the halls where they now walked, played on the fields where they now played, lived in the community where they now were growing up and died before their time. There were always two or three of my students who would notice that Ricky Propst died on his birthday. They would also notice my voice would crack and a tear trailing down my cheek.

I tried, I still try to help to help get your message out that you were real, that you were young, that you had futures, that you were "so many" left behind. I worry now that the wall is becoming a memorial to the Vietnam War and not you all who are on it. I worry now that as we, the people who remember, age out, the people left behind, the people rewriting history, will think or promote Vietnam as an honorable endeavor. I worry now that people will misconstrue your honorable, brave service and your forever sacrifice with an honorable cause.

So I am now asking you, "so many," to come haunt the hearts and minds of the young today to stand up and say no. Say no to a life ended too soon; say no to "so many" with PTSD or TBI; say no to fighting an "enemy" more misunderstood than threatening; say no to their war profiteers. If we don't go, they can not war. So I am praying to you "so many" please come change the course of this country so that this time we can choose NOT to go, not to war.

With that just remember

You "so many" are never far from my mind and you are always in my heart.

May God Bless You and Keep You.

Jim Wohlgemuth

Dear Doug Rawlings
To Whom It May Concern,

Thank you for your work in Vietnam: The Power of Protest conference and your work for Veterans for Peace. I immigrated to the U.S. under political asylum with my mother and brother shortly after the fall of Saigon. After the war, my father, who was a captain in the Army of Republic of Viet Nam, working as a judge in the Ministry of Justice, had to report to a Vietcong reeducation camp where he was a prisoner for nine years. I first saw my father when I was nine years old because he was taken away when my mother was pregnant with me. My father came to the U.S. with severe PTSD and I grew up with that.

I have spent my entire life processing and healing from the American war in Vietnam. In the past few years, I have been writing poems which serve, to me, as a sort of letter to those lives lost in the war and the pain and suffering as a consequence of the war. I strive to gather my fractured pieces as a result of the war, as in kintsukuroi art where broken pieces of pottery are glued back together with gold, and mend myself, to feel some kind of wholeness which I have strived for throughout my life through compassion and through doing what I can to bring awareness of the effects of the war in Vietnam.

I am attaching my poems (also pasted below) which you are free to share. I would be honored if these poem-letters can be placed at the foot of the Wall in Washington, D.C. I wish I could be there with everyone, but I will be there in spirit.

With infinite gratitude…gratitude…These poems were written in memory of the American War in Vietnam. They also tell my family's and my own experiences as a consequence of the war. Hopefully, these poems reveal the devastation, still felt today, of the American war in Vietnam and the necessity for peace.

Best and warmest wishes,

Teresa Mei Chuc
hòa bình

Mekong River

Today's flowers let me inside
into their vase-shaped bodies
Today, I swim this river
with its fish and turtles
and crocodiles
and I know the river
does not need a name
There are no memories
of dead bodies floating
bloated, lonely
or of massacres
Today, I do not feel
the blood of the dead
seep through my skin's pores
as I swim this sacred
water of my childhood
my hair wet
The sun sparkles
around lush green
rain forests and jungles
unkilled by defoliants
stretching out their
70-million-year-old
arms as they yawn
a douc langur monkey
peers out from behind leaves
its orange hair another sun
Today is bright
and hot and tropical
the palm leaves sway
and people in their boats
with baskets of fruits
and vegetables
and talk float like a leaf
along with the current
A woman sits
at the end of a boat

full of freshly cut bananas
her knees to her chest
wooden paddle in
her hands
she steers and stirs
the river

Vietnam Ghost Stories

Ghost-like beings roam,
carrying the bones of the dead,
their steps heavy with the weight
of fields and fields.
And the dead too –
stories Mother tells
of the ghost with a long tongue
that licks dishes at night.

The Gambler
The metal rod she holds is her wand
the deck is more than 52 cards
her suits: bombs used on both sides of the war - M14, đạp
lôi, mìn muỗi
she walks in the wild fields seeking the invisible
bringing it to the surface in a strange beauty of smoke and
explosion
the wager is her life or a limb
the shovel, a tongue that lifts the crumbling earth
to reach an unexploded landmine
she spreads out the dirt beneath her hands like cards
the decade the rain forest died*

the deer did not
stop running
leopards
climbed into trees
that could not

hide them
the douc langur
and the white
cheeked gibbon
cursed at the
metal gods
we flew
raining
on them
as they burned
from napalm
elephants
choked on the
smoke of gunpowder
and poison
their steps
a strange
rhythm
as they tried
to fly
the thunder
of bombs echoed the steps
of elephants
tigers exploded
as they stepped
onto landmines
in a forest covered
with leaves
dead from
Agent Orange,
fallen trees and
decomposing
bodies of animals
and people
the earthworms
were washed away
in monsoons
with soil that could
no longer grab onto

roots
the Javan
rhinoceros
and the wild
water buffaloes
that were still
alive
wandered
aimlessly
and weary
with M16s
and AK-47s, we
marched quietly
and steadily
not knowing
why we were
killing each other

*For ten years, the U.S. Air Force flew nearly 20,000
herbicide spray missions in order to destroy the forest cover as
well as agriculture lands in key areas of southern Viet Nam.*

Jumping Jack: The M16 Mines

In standing position
with arms to the side,
jump while
spreading the legs
and lift arms
above the head.
Jump back into
standing position
and up again,
spreading the legs
and lifting the arms
above the head.
Repeat
When a M16 landmine
is triggered, it will
spring into the air
and explode with
a capacity to level
everything in a
150 metre radius.
Deadly shrapnel
spreading
a further 350 metres.
Metal casings
from an unexploded
bomb can fetch
25,000 Vietnamese dong
or $1
for a poor family
in Vietnam.
Men comb
the forests and beaches
of Quang Tri
looking for the metal
that will feed their family,
risking their lives.
Children working

in the fields think it's
a toy they've found.
Nguyen was hoeing
a small piece of land
his parents gave him
when an unexploded
U.S. military bomb
was triggered
and blew off both
his hands.

those commemorated on the wall

I was 15 when you brave young men and women started to be deployed to Vietnam, but I was 25 when some returned, you did not. It wasn't as you imagined, how could it be, especially this war, it was unimaginable to so many. I am so sorry for what you suffered, so very sorry. At 15, I didn't know much but I knew this, we should not go, that was clear to me and so many of those around me. We really did try to get them to see the error, marching, speaking in loud voices which could be heard, but we were not heard.

Ten years later some came back, you did not. Then when some came back, not you, they came back to a country without a soul, they were blamed for the terrible atrocities of this war, how could that be, they were doing what they were told to do. Then more of them ended the nightmares and severe depression by taking their own lives than all those that were killed in combat. That is what wars like this do to our minds, it degrades the extreme value of life.

That happened to them not you. No, many of you were taken at the start of your lives, maybe before you got a chance to really live, and then to die without your family at your bedside. I hope you made your family new during your ordeal, bonding with those who were in hell with you. I hope you died with them at your side. Nothing about this war was right, nothing was won or really accomplished, as if winning even matters. Love matters, that is what matters, and I hope before you died I hope you were loved.

Deb Cayer

CLOCKWORK:
With machine like regularity and precision (Or imprecision).

I was nowhere near combat while in the Army during The Vietnam War. I was, however, over in Thailand during 1969-70 with the 219th MP Co., 40th MP Bn., USARSUPTHAI. Part of the support troops in the rear. So, in indirect and direct ways I and my fellow military police provided support to the U.S. Air Force. They were stationed at a number of Royal Thai Air Force bases. Some of it was MP's escorting munitions convoys from the port at Satahip to ASP's (Ammunition Supply Points). I wasn't personally involved with these convoys; I did stuff like work shifts as a gate guard at the nearest ASP to Camp Friendship where I was stationed for most of my tour. And I worked shifts at the Main Gate into Camp Friendship with two other MP's and three Thai Guards.

Right next door to the Army camp was the Korat Royal Thai Air Force Base with plenty of U.S. Air Force planes. In short order I became aware that these jets were making bombing runs primarily over Vietnam; and also dropping some tons on the Ho Chi Minh Trail; and other bomb deliveries to Laos and Cambodia. This was like a clock-work deal. The jets flew seven days a week, night and day, month after month. It was the routine.

The days clicked by, the bombs continued to be delivered, and the war lingered on. Yeah, I found it to be disturbing. There were others I knew who had the same reaction. God, it was just these endless tonnages.

I just don't think I ever really got over it; such relentless delivery of death, with the certainty of "collateral damage." But as we used to say: "Fuck it. It don't mean nothing. That's what's so sweet about it." Yeah; the human waste, the material waste, the money burned up in one-way bombs. So there it is and there it was.

A CLOCKWORK ORANGE: "It is an old Cockney slang phrase, implying queerness or madness so extreme as to subvert nature." – Anthony Burgess

FOR THE DEAD WHO LIVE ON, ON THE WALL

First let me say that I am very glad to continue to be a living veteran of the Vietnam War. I didn't serve in Vietnam; I was stationed in Thailand. My Tour Of Duty was June 1969-August 1970. So, today as I reflect on being a survivor of the war, I recall being enmeshed in "THE GREEN MACHINE". I was entangled, involved in, caught in, and ensnared.

I believe that my military duty caused me to receive a moral injury. Before being drafted and inducted, I was already against the war. I went in the Army because I couldn't seem to flee the United States, nor openly refuse induction. Perhaps I believed dumb luck would keep me safe; or I even might not be sent to Vietnam. Then off to Thailand I was sent.

So, I believe that war is always a crime. A fellow named Jonathan Shay introduced the moral injury concept as "an injury to an individual's moral conscience." As if becoming an anguished soul not necessarily experiencing a psychological disorder.

What can I say now? Maybe all I can do is continue to judge myself with some mercy, compassion. With gratitude that I've made it this far and have had a life after my own experiences as a support trooper during the Vietnam War.

I can't bring back the dead, nor live with hatred for those who perpetrated an unnecessary war that inflicted so much pain and suffering on so many. Perhaps, by my own humanity, I will always believe the Vietnam War was wrong; that it truly did subvert nature.

Robert L. Schlosser
Seattle, Washington
28 March 2015

I am a veteran of the anti-war movement

I am a veteran of the anti-war movement, not a military veteran.

As I reflected on the privilege and circumstances that kept me physically safe during the war and emotionally protected from personal loss, I remembered the death of my across-the-street neighbor in Indianapolis. His name was Brian John Devaney. He was a Canadian citizen who served as a Chief Warrant Officer in the Army Reserve and died in a helicopter crash in Laos at the age of 24. He was a month older than I was, but we never knew each other well. He was Catholic and went to parochial schools; I was Jewish and went to public school. Our families were dissimilar, but united in our difference from the majority environment of our community. Brian was athletic and cheerful, and his family was spirited and kind.

I was shocked when I heard of his death, and to my shame I don't remember if I wrote or visited his parents and siblings in their grief. I do remember thinking that he was Canadian, and surely didn't have to die in a war perpetrated by the US which I believed senseless.

I didn't know at that time that he perished as part of the "secret war" in Laos, and I don't know when that information was revealed. In a better world the neighborhood would have united to embrace and comfort his family (and I hope that some neighbors did), and would have joined together to prevent any more violent deaths in Vietnam or Southeast Asia.

In the last 15 years, I have had the incredible good fortune of visiting Vietnam many times to work on repairing war legacies. The welcome and caring I have received in Vietnam have humbled me greatly and helped me understand the importance of trying to make some small contribution rather than indulging in guilt.

I don't know what Brian believed or felt during his 18 months in-country, or whether his perceptions changed during that time. I do know that, thanks to this Veterans For Peace initiative and the encouragement to take responsibility for what we know and we have learned, I will not bury him again in my memory. As the best memorial to him and all the others lost on all sides, I will continue to work in friendship with Vietnam and towards social justice in US policies and practices.

Trude Bennett
Durham, North Carolina

As a citizen in support of the Full Disclosure project

As a citizen in support of the Full Disclosure project, I have personal stories to share.

Active participation in CALCAV (Clergy and Laity Concerned About Vietnam) was one of the activities that brought my late husband, Francis, and me together in 1968. (Then, as a married couple having left the clergy, we were so sensitized against war, that we became conscientious war tax objectors in the early 80's.) So when the opportunity arose to tour Vietnam, we immediately signed up. It was called a "Friendship Tour for building global community through cultural understanding."

This three week tour, however, was not a conventional one – not specifically because it was led by Tom Fox; editor of National Catholic Reporter (NCR) but because our guide, Tom, had volunteered as a civilian to work with war-displaced refugees immediately after college graduation. International Volunteer Services had flown him to Saigon for a month of intensive Vietnamese training, after which he had been sent to a camp in Tuy Hoa. He was a 22 year old, in the middle of a war. It was 1966. All at once, he was a Saigon-based journalist, a correspondent for NCR, and a stringer for TIME magazine and The New York Times.

It is difficult to refrain from saying more about Tom Fox, for example, how he had survived Vietcong shelling during the Tet offensive by lying low on a hotel roof in Tuy Hoa, and how he had met and married, Kim Hoa, a Can Tho, Mekong Deltborn social worker with the Committee for Responsibility. (The committee transported seriously war-injured Vietnamese children to the United States for treatment unobtainable in Vietnam.) Readers can learn more from NCR archives here: http://natcath.org/NCR_Online/archives2/2005a/ 012105/012105h.php This link includes a photo of the young couple, Kim Hoa and Thomas C. Fox in 1971: http://www.twhalloran.info/ page67.html

The presence among us of two Vietnam Veterans, Tom McNamara and Sam Luna, also gave our tour a singular flavor.

I took extensive notes, some written reports, and many photos during those three weeks. Once returned to Portland, I gave a one hour slide presentation to the Audubon Society's Travel Club. To share my most memorable stories from our Friendship Tour of Vietnam, now, I'm using excerpts from those notes.

Tom McNamara, a former Catholic chaplain in the Army, came to see how things were 30 years later. To Sam Luna, the tour was cathartic. He was able to talk to Vietnamese veterans of the war and achieve a sort of closure. In fact, Sam fulfilled what he said at the end of our tour about planning to share his experience through writing, and "to help vets experience some of the peace I have been blessed to experience."

He founded "Vet Journey Home." www. vetsjourneyhome.org/ and was honored for it along with 11 other veterans on May 24, 2012 by Secretary of Labor, Hilda L. Sollis. He was cited as one of the White House Office of Public Engagement's "Champions of Change" – "for his extraordinary efforts to end veterans' homelessness, boost veterans' employment, address problems with substance abuse and develop treatment programs for those dealing with post-traumatic stress disorder.

Vets' Journey Home Texas Inc. is a nonprofit organization that provides a free weekend retreat to veterans and active duty military personnel. The weekend is a safe place where participants can learn about what their war experience did to their bodies. http://www.dol.gov/opa/media/press/opa/opa20121067.htm

I didn't need the presence of Tom and Sam among us to experience grief of my own while touring the country our government had ordered bombed, thirty plus years earlier. Francis' and my objections to that war went deep. Only months before our wedding in 1972, having written an MA thesis on the Just War Theory versus Ghandian non-violence, I had represented the Catholic Church on a panel discussion about the war. It was aired by a TV channel in Portland, Maine. On his part, Francis, when still a priest in the mid-60's, had stood at court before Judge Gignoux in support of two young men. They then became the first Catholics in Maine to be given CO status exempting them from participation in the war.

So it was not surprising that tears spontaneously welled up in me several times while talking with some Vietnamese people. I made note of four instances: While talking with Huong, our guide, during breakfast at Cat Ba Island, after a memorable boat ride through Halong Bay. She mentioned the 1964 and 1972 US bombings of a 1902 bridge, but added that it had since been rebuilt for bicycles and trains. (We travelers had many occasion to appreciate the ingenuity of the Vietnamese people: they made use of the bomb craters to keep and harvest fish.)

A second one occurred during a conversation with two young clerks at a bank in Saigon where Francis and I had gone to get cash. One young man's face softened when he saw my concern. "Many died," he said. But a young woman said she blamed governments, not the US people. "Like in Iraq too," she explained. By then, all the tellers were caught up in our conversation. "The whole bank is engaged with us!" Francis whispered to me. Before we left someone took a photo of the two clerks, one on either side of me.

Francis' and my visit to the "War Remnants Museum" (like my whole trip to Vietnam, actually) was unforgettable. http://www.travel-fish.org/sight_profile/vietnam/saigon_and_surrounds/ho_chi_minh_-city/ho_chi_minh_city/619

I lingered in a few parts of it, especially the "Historical Truths," namely, the photographers' section, and the Children's Paintings on War and Peace section.

I took two photos that tell a story. One is a 3-4 foot statue of a mother bearing a deformed child with her hands covering her face. The other is a large children's painting releasing doves of peace into the heavens.

"They represent for me," I wrote "the light and dark of my own experience in Vietnam, first sorrow at the suffering we heaped upon the Vietnamese. And then, gratitude. The children's art represents for me the attitude of the Vietnamese who recognize the sad past is over now, and we Americans are their allies in helping their rehabilitation."

In fact, our Mekong River guide, Trang, sounded the same note after I engaged her in conversation. She told me that her father had been a nurse during the Vietnam War. Her family had to live in the cellar at that time, she said. She also explained that five people had to sleep in one bed but that a sniper's bullets came through and killed all five people. Then she assured me: "That's a sad story, but it's past now."

The most moving exchange I had, however, happened when I bought Graham Greene's The Quiet American from a man without hands. His open face and sense of dignity moved me so deeply, I reacted to take his stump of a hand to shake it. He offered it to me twice. He received my expression of regret for the Vietnam War – which they rightly call The American War – with such warmth and dignity, I felt ennobled.

One day we visited a special hospital for handicapped children. Tom had told us that the authorities were not eager for us to visit this Medical College, but that he had made way for us to go anyway. We walked up several flights in an old hospital building and gathered around a long rectangular table. Dr. Nguyen Viet Nhan, MD, PhD a slight middle aged man with an open, kind face welcomed us warmly. We sat riveted to hear his story.

He told us about his work in his Hue Medical College which (I believe) he founded to help poor children who suffer from various disabilities allegedly caused by Agent Orange or resulting from birth defects due to Agent Orange. Such disabilities, Dr. Nhan told us, sky-rocketed after the Vietnam War. Dr. Nhan works here as a volunteer in addition to his other regular job as a Chief of the Department of Medical Genetics. His "Office of Genetic Counseling and (for) Disabled Children," (OGCDC) helps poor patients who suffer from brain tumors, heart and eye problems hydrocephaly, cleft lip and palate, Meningitis, Septicemia, blindness and physical deformities of all kinds. To prevent further devastating suffering, Dr. Nhan emphasized the need for surgery as early in the victim's life as possible.

While he talked a young woman, perhaps in her early 20's, came in and gave him papers, perhaps copies of his Newsletter which he distributed. With our permission, she also took a photo of us for a souvenir. Tom had told us ahead of time not to give money while there but encouraged us when we returned home to donate over the web if we were so moved. I did. Their web address is still up and active: www.ogcdc.org.

Only days before the end of our three week tour, Tom had a treat in store for us. An octogenarian, Vietnamese scholar, a friend of his and Hoa would be giving us a lecture on the history of Saigon. Hoa was our interpreter. We sat in the garden eager to hear the professor.

He talked in detail about the history of Saigon, how originally there had been a wall to protect the city. But with a civil war, the French rebuilt a smaller city which made it easier for them to occupy. He said the French destroyed community villages in Saigon and remodeled the area as a French city in Europe. He then described how the city grew. . . .

I could include all the information in my notes here. They're details I only vaguely remembered, but for the notes. And I could share them with anyone who's interested. But what I did not forget, and want to relate now, is the following: During the question and answer period, Sam inquired whether or not any good had come from the Vietnam War. The professor did not hesitate. "No," he said. I saw and heard the anguish in Sam's voice when he pressed, asking again, "Nothing?" "No," affirmed the Professor. But then he paused, smiled, and added – "Well, maybe the marriage between Hoa and Tom."

I have too many stories to share. I would like to say much more about that Mekong River boat ride, and our overnight stay at the Bha Hung family's deltstyle compound. For accommodations, we slept in a bamboo house on stilts over the river. . . .

I would love to tell the story what happened during our private boat tour of Halong Bay, a World Natural Heritage. And there is so much more to say about the Vietnamese people. It's their open, eager faces, more than any thing or place, I'll never forget. Their graciousness was instinctive. They are passionate to learn English. In both Hoi An and in Saigon, I found myself repeating for two young women the correct pronunciation of words to which they pointed in their dictionaries.

When I prepared to give the slide show presentation of our tour of Vietnam, I made time to delve a little in the fascinating history and their culture, for example, not just the varied influences that shaped this unique, beautiful country – such as Confucianism and Buddhism, but also, for example – Caodaism whose temple we visited. This religion is an excellent example of Vietnam's religious syncretism.

Visiting the CHAM Museum in central Vietnam was another high point for me. Cham art, influenced by Hindu art, is also similar to An-kor Wat.

For this Audubon talk, Francis wore a handsome silk shirt I had bought for him in Saigon, and I wore a custom made dress.

I've saved a sweet story for last. (And all this was written then, in 2006):

"Picture me, an American woman being led across the suicidal streets of Saigon, each hand held by a child's hand. Small for their age, Hung is a 10 year old girl, and Long, an 11 year old boy. Our mission? I had agreed when asked, "Will you buy me some milk?" My heart swelled with joy and pride as we crossed two streets to reach a large department store. Wondering where the lunch counter was, I was taken aback when Hung stopped at an unlikely counter and pointed to a large cylindrical container of powdered "Ensure". "$20.00," the clerk asserted. Simultaneously stunned by the whole surprise and price, but equally shocked at what this meant – especially when Hung explained this would last one month in her family, to which Long added it would last even longer in his since he didn't have as many siblings as she, I eagerly handed over my credit card to buy a carton for each of them.

We then returned to their spot on the sidewalk where Hung sells postcards to tourists, and Long, his mother's cards hand painted on silk attached to glazed paper. When we hugged goodbye, Long reached higher and kissed me on the cheek. That kiss is seared there forever."

Elaine McGillicuddy
March 7, 2015

PS: The photo Francis took of me standing between Hung and Lang in front of the Continental Hotel in Saigon is on page 163 of my second book, SING TO ME AND I WILL HEAR YOU – A Love Story. Seven pages in that book (including two other photos) are devoted to the remarkable tour of Vietnam Tom Fox led for us. Its memory will never leave me.

I urge any and all – and especially Vietnam Veterans – to look up Thomas C Fox – Vietnam Tours. He began writing for the National Catholic Reporter almost, or virtually, at its founding, in 1964. Then Tom became its editor for many years, and is now publisher of NCR. But he is still, also, leading his friendship Tours to Vietnam. Look here:

http://ncronline.org/tour-vietnam-ncrs-tom-fox

As the war in Vietnam began

2 March 2015

Response to the War in Vietnam

As the war in Vietnam began I was a student at the University of Illinois in Champaign/Urbana. Having grown up in a Chicago suburb I was on one hand an upper middle-class kid for whom politics were not at all important. On the other hand my high school was one of very few racially integrated suburban schools and that, plus a few years working at a local establishment restaurant with a multi-racial staff, had made me increasingly aware of the complexity of American politics. I listened to Studs Terkel on late night radio, sang along with Joan Baez as her folk songs eased from our living room speakers.

At Illinois I learned Dylan songs, increased my exposure to racial and other politics through roommates who were, sequentially, Jewish, German, Iranian, African-American, and Japanese/Hawaiian. The seventy males in my housing unit came from twenty-six nations. When the teach-ins about the Vietnam War began in 1964 I attended them for the same reasons I attended large folk singing concerts: they spoke to my increasing concerns about American politics.

Nothing, however, prepared me for the international condemnation of the U.S. that I encountered when I began a year's study at the Universität Tübingen in West Germany. When a massive march protesting the war moved through the center of the city I watched carefully, stunned by the realization that these Europeans did not regard our political action in Southeast Asia to be either justified or wise. I had assumed the Vietnam War was our problem. It was not. The information provided on handouts and by speakers revealed more fully to me the dangers and the unjust nature of the war itself, the methods the U.S. was using to fight it, and the mechanisms for recruiting soldiers that fueled our actions.

I returned to the U.S. one year later, continued my education at Duke University (exempted from the draft as a husband and then as a father), began working as a civil rights activist and as an opponent of the war. I have carried these values with me ever since. My first trip to the Vietnam Memorial, where I saw the subtle power of Maya Lin's design as I descended into the darkness at the foot of the wall, brought me closer to all those who died in that conflict: Americans, Vietnamese, and many others. The experience deepened my grief and my respect.

I have returned several times since.

I prefer to state my positions in a positive rather than a negative fashion. I value peace and wish that our nation could and would foster peaceful, diplomatic solutions to local, national, and international conflicts.

Much of my work in the past thirty years has been in China, serving as an unofficial ambassador between our two countries, teaching, lecturing, assisting artists and writers who envision a world without war. I admire and strongly support the values and the accomplishments of Veterans for Peace. I pay tribute here to those who died in the Vietnam conflict and to those who wish to insure that we retain an honest and accurate vision of that war.

In solidarity,

John Rosenwald
Farmington, Maine

On July 18, 1968

Memorial Day 2015

Full Disclosure Project Letter

Veterans For Peace

On July 18, 1968 at grid square YD 385 157 in Quang Tri Province, Republic of Vietnam, I dug up the grave of a North Vietnamese soldier.

I was, on that day, running the point element of a patrol of the First Cavalry Division which was then operating in the mountains of western South Vietnam. After hours of heat, leeches and wait-a-minute vines, I walked the patrol into a concealed bunker complex. It was unoccupied.

Consisting of a broad oval of bunkers and fighting positions, it centered on a large meeting area, covered in thatch. Some distance away was what looked like a grave: six feet of mounded earth and at one end a flattened sheet of metal, probably from an ammunition crate. Holes punched into the soft metal spelled out something in Vietnamese, someone's name. This was reported to battalion headquarters and we were ordered to confirm the grave: dig it up.

It did not occur to me to disobey this order which was relayed to me by the company commander with something of a wry smile. I gave this repulsive mission to one of the squad leaders but soon pitched in to help. The shallowly buried man was wrapped in a thin sheet of black plastic and dressed in dark green fatigues. After weeks in the ground he was the consistency of cold, left over stew. Since his belt buckle was a fancy variation of NVA issue we established his rank as "Gook NCO". And that is what I reported to the company commander. I didn't have to tell him the body was badly decomposed; he could smell that.

Dig 'em up orders: the radio logs of our battalion (Second of the Fifth) and briefly that of another battalion show that 8 graves containing 18 bodies of North Vietnamese soldiers were opened during the period of July 1 to September 19 in 1968. I do not know if this practice was standard throughout the division (or throughout the Army) but given the reverent attention to body count during the war in Vietnam, I suppose it was. Nor do I know how long this practice was followed but on the apparent principle that body count trumps desecration, for that is what it was, I would guess that it was a long-term standing order.

No one bothered to write down the name that was punched into the metal sheet at the head of the grave I helped to dig up. I suppose there are people still alive in Vietnam who would like to know that name but it is not recorded in the radio log.

That man's grave remains vivid in my memory but over time that memory has been overborne by a desolate realization. These mandatory desecrations of soldier's graves reveal what the U.S. Army truly thought of its Infantry: expendable, 120 dollar a month privates, fit to endure any hazard, any degree of protracted misery, and any task however polluting and soul-corroding.

February 26, 2015
Dr. Jon Oplinger, Farmington, ME

Do I love you?

The Wall

Do I love you? YOU BET.
Do I think the war was worth it ? HELL NO.
Am I angry? HELL YES.
When I heard that a black granite wall was being constructed in Washington, D.C. to memorialize those who sacrificed the most during the Vietnam War, I felt nothing but anger. If anything, I felt that the memorial fund should have been used to put the lying war profiteers behind bars for the rest of their lives. Why shouldn't THEY, who start the wars, be punished? There will always be war as long as THEY are allowed to get away with it?

IF WE DON'T END THE MADNESS OF WAR, THE MADNESS OF WAR WILL END US ALL.

Sincerely,

Mark Foreman
US Navy Corpsman/3rd Battalion,
5th Marines, Vietnam 1968
Lifetime Member of Veterans For Peace

This letter, posted at The Wall

Vietnam Veterans Memorial
The Mall
Washington, DC

This letter, posted at The Wall on Memorial Day, 2015 . . .
. . . is framed in remembrance and respect for the two friends
I knew best whose names are inscribed on this black granite
memorial: Frederick Richard Ohler and Robert Randolph White,
both killed in 1968 when all three of us were serving in the U.S.
Army in Vietnam. I was the one who came home.

I share these thoughts with all the rest of us who survive
today – those who fought in a war that nobody wanted, which
few try to justify any more; and those who protested and helped
end a tragic policy that took the lies of 58,000 other young
Americans, and more than three million Vietnamese. Many of us
fought and, later, protested also.

Rick and Bob, I remember the 1968 Tet Offensive, when
your names were added to the list of American casualties, in
April. And I remember that day seven years later, in April, 1975
when the war ended as the tank crashed through the gates of the
presidential palace in Saigon. Amid a swirl of conflicting
emotions, that day for me was unforgettable because of a clear
hope that rose from the depths of my being: a new unshakable
confidence that welled up from all that sadness and loss, that
America had learned our lesson, that we would never embark
again on such a misbegotten foreign venture, that we would never
make such a tragic mistake, ever again. That lesson learned, for
me, helped to make the pain of your loss, and the suffering of
millions of others, somehow more bearable. I think that may have
been true for others who had survived.

Now, as your names and the polished stone reflect back at
us, the survivors – a steady stream of family, friends, sympathetic
visitors sharing more than three decades of loss and remembrance
since the Memorial was dedicated in 1982 – please know that we
continue our efforts, however feeble and inadequate, to learn and
apply the lessons of your sacrifice. Forgive our failures, but know

that we are trying, in so many ways, to mark and honor your untimely departure and to atone for the suffering, to help heal those who lost so much – Americans, Vietnamese especially, and people of goodwill around the world who labored mightily to stop the madness of that war.

Know that we continue to try, as futile as the endeavor may seem, to bring America back home and to restore the soul of our nation. Since you died in 1968, our government has wandered the globe in search of a false security built on military conquest and economic domination, when Americans have known, deep in our hearts, that we should be seeking peace.

Today, four decades after the U.S. war in Vietnam ended, believe me when I say that we will continue this quest, to rightly assume responsibility for the devastation we have left in America's wake in Vietnam – tons of unexploded bombs, and the toxic poison of Agent Orange. We pledge to continue our efforts, though shamefully inadequate, to help heal Vietnam. And to sustain American veterans and their families who are still suffering the consequences of that war.

Rest in peace, my friends. Look over us and our frail efforts, comfort us with the knowledge that your spirits guide us, and help us persevere as we strive to make your ultimate sacrifice a loss that was not in vain.

CHUCK SEARCY
U.S. Army SP5
519th MI Battalion
Vietnam June 1967-68

2015 will be the year of a special anniversary

2015 will be the year of a special anniversary for the United States and for me. It will be the fiftieth year since the beginning of our big military buildup in Viet Nam and since my service there with the 173rd Airborne. If our nation appears to be mired in endless foreign fiascos it is probably because we failed to remember the lessons of our criminal activities from fifty years ago.

One of our first confirmed kills in Viet Nam was a 12 year old Buddhist monk. Our artillery was firing near a village and one round was fired with the wrong data. We didn't use the term "collateral damage" back then but PR was still a concern. Our unit got a lecture on the desirability of performing our mission with quiet efficiency, as if killing people with artillery could ever be done quietly and efficiently enough to escape the notice of those being killed.

Before the US finally withdrew from Viet Nam it instigated the Phoenix program. A policy of torture and assassination that failed then but nevertheless was transferred to Guantanamo and Iraq and probably to wherever the US has the power to flout the standards of human decency. Obama's failure to prosecute the torturers is probably a good indication that it will continue.

As a combat veteran I have memories and perhaps a few remnants of damage from the stress of warfare. I sympathize with my fellow veterans who have PTSD but I never forget one thing from my service. I inflicted more stress than I suffered. We dropped 8 million tons of bombs on a nation smaller than California.

My wife and I went back to Viet Nam in 2006. This time I was delivering tourist dollars instead of explosives. My reception was remarkably kinder than the one I received in 1965. The lesson is pretty clear. It's time to punish the torturers and ground the drones. The US will never succeed in building our security on the bloody shreds of wedding parties, on the remains of shattered families, on the graves of children.

So on this fiftieth anniversary year I calculate that the 12 year old Buddhist would be 62 years old. Perhaps he would be a wise old man, a blessing to his village, but we'll never know. His voice was silenced but we can commemorate his death by being honest witnesses. By being voices for peace.

Sincerely,

Robert Tammen

None of us can quite get it right

Dear brothers and sisters:

None of us can quite get it right. We keep trying to figure out what our relationship to you should look like. Psychologists, sociologists, historians, poets, painters, musicians, sculptors have all thrown their hats into this ring of fire. It may be impossible. But we keep trying. For your sake. For ours. Along the way, we put you into the hands of a brilliant young student, Maya Lin, to build us a wall. She has come the closest. Along the way, some have wrestled with concepts like "survivor's guilt," "PTSD," "moral injury" to seek some clarity if not solace. They come close, too. You see, we care about you. We want to keep you in the conversation. We want you to know that we still think you can offer us a great deal.

Personally, I wonder this: did any of you cross paths with me from July of 1969 to August of 1970? Up in II Corps, up in the Central Highlands, down by the Bong Son River. Do you remember? I went one way, you the other. I survived, you didn't.

Along the way over these years, along the way, I wrote this for you:

THE WALL

Descending into this declivity
dug into our nation's capital
by the cloven hoof
of yet another one of our country's
tropical wars

Slipping past the names of those
whose wounds
refuse to heal

Slipping past the panel where
my name would have been
could have been
perhaps should have been

Down to The Wall's greatest depth
where the beginning meets the end
I kneel

Staring through my own reflection
beyond the names of those
who died so young

Knowing now that The Wall
has finally found me –
58,000 thousand-yard stares
have fixed on me
as if I were their Pole Star
as if I could guide their mute testimony
back into the world
as if I could connect all those dots
in the nighttime sky

As if I
could tell them
the reason why

—

So, okay, you would have thought that the grief from your loss and the many Southeast Asian lives lost would have compelled us to put an end to war. That we would no longer send young men and women into ill-begotten conflicts to appease the blood thirst of some self-appointed armchair avengers bent on protecting their warped version of the American way of life. You would have thought.

I'll spare you the details of wars mounted in our name since you left us. Trust me, though, that some of us have worked to stop them. We work to protect our children and grandchildren, to protect families we will never meet in lands far from here, to use your deaths as a means to say "no more." We have formed Veterans For Peace, partly in your memory, with the very lofty ambition of abolishing war. We oftentimes work in your name, for you. I'll admit that many times we feel like we are howling alone in the wilderness, but we will not desist. We owe that to you.

I'll be back, again and again, to walk alongside you for a short while. I will listen for your voices. I will touch your names and force myself to swing back through these many years and put myself in the place and time where and when we may have met. I promise you that I will take this opportunity to meld our spirits together, knowing that I grow stronger, in the doing so. And I will use that strength to abolish future wars. To stop the killing of innocents. In your name. That's the least I owe you. And the most.

Rest in peace.

Your brother,
Doug Rawlings

After 49 years . . .

A Letter To The Wall By John Grant

This Can't Be Happening

NOTE: I'm a member of a group of Vietnam veterans affiliated with Veterans For Peace called the Vietnam War Full Disclosure project. We would like to see a more historically accurate representation of the Vietnam War as presented by the Pentagon in its 50 Year Commemoration of the war, which is scheduled to begin with the 50th anniversary of the March 1965 Marine landing at DaNang. The government wants to commemorate the war as about "the defense of our nation's freedom," whereas Full Disclosure sees the anniversary as an opportunity for a national dialogue. The Vietnamese did nothing to us that required an invasion and occupation; all they wanted was independence from, first, the French, then from the United States. This is not a unique struggle for us in this country. The new government in Japan is becoming more militaristic and is suddenly making an effort to quash generally accepted historical accounts concerning imperial Japan's policies in the 1940s with the so-called "comfort women" in Korea and China. The Dutch a few years back went through a national dialogue concerning their brutal military occupation in Indonesia. As part of its mission, Full Disclosure has launched a Letter To The Wall campaign. Below, is my letter to the Vietnam Veterans' Memorial; it's an effort to see my service for what it was. The letters will be gathered and placed at the Vietnam War Memorial on Memorial Day 2015. For more information, go to the Full Disclosure website.

Dear Vietnam Veterans' Memorial Wall:

You're a wide granite gash in the earth, like the war itself, a man-made construction set within the order of nature. As I look back 49 years, I understand the war was a much more rude and shameful event than the grace of your shape in the earth might suggest. But you're what you are and where you are to recognize sacrifice divorced of politics. Speaking to you is speaking to the dead, and like a good hospice caregiver must do, one first needs to respect the dying and the dead. Addressing you is different than addressing the flag. Your dead were all part of a massive historic enterprise; but the simple fact at the root of all religion is we die alone and the ultimate providence of those named on your surface remains an eternal mystery.

I was in Vietnam as a 19-year-old kid. I joined the Army and became a radio direction finder in the Army Security Agency. Once trained in DF principles and practiced in Morse code, I volunteered to go to Vietnam, as did my older brother, a lieutenant in the Army infantry. I went with a company by troop ship from Oakland; it took 17 days and the ship anchored off the shore of Qui Nhon. In the morning, the entire company was loaded onto a large LCU, which chugged toward the beach. I'd watched John Wayne hit the beach at Iwo Jima, and I had no idea what to expect. They'd given us a clip of 7.62mm ammunition for the wooden stocked M14s we had been issued.

The LCU hit the beach with a long WHOOOOOSH. The high bow plate was slowly lowered, and we saw men in bathing suits sun-bathing and several blue air-conditioned buses with steel grates over the windows to take us to the Qui Nhon airbase, where they would load us onto a C-130 for a flight to Pleiku. I recall two things about the trip to the airbase. One, the teeming movement of people and poverty I had never seen before. The heat was no issue, since I'd been raised in south Florida above the Keys. The other thing I recall was looking out the window and when the bus stopped for traffic noticing a young kid, maybe ten, out the window. He seemed older than his age. When he saw me, he flipped me the bird.

Our company ended up attached to the 25th Infantry Division based in Pleiku. In an odd coincident, the second day I was in Vietnam, the 25th Division flew my brother back from an operation out by the Cambodian border; I hadn't seen him in two years. I was soon sent with seven other direction finders to firebases in the same area as my brother, all part of Operation Paul Revere. We were three teams of two, given jeeps equipped with PRD1 DF radios that we had used to learn DF principles at

Fort Devon, Massachusetts. We had been told the PRD1 was an obsolete WWII piece of equipment. When not using the jeeps, our teams were dispersed in the woods in armored personnel carriers or by helicopters. We envisioned ourselves romantically as foul balls sent to the boonies from the main company — a squad of rogues. We were kids and part of a huge army, and we felt we were special.

Our job was to spread out and locate tactical enemy radios, which amounted to a Vietnamese radio operator sending five letter coded groups of Morse code with a leg key along with a comrade working a bicycle generator. If we were lucky enough in the incredible mountainous terrain to get a tight fix from three bearings, we'd pass it on to division intelligence, who would process the coordinates and send out Air Force F4s, an artillery barrage or a unit of infantry. The Vietnamese knew we were looking for them, so the radio operators did their transmitting away from their dug-in headquarters. Over time, locating the same operator every day for a month, a pattern would become evident. We located them; others did their best to kill them.

We were REMFs — rear echelon mother-fuckers. On one operation, when my team partner and I were dropped by chopper onto a huge rock atop a mountain overlooking the border, I felt I was really out there. The half-squad of "grunts" also dropped onto the rock looked at the job of protecting these two REMFs as vacation duty from the normal task of humping the boonies.

After a year of this, I made it home without a scratch and without a bit of trauma. As I look back, considering all the names on your shiny black granite surface and what my brother and other combat veterans went through, in the spirit of confession, I have to say sometimes I feel unworthy to be called a "Vietnam veteran." Of course, I know that's not true, and I am a Vietnam veteran. I led a charmed existence with violence and horror going on all around me that never touched me. I know friends who suffered terribly. I've met vets who did horrible things and suffer for it. A friend earned a silver star for an act of incredible bravery. I'm friends with an African American veteran of the Battle of the Ia Drang Valley serving a life-without-parole sentence for a 1975 act of violence clearly rooted in PTSD. A federal judge ruled his conviction for First Degree Murder was a "miscarriage of justice" when what he was guilty of was manslaughter. The district judge was overruled, and Pennsylvania political leaders don't have the courage to address such an injustice. For some reason I remember a captain commanding an infantry company I spent time with. This CO was respected, even loved; he seemed like an ordinary man in an extraordinary situation. One of the grunts told me how the captain had crawled out under fire to save one of his men, only to find him dead — and how they had later found the man in tears embracing the dead man.

I'm a Vietnam veteran with survival guilt. It's my lasting bond to the names on your reflecting surface. Oddly, I do not know any of the 58,000 people attached to those names.

At a firebase I was at, the lieutenant colonel in charge of the battalion dropped leaflets daring the NVA to attack his firebase. He had mines dug in all around the camp. An NVA push was moving through the area. A guy on the perimeter let me look through his night scope, and you could see them as moving white shapes. I was pretty scared and got all my magazines lined up for a big attack. When the NVA decided to pass us by, the colonel ordered all the mines removed. One of the young privates assigned to that job blew himself to pieces just outside the perimeter near my little bunker. I watched a chaplain's detail pick him up in pieces and put him on a stretcher. I don't know his name, but I presume it's on your granite surface, even if his death was caused by his own team.

The closest I got to knowing a name on your wall was when, back in base camp, someone radioed me from the field that my brother had been killed. Friends fed me warm beers as I eulogized him; his wife had just had a baby. I was going to escort the body home. Four hours later, the Red Cross called to tell me it was another Lieutenant Grant. He was posthumously awarded the Congressional Medal of Honor. My brother became a lawyer.

Writing to you like this turns my mind to inglorious things. So I should tell you about base camp life and the whoring in Pleiku bars. Later, when the 25th moved north and we were attached to the 4th Division, a little constructed village of bordello/bars was set up outside the wire of 4th Division headquarters. Girls as young as fifteen worked there and were inspected regularly by division medics to avoid any down-time due to the clap. I was young, and at times the trysts with these girls felt innocent, even sweet. But now I know different; now I understand the erotic masculine power of being part of a massive imperial Army in a poor place like Vietnam. "The Tale of Thuy Kieu by Nguyen Du was published in 1820 and is considered the national epic poem of Vietnam; it is about a young woman who, in order to save her family, works as a prostitute — before she goes on to become a guerrilla fighter. It was not only REMFs; whoring was an epidemic in Vietnam, literally and metaphorically. Sometimes sexual tension was expressed in terribly abusive fashion, like the time a drunken infantry staff sergeant shot up a laundry/bar outside Pleiku and wounded one of the girls. Sometimes in the field, the mixture of this tension with fear and adrenaline led to violent rape. I sometimes see myself and my comrades in Vietnam as the worst kind of cliché American tourists in the world. Instead of cameras, we had guns.

As I imagine your long gash in the earth with all those names etched into your stone, I think of how I read Graham Greene's famous little novel The Quiet American when I was in high school. Besides my gung-ho militarist father, more than anything, I think Greene's vision of a sexy colonial world seduced me to want to go to Vietnam. It was a desire to "see the world," like the recruitment posters used to say. I had nothing against the Vietnamese, north or south. My ignorance was complete. I didn't want to kill anyone; what I wanted was to see an exotic place and meet people different than myself. I really think this was the case. The fact the huge historical enterprise you memorialize ended up consuming 58,000 American lives, several million Vietnamese lives and destroying much of Vietnam is, for me, the major tragedy of my time.

And I was there. I was a part of it.

In 2002, I visited Vietnam twice and made an 82-minute film about a wounded US Marine veteran living and working there. The experience was as powerful as my first trip. I now realize the film is really about what can only be called my love affair with Vietnam. Some psychiatrists will tell you love relationships are really complicated love/hate relationships. Given the history of US/Vietnam relations going back to fighting the Japanese with our Vietminh allies during World War Two, I think this is the case with America and Vietnam. The Vietnamese loved us in 1945, but something went terribly wrong.

As I consider your elegant simplicity and the great suffering you represent, I realize now, 49 years after my first connection with Vietnam, that I'm committed to the love side of that complex state of mind and heart. In a better world, the war would never have happened. Maybe I would have gone somewhere else in the world and done something I felt better about.

And you would not exist.

John Grant
Vietnam, August 1966 to August 1967

To All Vietnamese and Americans,

I am the daughter of a US marine who was killed on the beach-head of Guam July 22nd, 1944.

In 1967 after graduating college, I joined the US Navy Nurse Corps, went to Officers Indoctrination School in Newport, Rhode Island, and then began working at Oak Knoll Naval Hospital in California. Oak Knoll had been constructed during WWII to care for the marines wounded during battles in the Pacific.

I thought that I would become part of the healing process for the wounded; I thought that I would be able to undo the destruction of war and conflict in southeast Asia. We had an amputee ward at Oak Knoll where the guys had their limbs attached to meat hooks, their raw, open wounds hanging oozing infections so bad you could smell the sweet, sticky odor when you came into the unit. At night, they would talk with each other through their ongoing nightmares — "be careful, there's a land mine there; go slowly, there's a trip wire" as they wandered through the dense jungle — these youngsters, living on horror and fear. I was dedicated to getting them better and able to go out into life, but so many couldn't — the psychological imprint of what they had seen and done couldn't be cured by surgery and antibiotics, and the military didn't believe that war caused psychological pain and damage so severe it would haunt them for life. We were an extraordinary team — physicians, nurses, corpsmen and corpswomen — working long and difficult hours to heal our patients. I was training corpsmen who would be sent to the front lines, and so I became an instrument of war. I helped the military to function.

Like many others, Vietnam became a turning point in my life. It became personal, and I couldn't live with myself and continue to be part of this death and destruction — done in my name, by my government. GIs and veterans were organizing a march for peace in the San Francisco Bay Area in October, 1968. And so I joined them. We formed groups at Oak Knoll Hospital and would post posters and flyers announcing the demonstration — on the many barracks and wards. They were all torn down by morning. The nightly news had stories of the US dropping flyers on the Vietnamese, urging them to go to "safe hamlets."

So, along with a couple of friends, we loaded up a small plane and dropped flyers over multiple military installations in the San Francisco Bay Area, announcing the GI and Veterans March for Peace — and thousands showed up on October 12th, 1968. We spoke out against US involvement in Vietnam; we demanded to "bring the boys home." We spoke about the old men in Washington sending the young to die. And we thought we'd stop the war. We really believed that the American people and the US government would listen to us.

The fact that the war continued, that so many millions of Vietnamese and thousands of American soldiers lost their lives continues to haunt me and make me question what else we could have done. How could we have stopped this insanity?

As a child, I spent many Sundays visiting my father where he is buried in Chicago, Illinois. I watched my grandmother drop to her knees and talk to her son: "look, here is your daughter — see how she's grown" and I'd walk away from the grave, embarrassed and confused.

To all who have suffered, to all the family and loved ones who died and had their lives changed from the American War in Vietnam, I am so sorry we couldn't have done more. We tried — and we'll continue our struggle for peace and justice in this world in your name.

Susan M. Schnal

In early 2003

Vietnam War Memorial
Washington, D.C.

Respected brothers, Greetings.

In early 2003, as war with Iraq became more and more likely, two friends of mine and I attended a founding meeting in Chicago of a group that called itself Labor Against the War.

To my surprise, the meeting was held at the union hall of a local union of the International Brotherhood of Teamsters. One of my traveling companions was a Teamster steward. The Teamsters are not noted for opposition to the government in its conduct of United States foreign policy. I sought out a couple of shop stewards and asked them what was going on.

"It was the Vietnam vets," they told me. "They hit the mike at our local union meeting and said: We have seen this movie before."

I am an Army veteran. I am not a Vietnam veteran. I, too, had seen this movie before, but not in combat.

During the summer of 1964 I was the coordinator of Freedom Schools in Mississippi for what came to be called Mississippi Summer, or Freedom Summer.

During the first week of August, 1964, three related things happened in Mississippi.

1. The bodies of civil rights workers James Chaney, Andrew Goodman, and Michael Schwerner were found.

2. The Mississippi Freedom Democratic Party (MFDP) held its founding convention in Jackson, the state capitol.

3. At an improvised memorial service in Philadelphia, Mississippi, where the three young men were murdered, Bob Moses, project coordinator, told us about the Tonkin Bay resolution. At the time we did not know that the underlying "facts" of that event had been invented by the Johnson Administration. What angered Moses was that the United States could send armed forces to the other side of the world, allegedly to enhance democracy in Vietnam, but refused to send federal marshals to Mississippi to protect civil rights workers.

This was how I learned of the beginning of combat in Vietnam.

As a first-year assistant professor at Yale I found myself among longtime participants in American foreign policy-making. I debated Eugene Rostow at one of the Yale colleges. I came to know Yale chaplain William Coffin, a former CIA employee but an opponent of the Vietnam war. I took public positions against the war that were later advocated by Yale President Kingman Brewster and the historian who recruited me, Edmund S. Morgan. At the time, however, President Brewster said I was "giving aid and comfort to the enemy," words from the law of treason.

1965 drew me more and more toward outright, public, action against the war. Early in the year I chaired a meeting at Carnegie Hall in New York City, at which the keynote speaker was Alaska Senator Gruening. In April I was asked to chair what I believe to have been the first big public protest against the war in Washington, DC, organized by Students for a Democratic Society. In August, on the twentieth anniversaries of the nuclear bombing of Hiroshima and Nagasaki, I was arrested along with Moses, David Dellinger, and other "unrepresented people." We were arrested when attempting to assemble on the steps of the Capitol to state that someone else might be at war with the people of Vietnam, but we were not.

As American troops continued to land in Vietnam, to be stationed in bases like that at Danang, protest also escalated. Early in November a young member of the Society of Friends, or Quakers, burned himself to death within view of the Pentagon office of Secretary of Defense McNamara. (I am a Quaker.) In December, together with Tom Hayden and Herbert Aptheker, I made an unauthorized trip to North Vietnam in a desperate attempt to locate some clues, some openings that might help to make peace possible.

My trip to Hanoi cost me an academic career. Although not as sturdy at 85 as I was fifty years ago, I would do it again.

This is a small and inadequate way to express my solidarity with the thousands of young Americans and hundreds of thousands of Vietnamese who were killed in the Vietnam war.

Alas, such protest is still needed because like the Rostows and the Bundys, United States policy makers still pursue the irrational belief that they can physically present themselves in a foreign country about whose culture they know next to nothing, destroy its existing institutions and cause its civil service and military employees to lose their jobs, leave after a few years, and . . . create "democracy." The only thing we can be sure has been created is death and poverty.

In the prose poem, "The People, Yes," written by Carl Sandburg, a little girl attends her first military parade. She asks who are the marchers. Those are soldiers, says her adult companion. The little girl reflects. Finally she says, I know something. The response is more or less: Yes dear. What do you know? She answers: "Sometime they'll give a war and nobody will come."

s/Staughton Lynd

writing in support

I'm writing in support of the Vietnam War Full Disclosure Movement. Born in 1943, I was of draft age, though I did not go. I had a 1-Y classification based on significant myopia, correctable but leaving me useless without glasses. I still don't know how much the deferment was genuine and how much the work of my parents talking to my eye doctor; they were staunch Republicans and apparent supporters of the war, but concerned parents as well. My uncertainty is evidence of how little I understood the situation circa 1965.

Returning from study in West Berlin in 1966, I became engaged in the anti-war movement, especially as I lived in Cambridge, Massachusetts during Vietnam Summer. I remember reading Bernard Fall's history of Vietnam, which dramatically changed my view of America's role in Southeast Asia. I remember marching in a New York City protest, carrying an American flag which I meant to represent an ideal lost in the fog surrounding the war, but which also drew an angry response or two from those around me. I believe that it was this same march which began with men with American flag pins on their lapels — assumedly FBI agents–taking photos of us boarding buses outside Lowell House at Harvard.

I also remember visiting Carl Sagan at his Central Square apartment to deliver letters he would then share with those on a charter flight to Europe, encouraging them to speak with other Americans abroad, urging them to voice their concerns about American involvement. It was morning, and he was still in his bathrobe, hardly the scientist rock star of Cosmos. And I visited Noam Chomsky at his M.I.T. office, though the passage of years has erased what we talked about. Certainly his seminal New York Review of Books article, "The Responsibility of Intellectuals," had influenced me.

Despite my intellectual opposition to and activism against the war, it was not until 1972, however, that I returned my draft card, together with a respectful letter outlining my reasons for doing so, to my local draft board in Philadelphia. I expected blowback from this moderate action, but never heard a word.

Many years later, around 2000, I was involved in a resistance movement opposing the fingerprinting of school employees in Maine, and sent $25 to the FBI asking for a copy of my record. To my surprise, I was told that they had no information about me, which suggests either incompetence or sympathy from my draft board many years before.

And I remember interviewing returned Vietnam veterans in Somerville, Massachusetts, for a novel I was writing. It was at a neighborhood BBQ that Manny Kolidakis, one of these, heard someone set off a firecracker and threw himself to the ground in a Vietnam flash-back.

But of course none of this compares to what was being experienced by those who did go to Vietnam, whether willingly or through the draft. Or did not ever return. Still — and this persists fifty years later — I cannot talk about the war without choking up. It is my own private echo from that time, a sort of shadow of PTSD that, like the real thing, is always there, mostly submerged amid the hurly-burly of life, but never quite forgotten by that part of my brain that remembers how bad it was, how insane and twisted, how unconscionable. Perhaps the silver lining is how the experience of coming of age during the Vietnam War pulled me loose from my insular upper middle class background and led me to question and adjust ever after beliefs in ideas like patriotism and historical truth.

Bernie Huebner,

Waterville, Maine

Letters to The Wall 2016

Little By Little

by Daniel Shea

1968 Vietnam Veteran

5/27/16

I don't know when my opinion about war changed. There's no date, time or place certain, it just happened. It didn't happen suddenly like some epiphany. It was little by little, more like it revealed itself from something deep inside, something that was always there, but silent in its ignorance not knowing how to express itself.

It was more like an ember placed there by a mother's love and embrace. Whispered clichés of "Love thy Neighbor as Thyself" and "Thou shalt not kill" tenets of Bibles, Torahs, Korans and plain common sense.

These motherly pronouncements were part of a moral fiber that kept this internal spark fueled just enough for it to smolder.

Whispers fade as children grow older, play is loud with laughter and screaming, then comes the concentration of radios, movies and television voices telling you how lucky you are to live in this great nation and the noise of the world like a mighty storm drowns out that now faint lesson of love.

Teachers teach American Exceptionalism, Eurocentric history, our Country Right or Wrong while we stand at attention reciting the Pledge of Allegiance.

Parents like my own were living the American Dream, struggling from poor working class renters to owning a home, a car and credit at the local grocery store.

I was the oldest of six kids, three boys & three girls. We lived in a two bedroom house and by the time I started high school we outgrew it. We were like the Jeffersons (for those of you too young to know, it is a reference to a Black Family television series) moving on up from the hood to better neighborhood.

"Better" is relative. Our house was bigger with room for all of us, but the schools were not much better. The high school had its bullies and was self segregated by class and race. Teachers were mediocre and school bored me, so I dropped out and went to work.

The Vietnam War was raging on, the draft was licking at my heels. Work was hard labor and I saw no future on the horizon, the American Dream was in decline, so with abandonment I joined the United States Marines.

You want to know what Fascism is like, join the marines. Boot-camp will kick the Democratic shit out of you. I witnessed enough corruption, cruelty and racism while at Camp Pendleton.

Then came Vietnam. The war was a backdrop to firefights, snipers, mortar rounds and booby-traps, close calls with death, of which others – names long forgotten — were not so fortunate.

I often expected to see my own name on the Vietnam Memorial Wall as evidence that I too had been kissed by a sniper's bullet, or planted in the ground by a booby-trap. Now I am just a lost soul walking the earth dreaming up a surreal life refusing to accept my own end.

October 1969 I returned home to a civilian life. In short order fell in love and by June of 1972 was married. Vietnam was a distant shadow flickering in some deep cavern of my subconscious far from my reality. I had left the war, but the war never left me and on December 16th of 1977 it came rushing back into my life to wound my son with birth anomalies related to Agent Orange/Dioxin.

I was given three good years with Casey before the war ghosts of the past wrestled him from my arms, as he took his last breath, leaving me, his mother Arlene and his little sister Harmony to cling to each other as we cried out "WHY?"

Shouldn't Casey's name be inscribed on the Vietnam Memorial Wall along with my own, because a part of me ended when he died and that ember almost blew out.

Not right away but something was growing inside of me. I began to get beyond my own grief, to see that of the Vietnamese and the grief that all wars cause.

Mother's early ember of wisdom now began to catch fire, no longer flickering in the shadows but a sun shining a light, turning night into day and chasing the lies that sent me and so many others to a monstrous war that should never have been.

So for every name on that Dark Wall and all the names missing, my son's, the Vietnamese, the 22 veterans suicides a day, the Agent Orange victims and all the families who flood of tears, like mine ask "WHY?

Why Vietnam?

Why Afghanistan?

Why Iraq?

Why Any War?

I say No More!

Thou Shall Not Kill!

Thou Shall Love Thy Neighbor as Thyself!

Let these pearls of wisdom burn bright in your hearts and its roar silence the drums that beat for war.

I saw three wars today.

My first veteran was from remote Maine,
a small community that survived on fishing and fresh air.
He worked hard for his family more than 40 years.
Retired only to have his days filled with nightmares of VietNam.

Another, a Marine, came from a Bangor suburb.
He made the evening news when he took his 11-year-old son to
    Walmart,
bought a knife and threatened to kill himself and his blood. He
was stained from Agent Orange and his wife had found
    another.

The third knocked on our locked door.
Only 30 years old, his mind was bent from the horrors of his tour.
He had a shaved head, full beard, tattooed upper arms.
He was angry, full of rage, ready to fight. Still.

VietNam. Afghanistan. Iraq.
Pick a war. Only difference is the order in which they happened.
Seroquel, Zyprexa, Haldol.
Pick a medication. None will take away the pain, anxiety, stress.
I saw three wars today.

Respectfully submitted, Nancy Dykstra, Psychiatric RN at a VA
Maine Hospital

Written for Memorial Day 2016 for all the veterans that I have
been privileged to have in my care..

Thank you.

Viet Nam Wall, Panel 43 East

SONG BE', PHUOC LONG Province, Viet Nam

Dedicated to the Five A/1st-506th Parachute Infantry Regiment Currahees who were killed in our Song Be' battle:
Staff Sgt Chas Sanders (Squad Leader) Panel 43 East, Line #10, Name #3
Sp4/E/4 Thomas Pryor, Panel 43 East, Line #10, Name #2 Sgt Bobby McMillian, Panel 43 East, Line #9, Name #4 Pfc Juan DeMara, Panel 43 East, Line #5, Name #2
Platoon Sgt Jazreal "Jazz" Haywood, Panel 43 East, Line #6, Name #4
and to our four Rakkasans who were also killed when C Co, 3rd BN, 187th came to the aid of us Currahees.

Shortly after sunrise, about 0645, on 5 March 1968, our 29 person Platoon was beginning to "Fall In", to go outside the wire on yet another Counter TET "Search & Destroy" (S&D) Mission.
Dennis Lahiff and I were passing the pipe, while waiting on the other 27 guys from our Platoon to assemble for the S&D mission, when Platoon Sgt Haywood walked up on us, and for the umpteenth time, busted us for smoking the Hanoi Gold, and, some what miffed, but not surprised, he "punished " us by saying "Perry, you're walking Point (again), and Lahiff, you bring up the rear." Both "Point" & "Tail" are very dangerous, for very different reasons.
4 Star General William (Westy) Westmoreland, after his WW II heroics, served with the 187th Airborne Regimental Combat Team (RAKKASANS), in the Korean War, and later, commanded the 101st Airborne Division, in the late 50's. He was running the whole show, in Viet Nam, and he used our 101st Airborne Grunts as BAIT, in small unit actions, to get the Viet Cong to tip their hand (location wise) by ambushing us. Westy's theory was to use massive Air Power, and Artillery, to punish the elusive VC Guerrillas, and PAVN troops, when we could draw them into making "contact" with us, so we could call in Air Strikes & Artillery.

Talk about being used as expendable PAWNS.

While most of the American public, and ALL of the U.S. Military all thought Westmoreland was a genius, we bush pounding Grunts hated being moving parts in the profit driven Military Industrial game of Chess. But most of us were 19, 20, or 21 years old, and we felt we were invincible and invulnerable.

Airborne Infantry TO&E calls for a 5 yard space between each man, so that a 60mm or 81mm mortar round, or a hand grenade will only kill 1, or maybe 2 men. With 29 of us on this mission, our single file line was about 140 yards (1.4 football fields) long, weaving thru jungle thicket.

We left the perimeter wire, went down hill for a half mile, or so, crossed a small stream, then started up hill, thru really thick bamboo, for about 1,000 yards, then I came out by myself, on a clearing, with an abandoned & heavily overgrown Michelin Rubber Plantation to my left, and a row of Hootches, about 35 yards in front of me, that were strung along a dirt road.

Emerging by myself from the thick bamboo on the steep incline, I entered a relatively flat and sun bathed area. A young woman that I knew, rather well, from the far end of our Base-camp Perimeter, thought that I was by myself, and she ran out of her Hootch, towards me, signaling me in the Viet way to "come here quickly", then grabbed my arm, saying: "Beaucoup VC, maybe 90 or 100~ go back, you die."

(see the Pacific Stars & Stripes story, on the last page)

I always liked her, but I couldn't really trust her, so rather than go back, I grabbed her hand and we ran to her hootch. By the time we got to her door, 5 more of our Riflemen were out of the bamboo, and into the clearing, while the other 23 Troopers were still working their way up the slope.

On a 29 man Patrol, the VC Forward Observers would watch us, and count us, as we leave the Base Camp perimeter, and tell their Ambush team to let at least the first 7 or 8 men go thru, then, to look for the Radio Man's whip antenna, because he'd be assigned to the highest ranking NCO in the single file line. Kill the Communications capability & kill the brains of the Platoon, and then it's easy pickings.

(NCO's, Machine Gunners and M-79 Grenade Launchers were the next in line walking dead men).

Once inside the Hootch, the uncontrolled trembling & tears of my Lady Friend, and her Sister, who was the Mom of the adorable little girl clinging to her, made me realize that this wasn't just another walk in the woods adventure.

Although she was telling me the Ambush force was in the abandoned, overgrown plantation, to our left, the azimuth of my point man compass was telling me to keep going straight ahead. By now, about 15 or 16 of the other 28 members of my Platoon had emerged from the bamboo, and they gathered in a knot, drinking from their canteens and making quite a target of themselves.

As I went to the front door of her Hootch, an incredible wall of small arms fire, from the dirt road, all the way back to the bamboo jungle, erupted.

I dropped into a prone position, and turned to my left, just as 4 VC were charging out of the plantations' thick overgrowth, straight at me, but they were looking to their right, down where the bulk of my Platoon was. I shot those 4 Freedom Fighters with 2 bursts, the first, about 14 rounds, the 2nd burst, about 5 rounds. It seemed like the first 10 rounds went through all 4 of them, instantaneously.

I rationalize those deaths, to this day.

There were zero graceful, dramatic, chest grasping deaths, among those four men. The AR 15 M-16 is rated at over 800 rounds per minute, which is 14 rounds per second. The horrible, unnatural contortions, the flailing arms and legs, and the tremendous momentum-changing power of those first fourteen .223mm rounds that those four farmers caught, in the one second burst of my weapon, will never leave me. Then, there is the added guilt of my training, when my second burst pumped the final 5 rounds in that magazine into them, as they lay in a heap, ONE HALF of a SECOND, later.

I don't care who you are, "Thou shalt not kill" will forever weigh upon you.

My Lady Friend seemed frozen, but still trembling, as she stayed by my side, unlike her Sister, and her Niece, who stayed in their tunnel/bomb shelter. Although I could hear really intense fire, on my "7 o'clock," I had to level my fire, at 12 o'clock on the Hootch across the road, to keep the pressure on. The front of her Hootch gave She & I the advantage of hiding my rifle flashes, so the peeps across the road couldn't see where my rounds were coming from, because we had 12" high vegetation, but the incoming 7.62mm rounds eventually found both her and me. The rounds that killed her entered the top of her head, and her left shoulder, and the Viet Farmer only had to traverse about 18 inches to kill me.

I had a hollow, empty feeling when I felt her go limp, and saw where her head wound was, but a second or two later, I was pumped when I saw 2 M-79 "Willy Peter" rounds (white phosphorous incendiary) explode, bursting the Hootch into flames.

The 187th Parachute Infantry Regiment RAKKASANS, from our Brigade, were closing in on the road side of the Plantation, and they had suffered 4 KIA.

I was nearly out of my 24 magazines of ammo, so I stuck my head into the bomb shelter, and admonished the Mama and the Little Girl NOT to come out, again, until I came back for them.

I crawled up to Pfc Juan DeMara. Our Medic was trying to rinse off Juan's intestines, as he stuffed them back into his stomach. I took Juan's Grenades, and about 10 magazines.

Further down the berm, my Squad Leader, Sgt Chic Sanders, was already dead, from shrapnel & small arms. I took about 8 of his magazines. He must have thrown all his grenades, because they were gone.

I was about 20 yards down the slope, from the Hootch, when I saw Platoon Sgt Haywood, trying to rally the Troopers who fell back into the bamboo slope, to come back out, and carry the fight, when he got hit, and hit hard.

I knew Sgt Haywood was dead, too.

I ran & low crawled back to the Hootch, and covered my Lady Friend's body with mats, because I knew that her Sister and her Little Girl would be coming out of the bomb shelter, as the noise died down.

We had called for Air Strikes, hopefully with F-104 Phantoms, but we only got 1 Skyraider.

As with most ambushes, the actual Firefight only lasted 6 or 7 minutes, but the U.S. Artillery and Air Strikes pounded away, for over 2 hours. As though the ordnance exploding would make our survivors feel better. Such BULLSHIT.

I went back into the Hootch, to break the news of the one Sister's death, to the Little Girl's Mama. NOBODY wails, cries, and carries on more than Vietnamese folks, when they lose loved ones. I tried my best to calm & quiet her, so her daughter wouldn't come out of the bomb shelter, but she attracted the attention of a few of our troops who stayed all the way down at the bottom of the clearing, for the whole Firefight, by the bamboo forest. None of them knew what was happening up on my front end, of our position.

She was holding my left arm, and sobbing, hard, when SGT "REDACTED" kicked open the corrugated tin back door to her Hootch. He emptied a full 20 round magazine into the Little Girl's Mama, and while I still had her arms wrapped tightly, around my arm, her whole 90 pound body flew back, and her fingers lost their grip on my arm, her body was virtually cut in half, and her other arm was hanging by a bit of skin, because her bones were shattered.

It was all I could do to keep from shooting Sgt "Redacted."

He claimed that he thought this tiny woman was VC, and she was holding me prisoner. Our shouting brought more folks, (reinforcements) into the Hootch, and, at that time, orders came over the radio to place canisters of "Willy Peter" (white phosphorous incendiary, that would burn & asphyxiate anybody still in the bomb shelters). Folks in the bomb shelters are almost always NON combatants, including old folks & children.

I had to persuade the reinforcing Brass that I was 100% sure that a Little Girl was in "my" bomb shelter. One Officer even said that if the tunnel "is booby trapped, you'll deserve it," for sympathizing with the enemy.

(This is the first time I have tried to write about this 48 year old battle, and I'm up against a deadline to submit this essay, for Memorial Day, 2016, and I know I'd take at least 10 pages to write about going into the tunnel, and bringing out the Little Girl, because it was [and I'm finding, as I type] so incredibly emotional so I'm just going to cut & paste from the Pacific Stars & Stripes article, at the end of this essay.)

"During mopping-up and pursuit operations late in the afternoon, Perry remained near the home of the dead woman". (our "minders" wouldn't let the truth be told about Mama)

"Some of the houses still occupied by the Viet Cong were being destroyed and I was afraid they might get this one by mistake," he said.

He was sure the little girl was still in the tunnel. He did not know whether she had been hurt. He took off his gear and entered the hole carrying a candle.

"When I came around the last corner — there were three of them — I saw her sitting against the back wall crying and in shock," Perry said. "She recognized me immediately and ran over and threw her arms around my neck."

"He took the child back into the middle of the tunnel where there were a few belongings — a small transistor radio, three bowls and 25 packs of "PARK LANE" cigarettes." (Park Lane was a garbage brand of filter cigarettes that cost about 8 cents, per pack, and a small, innocent hustle, by many Vietnamese was to shake the tobacco out of the Park Lane, and repack all 20 in the pack with about 75 cents worth of high grade marijuana in each, hence, each pack would bring the hustler about $1.12 over cost, and the "loaded" packs sold for $2.00, each, a $1.17 profit, because Officers and rear echelon folks couldn't carry quarter pound baggies of reefer, like us Grunts could. In a country where $2 per day was a decent living, it was a very honorable hustle).

I kept 10 packs for myself because I had no idea what, or who, would take care of the Little Girl, and I put the remaining 15 packs and $20 "MPC" into a cloth bag, with her other meager possessions, and I brought her up, and out of the tunnel, and away from the Momma & Aunt's bodies.

All the gawkers at the tunnel entrance all started clapping & cheering, and chipping in C-Rat stuff, and chump change, as I brought her up, and out, but I felt incredibly dirty, and totally ashamed of our U.S. policy of Search & Destroy, because DESTROY (culture, family, relationships, keepsakes, etc., et al,) was truly the operative word.

A Lieutenant from the RAKKASANS came out, in a Jeep, and we drove the Little Girl to the Province Orphanage. A sad ending to a very sad day.

The Pacific Stars and Stripes article failed to note the 9 Currahees and Rakkasans KIA, nor the (very inflated) 56 Viet Cong bodies, 20 blood trails, + 2 POW's recorded in 506th and

145

3rd Bde "After Action" reports. May the ULTIMATE SACRIFICES of our BROTHERS never be forgotten.

Unfortunately, the sacrifices, horrors, and War Crimes that the people of Viet Nam suffered, at our hands, have apparently been forgotten, by the people, as the 1% Viet Nam RULING CLASS, reaches for riches, going by Barak Obama's whirlwind tour of Viet Nam, touting potential gains

Me? I forget NOTHING! PACIFIC STARS & STRIPES story

URL: http://377sps.org/stripes/march/24.pdf

Scroll down the page until you see: "Viet Mom Warns G.I., ... and Dies" (about ¾ way down the page)

PACIFIC STARS & STRIPES couldn't do ANY interviews, without a MACV "minder," and at least 2 officers "correcting" anything (and most everything) I said, that went outside the accepted Military Narrative for our War.

The typical "BODY COUNT" bull shit, throughout our war had to follow the minimum math ratio of 4 to 1 , or, better yet, 6 to 1 , or 8 to 1.

Our After Action Reports claimed 56 VC dead. Other than my FOUR kills, there were only 5 other VC bodies found.

We had 9 total deaths, the VC had 9 total deaths, BUT, the U.S. Military Rule of thumb was NEVER to admit to a numerical stand off. Always use the Military KILL ratios, in our case, 9 VC deaths, vs. 9 U.S. deaths ~ a stand off~ called for multiplying by the 6 to 1 ratio = 9 US deaths at 6 to 1 equals 54 "enemy KIA," then they always added a couple so the ratios wouldn't be too easy to figure out. Hence, the "56 VC deaths, as reported," in the STARS & STRIPES news accounts.

These daily LIES would start in Platoon & Company level reports, and, often get jacked up, even more, at Battalion, Brigade, Division, and Command levels. Hence, the high number of idiots in the Military Academies, and IVY LEAGUE schools, as well as Think Tanks, and NGO's, continually spouting BULLSHIT, even as I type.

I have spent the past 48 years opposing WAR & fighting for Equal Justice & Peace

I'm a certified Veterans Advocate, always trying to help kids suckered into the Military-Industrial-Political profit-driven

complex, as they battle the V.A. & DoD for EVERYTHING they are entitled to.
STAND UP
FIGHT BACK

bp (Bill Perry)

If you managed to read all the above, (Viet Nam Wall, Panel 43, EAST) then check out my other Memorial Day essay, called: (Viet Nam Wall Panel 32 East) Below.
Thanks for attempting to understand.
~VIET NAM WALL, Panel 32 East
Phuoc Vinh, Binh Duong Province, Viet Nam
10 Killed on our Platoon's 15th Day in Viet Nam
I was fooling around, outside the fence, with the 2 teenage daughters from our Laundry Hootch, when I could see our Platoon of Company A, 1st Battalion, 506th Parachute Infantry Regiment of the 101st AIRBORNE Division moving out, towards the flight line, 10 minutes before we were actually scheduled. By the time I caught up to our Platoon, my Squad & Fire Team took up all of Choppers #6 & #7, and I wound up in UH1B Huey #8, on the "stick," rather than UH1B Huey #6, where you guys were.
When our 10 Chopper "stick" took off, at 0800, it was a beautiful, mid seventy degree, sun shiny day. We were flying much higher than normal "tree top" altitude, maybe 400 feet high, and banking "right," when, from my perch by the door, I grasped my seat as we leaned way into our pitch & roll, and I could clearly see you guys in #6, as well as Choppers #1 thru #7. Suddenly, there was a huge orange, yellow, and black fire ball, and your ship went down.
I don't know whether the Aviation group flying the choppers that day were the "Kingsmen," the "Copperheads," or a 101st Aviation group, but ship #7 was unsteady, from the blasts' concussion, so our #8 Chopper "corkscrewed" down to evaluate what happened. It was pretty obvious.
Among ALL my PTSD triggers, "Survivors' Guilt" has me thinking about you guys, ALWAYS.

Staff Sgt Walter Brown   Panel 32 East, Line 020, name 4
Pfc Jimmy Lee Woolfolk Panel 32 East, Line 028, name 5
Pfc Eugene Miley   Panel 32 East, Line 025, name 3
Pfc Charles Carpenter   Panel 32 East, Line 021, name 2
Pfc Steven Nicholas Rad Panel 32 East, Line 026, name 5
Staff Sgt Leroy Everett   Panel 32 East, Line 021, name 5

Sgt "San Antone" Brown knew TO & E inside out, and was quite capable of keeping us out of trouble. Jimmy Lee Woolfolk was "Brownie's" RTO (Radio) man, and they were a great salt n pepper team. Brownie did a mean Sam Cooke "Born by the River."

Gene Miley was the first (wannabe) Black Muslim most of us ever hung out with. His logic was really hard to dispute.

"Old Man" Charley Carpenter (29 yrs) was from Oakland, California, and he regaled us with stories of these brave Oakland Home Boys of his, called the BLACK PANTHER PARTY. I was Lumpen Proletarian, and their ideas & ideals really appealed to me.

Steven Radu was the youngest of the crew, and back in Ft Benning's Parachute School, some NCO tagged him with "Dummy Radu," and it stuck. He was a Doors, Airplane, Joplin, & Beatles freak, and, like the rest of us, loved to party.

Leroy Everett sang Gospel tunes, 24/7, and was sort of an anchor when we'd get out of hand.

As with all Paratroopers, we had an amazing bond, from jumping out of perfectly good airplanes & jets, and partying in Hopkinsville, KY, Clarksville, Tenn, and all over Ft Cambell, KY.

The 2 Pilots, and 2 Door Gunners who also died on 19 DEC 1967 are also remembered, by me, but nowhere near as intensely as the six Brothers that I had trained with, jumped with, ate & slept with, and flew , together, to 'Nam with.

Exploring the wonders of Phuoc Vinh, Ba Moi Ba, Cambodian Red, and "the field" created an incredible bond. A bond that is still there.

At our 1st Company "A" reunion, around 2004, (37 years after the fact) we read what the DoD report calls "Casualty Type," and here's their quote: "Non-Hostile, Died while Missing,

148

Air Loss, Crash Landing Helicopter — Non Crew." We had always thought you guys were brought down by hostile indirect (mortar) fire ("missing" denotes the time it took to recover you).

I went down to the National Archives, in College Park, Maryland, to see why a helicopter, downed in a "hot" war zone, was listed as NON Hostile. On my second day there, I cross-referenced all communications from Division, Brigade, Div Arty, Alpha Company, & Battalion S-2, S-3, & S-4, and other sources, and it became very clear that it was our own 155mm Artillery that brought you guys down. I was stunned. It's really cold, inside the Archives, and the blood drained out of my head, and I had to run out of the Building, into the hot midday sun, to gather my soaking wet self together again. I was devastated.

At the 2005 reunion, I only told Dennis Lahiff what I had learned, b/c we were the ONLY original 1967, 1968 "Airlift" Currahees at the reunion, and we didn't want the others to contact the families, and throw them into turmoil, but, now, 49 years later, it just MAY get out there.

Picturing you six brothers, as if you were sitting here, having a beer with me, it just dawned on me that 4 of you are African American, which is a high lighted 'Nam fact among historians, but as we used to say "it don't mean nuttin'," b/c that's the way it is, with EM, in AIRBORNE units.

You wouldn't believe how our country has so damn many know-nothing book freaks who have us involved in 7 "hot" wars, as they frighten the taxpayers into buying more and more weapons systems in their unholy drive for Global Hegemony.

I wish you guys could somehow influence them to stop lying, and start caring for LIFE.

Please know that I Love you, miss you, and will never forget you.

Wild Bill (Bill Perry)

To: Barry Vorath Hopper,

Barry Vorath Hopper,
January 25, 1970,
Montrose, PA

May 2016
Dear Barry,

It has been 46 years since we lost you. My two children know your name, your childhood pranks (lots of material there) and that you died in a useless war that was wrong. Yes, I have children: Ari who is 12 and a redheaded baseball slugger. He shoots a 22 and loves the woods like you. He loves the story about you getting an 8-point buck with a bow and arrow just before you were shipped out for Nam. I have a daughter, Ella, who works with Doctors Without Borders in Africa. She was on the cover of Time Magazine as an Ebola fighter. Yes, I am a prideful mother. My missing you emerged when they were born and for every achievement since. I think, "Uncle Barry would have loved this."

As I keep your memory alive through my kids I feel that I am teaching them to "question authority." I want you to know that I spent my 4 college years fighting against the Viet Nam war. They told us we were just stupid kids and did not understand international affairs. We pushed back and that pushing, to some degree, probably helped to end the war. That loud and vociferous pushing did end the draft.

So many of you were used as pawns by selfish old men. Many of you that have survived are now on the street, living a hopeless existence. Do we honor our veterans? Only in the newspapers, but elsewhere your comrades are forgotten and swept under the social rug. Years later the folks behind this ugly moment in US history wrote books admitting that the protesters were correct. Little comfort that is for us now.

I am writing this letter to you to be left at The Wall. Silly perhaps, but what else can I do? We have all gone on without you. We were just kids then. Suzanne became a nurse; Patty a journalist; and I reached my goal of becoming a PhD sociologist and college professor. You were a medic when you died and we were all betting on you becoming a doctor. Your goals were cut short in 4 lousy months in Viet Nam and I am still totally pissed about it. I cherish my anger and keep it burning way down deep in my core because that is what they left me after taking you.

I have just retired from 40 years of teaching at the university level. I want you to know that I have consistently put peace and respect out there as an option. Good college professors do not preach, as our job is not to tell them what to think, but to teach them how to think. But I do ask them to think through peace and non-aggression as a viable option. I do this for you and our entire generation. I worked hard to fight against the war and the draft when in college and I want you to know that I never stopped. My protests changed as I have moved through life, but I have never stopped and this is fueled by missing you.

Now you are a name on a big black wall for all future generations to see. You are also in our hearts and minds. Going to my 50th high school reunion in September where some are sure to say, "Remember Barry?" The tears still flow.

With love,

Betsy Watson, PhD
Professor Emerita

I graduated high school in 1968

I graduated high school in 1968, and turned 18 in the fall. I was already absolutely against the ridiculous war in Vietnam and had marched against it. I remember turning 18 and thinking about what I would have done if I had been a male and faced the draft. How horrible it was for young men of my generation.

The war was wrong and purposeless, and now looking back more than fifty years later, I am saddened still by the tremendous loss of both military and civilian lives to no purpose and the continuing consequences for the many who were wounded in the war, or suffered PTSD as a result of the war. And now in 2016, we still persist in sending young people to fight and kill primarily to benefit the corrupt and wealthy corporations and politicians.

Did we learn nothing from the horrible devastation of the Vietnam War?

K. Cutler

To All Who Visit This Wall of Remembrance:

When I visit this memorial, and others like it, the individual names draw me immediately. I look at one name and spontaneously imagine one person — a body, young and healthy, a face smiling, someone who is loved. I think of the tenderness of that body's flesh, and the tenderness of the relationships that surround him, or sometimes her. And I feel the irreparable rupturing of that body, those relationships, that life by an old dispute that is also dead. The dispute ends, one way or the other, but the ruptured lives remain irreparable.

Then I see the next name, and next, and next. Then I see hundreds. Then I am silenced by the weight of the completely senseless, useless waste. One precious body, facing an equally precious body, trying to kill each other?

At this wall, I turn to imagine the companion wall that should be out on the mall, six times as long, with the names of 3 million precious Vietnamese lives lost. This wall tells me all over again why we must never, never accept war. Who decides? How dare they? Never again.

I was in high school when opponents of the war took to the streets. Seeing them take action and make a difference defined my sense of the world I live in. I have tried to be faithful to their lesson and to the horrible price paid by all whose lives were touched by this one war.

V. Druhe

Here is my share

Here is my share concerning both the Vietnam War and the Vietnam Era. This share will look at things from the perspective of being a Disabled Veteran and also now being 65 years of age.

After being in USMC and then USAF between 1968 and 1976, it is imperative you understand the cultures and events of that timeframe, particularly 1969.

What I particularly want to share about that is that many of us went in at 17 as South Side Chicago high school dropouts, poor, with no skills nor hopes. We were not drafted.

We knew nothing of the 'Military-Industrial Complex" and only were very dimly aware of the "Domino Theory."

What I know, from personal experience, is that between a 1968 Thursday afternoon and the following Monday evening, I was in a terrorist training camp known as Recruit Depot MCRD San Diego California.

I clearly recall being told numerous times that the purpose of this was, in some versions, that the purpose of this camp was to drain me of everything I knew, had learned, and kept inside my head, so that I could be rebuilt as a United States Marine "thoroughly indoctrinated in love of God, Country and Corps."

I held back ever so slightly and kept a tiny journal listing the many times I heard "KILL!" in things like the chow hall line or marching in formation and such. Every class started with variations of its "kill THEM before they kill YOU!"

One would not DARE to ask 'Why?' Physical assault and psychological warfare and ostracism would be heaped on your head for hours and days for asking that simple question.

I also recall a Major with close-cropped gray hair pulling me alone out of a formation and wrapping his arm around my head and shoulders walking me away a piece and saying "private, you do understand that what we are trying to do here is make sure you understand that we have to kill them there before they kill us here, right?" I answered, loud and clear, "Sir! Yes Sir!" "You wouldn't want your Sister or your Mother molested by them in anyway, would you?" "Sir, No Sir!" "Well, get with the program and square yourself away." "Aye, Aye, SIR!"

And off to Vietnam I did fly. There, I was a FAC/TACP 1-4 radio operator. Forward Air Controller/Tactical Air Control Party, 1st Battalion, First Marines, First Marine Division. A 'Blood and Mud'-Marine with a radio link that all of Marine Aviation relied on for the good of the Marines on the ground.

Three years to the date and hour that I signed the papers in 1968, I was handed my DD214 indicating an Honorable Discharge at noon of June 1971 at Quantico MCB in Virginia. I was still only 20 years old. That very night I had acquired a job on South-side Chicago driving a tow truck in my Class A summer-tan uniform. It was the beginning of trying to 'untuck' myself. It is amazing to me how greasy and black that honorable uniform got by midnight that night.

I could easily write a 300 page narrative-novel about the days in Vietnam and the subsequent days in the US Air Force. At the end of the Air Force days, I began to hear terms like schizophrenic, bi-polar, manic-depressive Survivor's Guilt and some new thing called PTSD. In April of 1975, I spent an entire month of 12 on/12 off supporting aviation operations during the Fall of Saigon.

A second Honorable Discharge followed and I was helped in getting a job in the mail room at VA Chicago. A chance event occurred: a fellow Vet asked what I was doing with my benefits; WHAT benefits I asked. He got me in contact with a Vocational Rehabilitation Program Officer (civilian) at VARO (Veterans Administration Regional Office) and they tested me every morning and afternoon for a week and more.

Turned out I should never have been allowed in the Marine Corps in the first place. And the Air Force could have been held responsible for re-enlisting me. After many hearings, it was decided by all that I should be rehabilitated.

Two Bachelor's and one Masters degrees later, I was a Senior Professor for DeVry University for 32 years. My problem is not that I may be nuts, but that I fully and comprehensively understand just how much of our history is built on LIES and coercion. And the consequences (and the consequences avoided) thereof.

My Wife urged me to respond to you and 'just write a note.' I hope I've done just that and no more than that.

I hope this helps your endeavor.

Dan Sea

Dear Dan

21 May 2016

Dan Yazzie,
The Wall
Washington, DC

Dear Dan,

You were a wiry Navajo from somewhere off on the reservation in New Mexico or one of the adjacent states when I met you in Basic Training at Fort Bliss in El Paso, Texas in the late winter and spring of 1968. About a third of our company were Navajo and I was always a bit jealous of them for having their own private language that was inaccessible to the drill sergeants (as well as the rest of us). You were in a different patrol from me, so I didn't really know you. The basic training regimen didn't leave much time for socializing and I'm not sure I ever even spoke with you. You were a pretty quiet guy, and did whatever was asked of you quietly and proficiently without complaint. What I remember most about you is that you were really fast on your feet, and seemed capable of running forever. I considered myself somewhat of a runner, but at the tests at the end of Basic Training you ran the mile more than a minute faster than I did. A couple of days later, just a day or two before Martin Luther King was assassinated, our basic training session was over and you and just about everybody else went off to AIT. The Army seemed to be uncertain as to what to do with me, but I was eventually sent off to a backwater in Georgia and several months later found myself in Vietnam.

I had a pretty easy time of it in Vietnam. I was in the HQ company of an engineering battalion whose main assignment was to pave roads. We were at Phu Loi camp, a few miles out of Saigon, which was pretty secure during the year I was there. A couple of rockets came into camp, but no one from our battalion got hurt at that camp from enemy activity all year. However, a group of guys in a tent at an auxiliary camp at Lai Khe got hit by a rocket one night and several of them were seriously wounded. Another guy drove his truck over a mine and became the only fatality from our unit for the year that I was there. He was from Delta company, who I had no contact with, and now I don't even know his name. I only know that he had joined the army with his brother and that he and his brother did everything together and got the same assignments together. On that particular day his brother hadn't felt well and went to sick call, while he went to work and got blown up.

It wasn't until recent years that I began to wonder about the fate of the people I had known in the Army, and started checking the Vietnam Memorial database for the few names that I was able to remember. It was there that I found your name, killed in Vietnam in May 1969, just over a year after proving yourself to be the fastest man in our basic training company. I wonder about your wife, parents, siblings, extended family and other loved ones left behind and how their lives were forever changed by your death. Then I think about all that grief and sorrow multiplied 50,000 times over, and wonder how the course of the Nation, the course of all our lives, would have been different if our policy makers had been more far-sighted and avoided escalating the war in Vietnam in the first place.

Sincerely,

Alan Batten

Dear Reader,

My name is Amy Martin (nee Rider) and I live in Northern California. My father Donald Rider served in Vietnam during his 20 years of service to the USAF.

I was not born until after my father's retirement in the latter 1970's. I only ever knew the scarred man he was. He bore the depression, the PTSD and the heavy weight of the memories made there. Medications, eventual therapy and good ol' talkin with other service members eased some of the burdens. I loved him despite the temper which arose often and learned not to resent him because much of what he experienced was beyond his control. He was the most perfect father to me despite his imperfections.

He wouldn't speak much about the time he served in Vietnam to his family. One name was brought to our attention though and I think the loss of this young man affected my father's future beyond what we will ever know. Roy Leo Lede – his name is here on the memorial. A 20 year old kid that worked beside my father. My dad never understood how someone with so much life ahead of him could be taken. My father wished he'd been taken instead, but then I wouldn't be here writing this letter today.

This letter is in support of peace and honor. These veterans had to endure, sacrifice, fight, heal and serve so they are deserving of all of our respect.

My father passed nearly 4 years ago from health issues tied to his time in the service. Since he left I direct my thoughts and attentions to homeless vets in particular. I have a tender spot for their plight. I know the mountains my father climbed to maintain a "normal" life and I recognize that those living on the streets are still fighting to live. If all I can provide is a smile, I'll do that. If I can do more, I will. I stay close to my father by helping out those he might have fought/ worked beside.

I'd like peace, just so that those involved could breathe/live/sleep better. I can't fathom why we let young people go destroy themselves and others in faraway lands. So much work is needed here in the USA, the energy put into war could be redirected into building up our people and our land.

How long will we fail to see all the offerings a peaceful world might provide for future generations?

Rest in peace Vietnam veterans and thank you for your service. I am sorry for any suffering put upon Vets alive or dead.

Respectfully yours,

Amy

A new friend invited me

May 25, 2016

A new friend invited me to add my voice to the many letters delivered to the Vietnam Veterans Memorial Wall in Washington, DC on May 30, 2016. I keep trying and failing to put my thoughts and feelings into coherent expression – too intellectual, too abstracted, too angry, too despairing… What do I want to say and how can I possibly say it?

When I think of the Vietnam War and the Vietnam Veterans Memorial Wall, I'm often brought to a place of impotent despair and tears. I was a girl during the war (I turned eleven in 1969), growing up just outside of DC, and the social, political, and moral upheaval of the time left an indelible mark – both difficult and positive – as I struggled to develop personal standards of behavior and belief.

Two things have stayed with me, especially, from the Vietnam War era. The first is the imagery. Seeing those photographs – as a kid and still now – leaves me grief-stricken and disconsolate. Exhausted GI's with "thousand yard stares"; a terrified girl running naked down the road; convulsive napalm explosions; a grimacing, flame-covered Buddhist monk; crying children, crying women, crying soldiers; dense, beautiful, confining jungle and scorched and defoliated countryside; the black, reflective face of the Vietnam Veterans Memorial with its 58,000 names and then also the coincident, unmemorialized names of the thousands upon thousands of additional casualties of that fateful time. It was beyond my capacity to process or integrate as a child and I've not made much progress since. I deeply appreciate those images, as alarming and profoundly haunting as they are – we should be horrified and frightened and angry and acutely provoked by them as well as by the on-going specter of America at war.

The second thing that has stayed with me is the ubiquitous unrest and deep-seated conflict of that time. Assassinations, civil rights demonstrations and violence, anti-war demonstrations and violence, the feminist revolution, hallucinogenic drug use – all forms of social and personal disruption and reorganization. Growing up close to DC amplified that experience. And not only was the turmoil in the streets of our neighboring city, but the unrest came flooding into my own living room as my mom and dad and older brother argued and fought and shouted and cried over the war with its terrible and unimaginable possibilities. My parents were ordinarily mild-mannered people but the war and the widespread social upheaval and my brother's appropriate rebellion all conspired to make it a time of intense family conflict, hostility and aggressiveness. It created in me a consequential and long-lasting sense of fear, confusion and anxiety.

I was a sensitive kid and regularly overwhelmed by the pervasive crisis and conflict – outside on the streets and inside my home. I was often frightened and a lot of that fear and unsettlement has stayed with me into my adulthood. My first political memory is JFK's assassination. Then there were the dogs tags we wore in elementary school so that our bodies could be identified if DC were attacked with nuclear weapons. And then the sweeping cultural revolution. And more assassinations. And beautiful, artful, terrifying photographs of it all. And my family – embroiled, embittered, bewildered.

As part of my coming of age process, I developed strong ambivalence toward authority, employment, gender, politics, economics, medicine, even ancestry (looking to the past) and lineage (looking to the future). I believe that the tumultuousness and uncertainty of that time is part of the reason I chose not to have children. I don't see the world as a particularly safe or sane place. There's a way that I only have one foot planted in this world, even now, and I think that growing up during the 1960's and the Vietnam war had a profound impact on my capacity and willingness to participate in the American collective.

I see the faces of some of the young men and women coming back from Iraq and Afghanistan and my heart breaks with sorrow. How have we not learned our lesson from Vietnam? How can we keep doing this – to our own children, to children throughout the world?

Trying to write this letter has been a painful exercise of falling back into the dark abyss of our unlearned lessons, our arrogance and our unconsciousness, and trying to climb back out to write, to reflect and remember, to search for some seed of hope, some point of recommitment to justice and atonement and our shared future. Even now, this letter – in its umpteenth iteration – seems a wholly failed attempt to convey what I feel and remember and hold sacred from that time.

Finally, in the end, perhaps all I need to say is that I'm still so deeply sorry for all that terrible loss.

With sorrow and gratitude,

Elizabeth Ratliff Schecher

Please deliver

Please deliver to the panel where HM2 Larry Jo Goss' name is found- Memorial Day 2016

Dear Dad,

I so wish I could be in DC today to deliver this letter in person. My husband, Eric, is amazing. Oh how I wish you could know him. He offered to drive me 10 hours so that I could be at the wall this weekend and meet other adult children whose father's also died in VN. I really want to meet them but feel it's important to be home with our two youngest kids who still live at home during the summer.

I could go on and on about your grandchildren. Mom says she sees different parts of you in them. It's such a blessing to know that parts of you still live on in them and in me. The biggest part of you I see in my mom though. She has never stopped loving you. What an impact you made on her life, dad, in the short time you and she were together. Oh, how I wish you would have never had to leave. It's been 48 years but the sadness remains. There is not a day that goes by that mom or I don't think of you.

I've learned to be proud of your service but must admit that for many years I wished you would have fled to Canada so that you and mom and I could have been together. We would have been quite a team. You and I, so much alike — assertive, driven, and full of energy. Mom so sweet, calm, and loving. She would still, to this day, give away everything she had if she knew someone was in need. You and her would have been a great team!

The three times I have been to the wall, I wondered if you could see me. It's such a mystery — on this earth — to know about Heaven. Are you already there? Are you "asleep" until the rapture? Do you "watch over me"? People say things like that but I don't know if it's true. I wish it was but I can't tell. This whole idea of feeling your presence is also something foreign to me. I don't know if that's because I have no memory of you or if it's because I'm not sure it works that way after someone dies. I'm a little bit stubborn and resist thinking something is true just because I want it to be. I have this really inquisitive mind that tried to figure things out. I want to know what is true. I operate much more on fact than feeling. When I was little I wished that you were still alive on every birthday cake. I think this continued (though to a lesser degree) even as I got older. It wasn't until I found Dr. Behrens in 1995 that I knew for sure that you were really killed in action on Valentine's Day of 1968. What a terrible day to die. What a terrible way to die. It makes me so sad to think of the way you died. Dr. Behrens identified your body by the wallet you had in your breast pocket. The one that had the picture of mom and I right by your heart. In one of your letters you said you always kept it there so we were always with you. Oh how true your statement was. Mom and I were with you that day in love and a part of both of us died when you took your last breath. Neither of us will ever be the same because we love you so much.

As I type this it sounds confusing to me to talk about loving someone I do not remember ever meeting. Love is something I take very seriously. I don't say the words "I love you" lightly and never say them if I don't really mean it. I know there are different types of love and that God calls us to love everyone. I try to be obedient to God in all I do. The way I've made sense of all of this is to think about there being different types of love. The love I feel for you dad is extremely powerful. It won't go away even when my sadness at times wishes it would. If I could just tell myself that you weren't that great of a guy or that you wouldn't have been that great of a dad, I know I would be less sad. The truth is, though, you were that great of a guy and you would have been an incredible dad and husband to mom. My sadness even increases when I think about the kind of grandpa you would have been to your five grandchildren. This doesn't even include the other child I know you and mom would have had and the grandchildren that may have come from that child.

I am such a positive person that I know I need to make a right shift before this letter comes to a close. Do you know the thing I am most thankful for when I think about you? It's the genes you gave me. You and mom are both very positive people and you both have a great sense of humor. I know I'm talking about you in the present but the image I have in my head of you never dies. That image is of your smile.

Do you remember when Ray Felle captured video of you near Valentine's Ridge five days before you were killed? Your personality was so evident in that 7 seconds of footage. You stopped and made eye contact with him. You said something to him, because you are so conversational and then you smiled and waved at the camera before quickly turning and walking quickly away. It was as if you knew you had a task to do and you were "on it." Focused to get the job done but not without a smile on your face and a good attitude all along the way. What a gift you left us. A great example of how to live.

If I believed for one second that you would be able to see this letter being walked to the wall on Monday and delivered by your panel, I would be there whatever it took. I'm not sure it works that way so I will send the letter so it can be delivered and stay home and love on your grand-babies who are now 16 and 18 years old!!! I'll tell you all about them someday.

I love you, dad. Please know that on this Memorial Day and every day I remember YOU! You influence the way I live my life. You taught me to not waste a single minute because we have no idea how many we have left. You taught me to work hard, to set high goals and go after them with all of my heart.

Thank you for falling in love with mom. She was a wonderful nurturer who spent her life trying to be a mom and dad to me. She talked about you often and did her best to help me "know" you. She did a great job!

I've searched far and wide to attempt to find out exactly how you died. I know it won't bring you back but something inside of me has felt a strong need to know. Lawrence Hoff sent me an e-mail a few years ago. His story was difficult to hear. I wish I knew if it was true. I now have Hoff's account and Marty Russell's, the corpsman who helped you treat the wounds of Camron Carter. The pieces have not all fit together but I keep hoping there will be more to come to bring clarity to the story of how your final hours were spent. Something inside of me thinks Hoff's story is true but no one else has confirmed it so I'll do my best to keep my mind open. More importantly, I'll live in the present, most of the time, because I know that is what you would want for me.

You are my hero dad. Not because you died saving the lives of wounded soldiers (Marines and Navy corpsmen) but because of who you were. Because of how you lived in the 21 short years you were given. Mom and I will carry you in our heart all the days we have left on this earth. At the end of our time, I pray that we are reunited with you in heaven. If you are already there, I know you know how amazing Colton will be when he gets his new body. If we all arrive at the same time (after the rapture) it is going to be one amazing day! Either way, I look forward to praising Jesus with you and spending eternity around God's throne. We will be together. Oh how sweet that will be!

Thank you, dad, for everything. Your service and more importantly your love for mom, for me and for your country and for those you gave your life to protect and help.

Eric and I have a saying. It is that we love each other more today than yesterday and less than tomorrow. I know it doesn't make any sense but it applies to the way I feel about you too. MTYLTT!

Your Darling Daughter (that's what you called me J)

Lori Jo Reaves

Feeding the Beast

"Non-violence means avoiding not only external physical violence but also internal violence of spirit. You not only refuse to shoot a man, but you refuse to hate him." Martin Luther King, Jr.

Hate is a beast that must be fed everyday to stay alive.
I groom and feed the beast with my hateful words and actions.
I groom and feed him when I let the homophobic joke slip by.
I groom and feed him when I take the bait of racism and pass it on.
I groom and feed him when I use silence, anger or threat to get my way.
I groom and feed the beast of hate when I vilify those who are different from me. I groom and feed the beast of hate when I let others think for me or tell me what I "should" do to keep it all under control.
I groom and feed the beast when I hide my shame and assume that I stand outside the human condition.
I groom and feed the beast of hate by my lack of self-examination or self reflection.
I groom and feed the beast of hate when I harden my heart against forgiveness.
As long as I keep the beast as a pet, my life will know violence. All war everywhere will be my own private war waged in the recesses of my heart and soul.

Patricia McConnell,
May 23, 2016

On April 18th of 2016

On April 18th of 2016, the unit I served with in Vietnam, Alpha Battery 1st Battalion 11th Marines, had a reunion at the Wall.

On April 18 1966, my third week in Vietnam, our unit was attacked and overrun by Vietcong Sappers.

We had 5 men killed and 28 men wounded out of 90 of us. That day changed who I was and who I would become. My first friend in the unit was Terry "Jake" Main – he was also from Florida. He was killed on April 18.

The morning after the attack, the dead Marines were laid next to a bunker and were covered with ponchos. I pulled back the ponchos from each man to see who they were. My friend Jake was one of them.

I realized that I was in a place where people were trying to kill me and my friends and that there was no do-overs; if I was killed that would be it.

I had believed that we were there to help the South Vietnamese protect themselves against the North Vietnamese. But the people who had just laid waste to my unit were South Vietnamese.

It became obvious to me that my real purpose was to keep me and my friends from being killed or injured. It was no longer about politics – it was about survival.

I ended up spending 20 months in Nam and received 2 Purple Hearts for being wounded twice.

Now 50 years later, I reflect. As I look at this Wall, I think about all of the sacrifices we made, the pain, the suffering, the loss of very special friends. I think of those of us that "survived," with our broken bodies and searing memories.

My psychological wounds are much more intense than my physical wounds.

I wonder what did we buy with all of this sacrifice?

All I see is a Black Marble Wall.

This was a very expensive Wall.

If my country would have learned from Vietnam, to never repeat this again, then our sacrifices would have bought something invaluable.

My country did not learn anything from our sacrifices in Vietnam and this is what causes me the most pain.

We continue to repeat the same mistakes over and over. We continue to behave as if we can make the world better by killing those that disagree with us.

When we killed people in Nam or when one of our own was killed we would say, "The gooks Wasted him or we Wasted some Gooks."

I never realized how profound the use of the word "Waste" was. Yes, it was all a tragic waste and that is what I see when I come to this Wall.

Scott Camil
Sergeant, USMC
– 1965-1969- Vietnam 3/66-11/6

FROM A VIETNAM VETERAN

TO WHOEVER READS THIS

Thank you for coming here today and standing before this black marble plowshare

Where you stand is Holy Ground

If you can, find a quiet place, be still and be willing to simply listen and let this wall and the names written on it speak to your heart.

Take your time.

When I first stood before this wall it felt like a punch in the gut. I was one of the lucky 'Vietnam Veterans' who spent two years out of harm's way. I had no family members or friends among the names on the wall. Still I felt at a loss facing all those 58,000 names and in the middle of them, my own reflection. There were no lofty words or heroic images to tell me how to feel.

Perhaps you feel, as I did, only inadequacy or emptiness or a vague sadness. It's true that nothing we can say or do can restore these dead to life or take away the grief of their loved ones. What has helped me has been finding a sense of purpose and hope through working to promote peace through Veterans For Peace, an organization dedicated to exposing the folly of war so that we do not have to continue to build memorials with the names of our children and grandchildren inscribed upon them. I sincerely hope that your visit today will help you to be a peacemaker in all that you do.

Harvey Bennett

Memorial Day, 2016

To The Wall Memorializing The Names of Our Vietnam War Dead,

You must know this, as we all must be reminded... there are many, many names of our brothers and sisters who were 'killed' in or by Vietnam but who did not die until many years later, and who are still dying to this day.

I write to you about a good man named William Patrick Ferrie whom I came to know during our tour of duty in the First Gulf War, then known as Operation Desert Storm.

I was the XO of a medical company in the Colorado Army National Guard. Pat was a Staff Sergeant in the Army Reserve from Helena, Montana. Pat was augmented to our company as the chaplain's assistant. He did so voluntarily; he was not ordered to active duty. Due to our company's deployment to four far-flung locations in Saudi Arabia, Pat and I spent a lot of time together driving around the desert checking on the welfare of our folks.

Dear Pat,

I enjoyed your company and our work together very much. You impressed me as a caring husband to Kate, and father of two daughters. Your commitment to working in the marriage preparation ministry of your church also stands out in my memory of your character. You mentioned your time in Vietnam as a radio operator in an infantry platoon, but I did not detect the anguish I came to know you had as a result of your time there. What I did perceive was a desire to serve again in what we were led to believe was a just cause, and then have some kind of positive closure in contrast to what your Vietnam experience was like.

Who could have known that our encounter in the desert in March 1991, with the Bedouin man maimed by some unexploded ordnance that detonated as he scavenged through a trash pile would have resulted in your being sent home before the rest of the company? Even though you were not a member of our unit before mobilization you had quickly befriended many and earned the respect of all through your service among us. Just before you left us there you mentioned having been diagnosed, again, with PTSD, which was the first I had known of that being a part of your life.

When I received the phone call from Kate in May 1992 letting me know that you had died she spoke next of your fondness for all of us and the time we spent together in Saudi Arabia. She told me of your disappointment that you could not come home with us, your continuing struggles with PTSD for all those years after Vietnam and especially so after Desert Storm, and the night that your life ended as a result of it all.

Pat, the Department of Defense is currently spending millions of dollars rewriting and publicizing their version of the history of the Vietnam War. The voices of those whose names are on The Wall cannot be heard in contradiction to what the Pentagon wants the American public to remember and think about that war, all the wars now being fought in our name, and to set the stage for wars yet to be waged. Your name is not, and the names of thousands like you are not, even on The Wall. But they should be. You all were killed there as surely as if you had died in an ambush.

It is my hope and prayer that your sacrifice to the Vietnam War as told by this letter will somehow make our nation come to our moral senses and cease the pursuit of empire and all the death and destruction we are causing in our world and to ourselves.

Rest in the peace that this world knows nothing of in this age.

Semper Fidelis et Pacificus,
Gerry Werhan
Veterans For Peace
Chapter 099 – Asheville, NC

In Remembrance

May 22, 2016, Letters to The Wall, Memorial Day, 2016.

In Remembrance of:

Sgt. Glenn Alan Lovett
Vietnam, KIA, March 7, 1970.
The Wall, Panel W 13, Line 93

Dear Glenn,

It has been 46 years since Vietnam, when you were fatally taken from your family, wife, one year old daughter, your mom, dad, sister, brother, and from your friends, one was me. We were infantry. First the 82nd, then the 101st. We did not know why. War would be a lie.

So many years ago though it seems like yesterday. When we were in the same unit you would share the news from your family with me, and when at base camp, your cassette messages from your wife. Happy news of how they all were doing, how the love of your life one year old daughter "was growing like a weed". You loved, missed them, looked forward to going home to them, to the farm in Ohio.

I received a letter from you after we transferred to the 101st, from your company to mine. My letter of reply to you was shortly returned to me at a fire base. An official letter from the Army, with mine to you, offered regrets and told me you had been killed. A week later I received letters from your family of the trauma and sadness of your loss, about the funeral, about their knowledge of our great friendship as brothers in war. They wrote to make sure I knew of your loss and with prayers for my safe return home. I wrote back of the wonderful person of Spirit you were, of how much you loved them all, how sorry I was, and I sent prayers for comfort for them and thankfulness that we were friends.

46 years it has been. Twice the years of the 23 that you were there in Ohio, at home in peace, a blessing to all who knew you

on this earth. I went to your company when I was back at base camp to ask what had happened when you were killed. They told me that your company was in the mountains, the point man was shot and wounded, that you as slack man, next in line, ran forward to help him. You were killed in your effort of sacrifice to help him.

Those who return home always know the guilt of not being able to bring our buddies back. You gave again, as you had all your life, this time giving your life for that wounded soldier in front of you. Wars, needless wars, another war we now know as lies by those who sent us, wars which continue to kill through these many years. We have Nams still, in the middle east, subversive political war mongers of killings, torture, war crimes, suicides, sufferings that take innocent children and loved ones of sovereign nations, as you were taken. The peoples, the many more taken by the betrayals of our abused power policymakers of violence, of no conscience, of political and special interests' atrocities.

Glenn, I'm sorry I have not written before, though I have visited you and those at The Wall many times. Know you are never forgotten but remembered in all hearts that knew you, Glenn, a brother for peace. I know you are in peace now. After The Wall was built, I wrote to your family again, then 25 years after your sacrifice. I met your loving mom, dad, wife, and that little one year old who had become a nurse, who has now blessed you with a beautiful granddaughter. What a family you were, are, and always will be.

Your mom, dad, and sister are with you again in the heavenly home of your faith. Know that we always shall remember, love you, and will one day all be blessed to see you all again. Bless you, my friend, my brother for peace. The power of truth and peace will bring us home to you, to our families, to brothers and sisters for peace, and that power of love, of humanity, will serve to see that wars end.

Thank you, my friend, my brother.

Til then and always… peace.

Wade Fulmer

Celebration of Memorial Day in the US

MEMORIAL DAY, MAY 30, 2016
PORTLAND, OREGON VIETNAM MEMORIAL,
S. Brian Willson

Celebration of Memorial Day in the US, originally Decoration Day, commenced shortly after the conclusion of the Civil War. This is a national holiday to remember the people who died while serving in the armed forces. The day traditionally includes decorating graves of the fallen with flowers.

As a Viet Nam veteran, I know the kinds of pain and suffering incurred by over three million US soldiers, marines, sailors, and airmen, 58,313 of whom paid the ultimate price, whose names are on The Vietnam Wall in Washington, DC. The Oregon Vietnam Memorial Wall alone, located here in Portland, contains 803 names on its walls.

The function of a memorial is to preserve memory. On this US Memorial Day, May 30, 2016, I want to preserve the memory of all aspects of the US war waged against the Southeast Asian people in Viet Nam, Laos, and Cambodia – what we call the Viet Nam War – as well as the tragic impacts it had on our own people and culture. My own healing and recovery requires me to honestly describe the war and understand how it has impacted me psychically, spiritually, and politically.

Likewise, the same remembrance needs to be practiced for both our soldiers and the victims in all the other countries affected by US wars and aggression. For example, the US incurred nearly 7,000 soldier deaths while causing as many as one million in Afghanistan and Iraq alone, a ratio of 1:143.

It is important to identify very concretely the pain and suffering we caused the Vietnamese – a people who only wanted to be independent from foreign occupiers, whether China, France, Japan, or the United States of America. As honorably, and in some cases heroically, as our military served and fought in Southeast Asia, we were nonetheless serving as cannon fodder, in effect mercenaries for reasons other than what we were told. When I came to understand the true nature of the war, I felt betrayed by my government, by my religion, by my cultural conditioning into "American Exceptionalism," which did a terrible disservice to my own humanity, my own life's journey. Thus, telling the truth as I uncover it is necessary for recovering my own dignity.

I am staggered by the amount of firepower the US used, and the incredible death and destruction it caused on an innocent people. Here are some statistics:

- Seventy-five percent of South Viet Nam was considered a free-fire zone (i.e., genocidal zones)
- Over 6 million Southeast Asians killed
- Over 64,000 US and Allied soldiers killed
- Over 1,600 US soldiers, and 300,000 Vietnamese soldiers remain missing
- Thousands of amputees, paraplegics, blind, deaf, and other maimings created
- 13,000 of 21,000 of Vietnamese villages, or 62 percent, severely damaged or destroyed, mostly by bombing
- Nearly 950 churches and pagodas destroyed by bombing
- 350 hospitals and 1,500 maternity wards destroyed by bombing
- Nearly 3,000 high schools and universities destroyed by bombing
- Over 15,000 bridges destroyed by bombing
- 10 million cubic meters of dikes destroyed by bombing
- Over 3,700 US fixed-wing aircraft lost
- 36,125,000 US helicopter sorties during the war; over 10,000 helicopters were lost or severely damaged
- 26 million bomb craters created, the majority from B-52s (a B-52 bomb crater could be 20 feet deep, and 40 feet across)
- 39 million acres of land in Indochina (or 91 percent of the land area of South Viet Nam) were littered with fragments of bombs and shells, equivalent to 244,000 (160 acre) farms, or an area the size of all New England except Connecticut
- 21 million gallons (80 million liters) of extremely poisonous chemicals (herbicides) were applied in 20,000 chemical spraying missions between 1961 and 1970 in the most

intensive use of chemical warfare in human history, with as many as 4.8 million Vietnamese living in nearly 3,200 villages directly sprayed by the chemicals

• 24 percent, or 16,100 square miles, of South Viet Nam was sprayed, an area larger than the states of Connecticut, Vermont, and Rhode Island combined, killing tropical forest, food crops, and inland forests

• Over 500,000 Vietnamese have died from chronic conditions related to chemical spraying with an estimated 650,000 still suffering from such conditions; 500,000 children have been born with Agent Orange-induced birth defects, now including third generation offspring

• Nearly 375,000 tons of fireballing napalm was dropped on villages

• Huge Rome Plows (made in Rome, Georgia), 20-ton earth-moving D7E Caterpillar tractors, fitted with a nearly 2.5-ton curved 11-foot wide attached blade protected by 14 additional tons of armor plate, scraped clean between 700,000 and 750,000 acres (1,200 square miles), an area equivalent to Rhode Island, leaving bare earth, rocks, and smashed trees

• As many as 36,000,000 total tons of ordnance expended from aerial and naval bombing, artillery, and ground combat firepower. On an average day US artillery expended 10,000 rounds costing $1 million per day; 150,00-300,000 tons of UXO remain scattered around Southeast Asia: 40,000 have been killed in Viet Nam since the end of the war in 1975, and nearly 70,000 injured; 20,000 Laotians have been killed or injured since the end of the war

• 13.7 billion gallons of fuel were consumed by US forces during the war

• If there was space for all 6,000,000 names of Southeast Asian dead on the Vietnam Wall in Washington, DC, it would be over 9 sobering miles long, or nearly 100 times its current 493 foot length.

I am not able to memorialize our sacrificed US soldiers without also remembering the death and destruction of civilian infrastructure we caused in our illegal invasion and occupation of Viet Nam, Laos and Cambodia. It has been 47 years since I carried out my duties in Viet Nam. My "service" included witnessing the aftermath of bombings from the air of undefended fishing villages where virtually all the inhabitants were massacred, the vast majority being small children. In that experience, I felt complicit in a diabolical crime against humanity. This experience led me to deeply grasping that I am not worth more than any other human being, and they are not worth less than me.

Recently I spent more than three weeks in Viet Nam, my first trip back since involuntarily being sent there in 1969. I was struck by the multitudes of children suffering from birth defects, most caused presumably by the US chemical spraying some 50 years ago. I experienced deep angst knowing that the US is directly responsible for this genetic damage now being passed on from one generation to the next. I am ashamed that the US government has never acknowledged responsibility or paid reparations. I found myself apologizing to the people for the crimes of my country.

When we only memorialize US soldiers while ignoring the victims of our aggression, we in effect are memorializing war. I cannot do that. War is insane, and our country continues to perpetuate its insanity on others, having been constantly at war since at least 1991. We fail our duties as citizens if we remain silent rather than calling our US wars for what they are – criminal and deceitful aggressions violating international and US law to assure control of geostrategic resources, deemed necessary to further our insatiable American Way Of Life (AWOL).

Memorial Day for me requires remembering ALL of the deaths and devastation of our wars, and it should remind all of us of the need to end the madness. If we want to end war, we must begin to directly address our out-of-control capitalist political economy that knows no limits to profits for a few at the expense of the many, including our soldiers.

S. Brian Willson, as a 1st lieutenant, served as commander of a US Air Force combat security police unit in Viet Nam's Mekong Delta in 1969. He is a trained lawyer, an author, and has been an anti-war, peace and justice activist for more than forty years. He currently resides in Portland, Oregon.

You, Dear Wall

You, Dear Wall, are crowded with the dead
of my generation of my Country.
Some of you I knew. Most not.
Does it matter, Dear Wall,
That you only name the fallen from my country, and not
The agonized wandering souls of Vietnam?
Could you grow to fifty times as big?
Would the Mall hold you?
Would our souls?

Paul Cox

What had started out

1973.

What had started out as a few military "advisers" (or so we were told) had turned into hoards of U.S. military combat troops stalking and killing unarmed Vietnamese citizens by the hundreds of thousands, dropping bombs and napalm and bodies with no end in sight. And the body bags kept arriving at our airports and kids from Iowa and South Dakota were dying and the lies kept coming and I had two little boys who I swore would NEVER grow up to be soldiers and so, one day, when our younger son was three, his father and I took him to Washington, DC, to march, as we had marched so many times before, for an end to the war.

It was springtime in the Capital, and the azaleas and the cherry blossoms were in bloom and the sun was shining, and there were thousands upon thousands of us who came to march for an end to the war.

I was married at the time to a pediatrician, and so we joined the contingent of Physicians for Social Responsibility, and we marched next to Ben Spock, the famous "baby doctor," at the front of the line, and we introduced our little one, our Adam, to Dr. Spock. Adam held out his left hand for a hand shake and Dr. Spock said, "A lefty! Don't worry. He'll grow out of it."

Adam never grew out of it, and I never worried. Not about that. I worried that one day his number would come up and he'd become another kid from who-knows-where coming home in a body bag. And so we marched for an end to the war.

We marched. And we marched. It was hot, and we marched. To a three-year-old, the route must have seemed a million miles long, though in reality it was probably no longer than from the White House to the Pentagon, or maybe it was the other way around. And all along the route, our three-year-old kept asking "why?" and we explained over and over that we were marching for an end to the war.

Finally, the march was over. We were hot. We were thirsty. We were tired of marching for an end to the war and tired of trying to explain "why." But it was over! At last! And then it came… the one final question. Adam turned to us then and asked, "Is the war over now?"

It's been many years, and many more marches, since that one in 1973, and Adam's question still haunts me. Did our marching end the war? Did it make a difference? Does it make a difference? Do our marches, our letters to the editor, our petitions, our rallies, our lobbying, our meetings, our vigils, our songs, our chants, our poems, our putting our bodies on the tracks and in the streets…. Are the wars over now?

I don't know if we made a difference then. I never can be sure of that. But I do know this: Adam now has a child of his own. And for him, and for all the children and grandchildren of the world, and for all of you whose names are engraved here on this wall, the American War on Vietnam taught me that there's nothing else I'd rather do, nothing else I can do, but keep on marching for an end to war.

Vicki Ryder

The Wall That Separates Us

The Wall That Separates Us

I truly believe if the people on this memorial could
come back to life, they would all be in the antiwar
movement.
Since Vietnam, the United States has been involved
in war after war after war.
More Vietnam veterans have committed suicide
than were killed in Vietnam.
Why?
When politicians and the rich in America start sending
their kids to war, I'll start believing in noble causes.
I honor the dead on this memorial,
but I do not honor the lunatics who
sent them to die.
While the churches in this country pray
for peace, our economy worships war.
I saw some people on this Wall take their
last breath, and I do not want to see the next
generation do the same.
I did not serve in Vietnam for the cause of freedom,
I served Big Business in America for the cause of profit.
Every American soldier on this Wall now knows this.
I deeply honor Vietnam veterans who are here today,
and those who were in the antiwar movement who
tried desperately to stop the war.
I came back as I said I would,
to face the pain that I should.
Only this time the tears will flow,
like I couldn't do years ago.

Mike Hastie
Army Medic Vietnam
May 15, 2016

Photograph by Mike Hastie
Medevac Helicopter An Khe, Vietnam

JOHN LEES (3W-83)

I talked to John Lees the other day
in the garden of the Vietnam Memorial.
He remembered me and my new son
I remember his farm, his high school sweetheart's daily letters.

It's been a long time, John
since we staggered back to the barracks
counting the long days.
He laughed and said we didn't know then
how long it really would be.

We traded stories: who went, and who didn't
who came back, and who didn't; who came back
with so much baggage they would have been better
not coming back.

I wondered if it was worth it
and John got mad: it's never whether it's worth it
he said, it's what we did, and what's now.
He said his sweetheart is married, has three kids
his mother gone to cancer, his father to farmer's lung
his farm part of a company his brother works for.
He said what makes him mad is to think we did it
so there could be more homeless on our streets
so there could be less clean air and clean water
even in his precious Iowa
so there could be more rich politicians standing trial
so there could be less spent on bread and more on bombs.
He said now there was less caring, more grabbing for power.

I didn't know what to say so I asked him about the flag
and the Supreme Court, if he'd heard about that.
He seemed to ignore me and said
if we fought for anything it was to make it better
for those who've had it stacked against them
that's why so many blacks died there, for their

brothers' and sisters' jobs, for all people
to control their own bodies, their futures, in their own ways.
Perhaps we even fought, he said, for those nine black robes
to chip away at all that.
Freedom, he said, what's that?
Freedom to invade, to destroy?
Freedom to enslave, freedom
to give up freedom?
He laughed, his anger turned back on him
twisting inside out.
I even know about China, he said
in China they fought for the freedoms
your President wants to take away.

He stepped back towards the edge of the park
towards where the shadows had disappeared
and where the shadows grew again
past the flowers and the lunches
past the sons and daughters of the veterans
past the veterans themselves and the great crowd
of the sons and daughters who would never be.

Your flag, he said, your fucking flag
I didn't die for your fucking flag
I died for your freedom to burn it.

Dan Wilcox

Red Rage

Red Rage

It was in a philosophy class, I'm sure, where a young, bright instructor gave a clear and cogent argument against the war in Vietnam still being waged by our country. It was 1969 or 1970.

He was so correct; so right on, that I could not enhance his argument in the least.

The red rage was that he had no right to know that. I knew that. But he had not earned that right in the manner I had. A few short weeks or months earlier I had gotten back from that country and did not know how to endorse his observations without smashing him in the face while saying, "You're so right!"

It did not seem to be a wise course of action, if I wanted a good grade.

Looking back from forty-seven years later, it might have been nice, if I could have just written what goes before and given it to him. Perhaps the intervening years might have been different. Keeping silence seemed to my rocked world a wise course for survival. I wasn't positive that the military might not try to grab my ass out of civilian life and thrown me back into their mad house. Anything seemed possible.

In the 2nd Battalion, 1st Marines area of operations (AO), when they didn't like having a World Council of Church's leper colony in their AO it was a simple matter. On the given day they marched past the site with two tanks and a company of Marines. Since it was a "no fire unless fired upon" zone, a squad of a few jarheads were sent around the colony on the east (ocean) side, who then called their platoon to see if they should take a few Viet Cong under fire who they saw running around in the colony. Shooting through the colony their rounds went over the main force, which was fortunately (by plan) on lower ground. Now that the main force was receiving fire, they commenced firing back. Quite a few rounds later (they needed a re-supply) the colony was in shambles and the lepers would need to be moved closer to DaNang. Problem solved.

I'd personally marched through major taboos in our culture since returning and no one said shit. Although my Dad did said, "At least your taste is improving." I knew that smoking dope had possible legal consequences, too. But that didn't slow my involvement. Chasing and reading, working on classes, working for "the man," chasing and using held my attention. That was it.

Protesting the wild war was a step too far for me. Drinking and hanging with other student veterans, who didn't want to have anything to do with the insanity, maxed out my ability to respond.

Maybe I could have told that college instructor about going into a village in Vietnam with a company of Marines and asking one of the officers who the Vietnamese person with us, was. Outfitted with a white shirt and six gun strapped on his belt, he didn't seem to be one of the villagers. And clearly didn't live there as he had come with us. I was told he was the mayor of the town.

Being the strongmen for this guy really had lighted up my sense of patriotism and sense of pointlessness to the blown-up troops, officers or enlisted. Great use of our national tax moneys. Dying for "the man," who happened to be Vietnamese. Wow. Thank me for that service!

Oh, and speaking of blown-up, there was the time I managed to get my own ass blown-up. Not even a scratch on my body. The other ten Marines were not as fortunate when some defective ordnance went off, when it wasn't suppose to. Thank you, armaments manufacturers! How much did your profits go up from cutting that corner? I wonder if that attitude was part of the one so many Presidents since Ford have wondered about the problem with "the Vietnam Syndrome?" You know for sure that those Commanders In Chiefs (CIC) were not really talking about any of the "mental issues" associated with fighting that pointless war.

After all everyone knows that post traumatic stress disorder didn't appear in the Data and Statistical Manual of Mental Disorders until five years after that country was united and the last Americans flew away. Yes, five years after the war was over; suddenly there was a disorder called PTSD (post traumatic stress disorder). Don't you know that veterans of the America war in

Vietnam were instrumental in getting it recognized for their brother veterans' benefit. Thanks again all you caring mental health care workers! We knew you had our backs on that one.

But I drift.

Last year in a "Full Disclosure" note I mentioned a "back story" to an operation just before Christmas 1968. Before we boarded the choppers to complete the cordon on that cordon and search operation, a number of us noted a psyops plane flying around south of us. When we asked the Vietnamese interpreter what was being said, he reported that they were saying that the Viet Cong were surrounded and should give up. Unfortunately, we were not there, yet; and would not be for another hour or so.

One can bury a lot of booby traps in an hour.

A number of "short timers" who were in the rear in preparation for going home went home sooner than expected that day. And the one boot platoon commander who is named on the wall was part of the parties that bought the farm from deeply buried dud 105 artillery rounds they scavenged to use against us. Yes, the Vietnamese are nothing, if not resourceful.

Their culture has had a long history of opposing invaders. Possibly our politicians didn't know that when they decided to back the losing French enterprise in 1954.

Oh, and the commanding officer for the battalion even came out to visit his operation on the second or third day. As a leader of infantry he arrived inside the middle of three tanks. When the company commander went to speak with him. He had to walk to the back of the tank and pick up a field phone on the back of the tank to talk to him. The lite colonel never did get out of the tank. Too many booby traps, I guess. And he was too short himself to risk it.

Would that have been the Operations Officer or the Commanding Officer, who should have called off the psyops plane? One assumes that after action reports comment on this question.

But it was a dumb war anyway. If there was ever a non-dumb war. Or ever will be.

Seven years later (after my return), I finally finished the two quarters of college work I had left when I was kicked out in 1966. Eight years after that I stopped using dope and began attending to what it would mean to have a career. I guess I just wasn't cut out to be a tough, heartless killer for christ and the rest of the patriotic bull shit. I still cared about people. Like the time I came across a wounded North Vietnamese medic, who had been taken captive, because they left him behind. He was on a stretcher on the ground with a Marine guard with a rifle near him. I casually walked up to him smoking a cigarette. We looked one another in the eye. He signaled he would like a cigarette. I didn't think the threat of cancer was a big deal in fulfilling his wish and gave him one. We had a few puffs and then I walked away.

I have no idea what became of him. But one Marine gave him something, without a string attached to it. At the time I recall thinking that the Marines around me may have wondered what I was doing. I was clear about demonstrating a human kindness in the midst of senselessness.

When my wife and I were in Vietnam in 2014 with Chapter #160's fund raising tour, I had a brief sense of me pissing into the hurricane with that kindness. But I did it without missing a beat. It just needed doing.

It was such a fucked up war. The second "Asian anticommunist" war. Both had questionable beginnings. And both likely arose out of the "China Lobby," with that whole questionable origin. Or hadn't you heard about the doubts about the origin of the supposedly civic organization's history. Secret funding goes lots of secret places, for lots of secret reasons. Study the China Lobby. It's good use of your time in developing perspective on this democracy.

I believe the truth will out and the careening course of our democracy can straighten out for a short period again.

I hope so.

Ron Staff

I'm so sorry

Dear Brothers and Sisters of The Wall —

I'm so sorry your young lives were cut so short. I've tried to physically approach you at The Wall to offer my prayers and condolences but am unable to get within fifty yards without breaking down. So this letter is being delivered to you by Veterans For Peace on Memorial Day 2016.

We all live with the racism, lies and atrocities committed by our country in Viet Nam. I'm so sorry you had to die for it.

Charlie Sisson, USMC

Viet Nam 1968-1969

Letter to Dave Brostrum.

This letter is to a Coast Guard Academy classmate who while serving as a Patrol Boat skipper in Danang in 1966 was killed with "friendly fire" by the US Air Force.

I also drove one of those 82 foot Patrol Boats, with a crew of 9, harassing fishermen and passenger vessels plying the coast of Vietnam. Fortunately, my boat was only shot at a couple of times, and we suffered no physical casualties. I don't know about how the crew has made it mentally through the last 40 years.

Having left Vietnam in late 1966, I returned to the states ignorantly believing that the "war was going well... more roads were open... etc", only to see, just a few months later, the Tet Offensive, to me a real turning point in the War, as I began to realize how brainwashed I had been during the 50's and 60"s. Years later reading the Calley story showed me how men get caught up in the excitement of war, get really crazy and really lose their humanity. By the time I left Vietnam the rebellion was beginning, and there were already stories of coasties and fragging.

I credit my spouse at the time, who said that humans had been trying for thousands of years to resolve conflict with violence, and that it was time to find another way.

Later the Pentagon Papers exposed all the lies behind the war, from the Gulf of Tonkin on. Unbelievably, the US hasn't seemed to learn any of those lessons from that time...how the government lies to us, and how our democracy exists in name only.

Dave, you were a great guy, caught up like the rest of us in Imperial America. May you RIP.

Bud Haas
Bradford Vt
Member, Will Miller Green Mountain
Veterans For Peace, Chapter 57

I write to the Vietnam Memorial Wall

To Whom It May Concern,

I write to the Vietnam Memorial Wall as the United States is in the midst of the 50th Anniversary Commemoration of the Vietnam War.

President Obama's effort to focus the commemoration on injustices suffered by the troops who served in Vietnam is a disservice to history and to prospects for peace in our future. On commemorative occasions of World War II, the world expects and receives words of remorse and contrition from the leaders of Germany and Japan, two aggressor nations in that war. The United States, if it had any objective view of history, would do the same in its commemoration of the Vietnam War. It would disavow any future acts of aggression and completely acknowledge the commission of war crimes and atrocities.

Any injustice suffered by American troops upon their return from Vietnam pales in comparison to the injustice of sending them there in the first place. Halting the spread of communism is not a permissible use of military force under international law.

Obsessive veneration of the troops is a predictable characteristic of a militaristic nation. It serves to distract attention from the criminal architects of the war (Johnson, McNamara, Nixon, Kissinger et al.) and obviate the suffering of the truest victims of war; in this case, the people of Vietnam.

During this fifty year commemoration, let's dispense with the platitudes and work to repair the damage done to Vietnam, Cambodia, and Laos by America's indiscriminate war machine. I call on my country to do everything in its power to dispose of unexploded ordnance, clean up the contamination caused by Agent Orange, and care for the victims of both in Southeast Asia.

With Hope for Lasting Peace,

Mike Madden
Veterans For Peace, Twin Cities Chapter 27
United States Air Force and USAFR (1973-78)

Ten of the people who were in my company

Ten of the people who were in my company during my time in Vietnam are on this Wall. Every time I hear Iris Dement's song "There's a Wall in Washington" I start to cry.

I just realized I didn't say "The names of ten of the people" but "Ten of the people." That's because when you know people they are more than names on the Wall, they are the things that you remember about them.

One was given the Congressional Medal of Honor, posthumously, for falling on a grenade and saving the people around him. We lost two other people that day.

One was a Mennonite, a medic who didn't carry a weapon, killed in his sleep by a grenade thrown through a hedgerow near Cu Chi.

One was a friend of mine, killed by a mine in a hedgerow, also near Cu Chi. He's always on my mind. I could have prevented that if I'd been mature enough to know that I could have called a halt and had him removed from the field. He seemed to be having a breakdown while he was walking point and as his squad leader I could have stopped it, but I didn't know what to do, so I did nothing and he died.

Two were killed by our own artillery. I wonder if the artillerymen were told about what they'd done.

Three were killed in a little village a few days after the Tet Offensive started. After they died we were told to pull back and get behind some APCs. The Air Force came over and started 12 hours of bombing with HE and napalm and burnt the whole village to the ground. At about the eighth hour of the bombing, in the dark, in the lull while the F-4s went back to reload, a young girl came out holding a little baby over her head, saying the same thing over and over in Vietnamese, None of us understood it, She was probably saying "Please don't kill my baby, please don't kill my baby, please don't kill my baby." She walked past us into the dark.

In the morning we stayed in a circle around the village while they brought in Charlie Company to search the rubble. They counted 192 bodies. Just one more atrocity to add to the thousands of big and little atrocities that we did in Vietnam. We came to protect them from the evils of Communism and instead we killed them.

Was that war one fucked–up mess, or what? How could we have been so stupid? But unfortunately, I don't know about you guys, but yes, I was that stupid. But I'm better now. And we keep going, trying to warn other people about the dangers of war and militarism.

My brave and beautiful brother Ken should be on this Wall. He was in the 4th Infantry Division in the Central Highlands. In May '69 he was wounded in a firefight. His left leg was broken by a bullet and he lay there for 8 hours while the fight went on around him. Our own artillery hit him and broke his right foot (Lord, have mercy). He suffered for years. He killed himself in 1994. I want everyone of you who reads this to get through your sorrow. We don't have a Disorder, our society has a Disorder, and we can help them fix it.

I speak in high schools and colleges about Vietnam and Afghanistan (two sides of the same Western arrogance coin). We are trying, as Martin Luther King, Jr. said, to save the soul of America. I've given out about 3 hundred copies of his "Beyond Vietnam" speech in the last few years. As I hand it to people I say "If you read this, it will change your life for the better."

I think when I speak in classes from now on I'm gonna bring a good portable sound system and start out by playing Iris Dement's song. Around the middle I think I'll play John Prine's song, "Your flag decal won't get you into heaven anymore." I think I'll end by saying that if we're going to save the soul of America, first, we got to get some soul, and hand out "Beyond Vietnam" and end by playing Marvin Gaye's "What's Going On?"

Sisters and brothers, we are doing something that needs to be done, so let's keep going. But take some time to watch the clouds, and watch the river flow, and watch the children play, and remember the beauty of life. That's what we're working for.

Bill Distler
Vietnam, December '67 to September '68
Delta Co., 2/ 506th

Peace to those

Peace to those who for a moment lived inside the Vietnam Wall, but have made the crossing.

As Michael Norman said, "To touch the Wall is to touch the dead, to get close to them." But those names should not have been on that or any Wall. Mankind always builds Walls, Walls that divide us into "Us and Them," "Good People and Bad People," and creates cultures of "Others," of whom we are all a part. As Robert Frost said, "Something There Is That Doesn't Love a Wall, That Wants It Down." And the ultimate Wall, is the Wall of War to honor, respect and touch our dead. But it is time to STOP WAR, to tear down such walls and honor those that are alive, who refuse to create war, which is all of us "Others!!"

Peace, Judith Sandoval,
VFP Chapter 69

Last year was the 50th Anniversary

Dear Vietnam Veterans' Memorial Wall,

Last year was the 50th Anniversary, 8 March 2015, of the "beginning" of the war with the landing of Marines at Da Nang.

The so-called Gulf of Tonkin Incident occurred on my 18th birthday as I was getting ready to begin my freshman year of college. I finished out the year, but the main thing I learned there was that I didn't like chemistry after all, even though I was good at it.

What to do?! My grandfathers were both Army vets, one from WWI, the other from the Spanish-American War, my father was a Navy officer and my mother was a Navy nurse in WWII so I enlisted in the Navy in September '65, "chip off the ol' block" so to speak. The recruiter put me on delayed entry so I reported to Great Lakes Naval Training Center on 6 January '66.

After Basic I was sent to the Memphis Naval Air Training Center in Millington, Tennessee. I'm from Nebraska and lived and enlisted in northern Ohio, but after Basic Training north of Chicago during the coldest months of the year I didn't mind being sent to Tennessee.

Duty there was good, it was near Memphis after all. A couple of my buddies and I decided to take a day trip down into Mississippi one summer day. One of them had a '39 Ford with a rusted out floor pan, but it ran so we didn't care; all three of us were still 19 so it was an adventure. Before we got very far into Mississippi we heard on the radio of civil rights troubles so we decided we'd be better off by grabbing a burger somewhere, and heading back to base. We found a little place down a side road and went in. We got the "look" from the proprietor/cook. She must have thought we were bringing the civil rights trouble right to her, me being white, one of my buds African American and the other a Native American. It was about a year after "Bloody Sunday" in Selma. But she served us, we had fun, and returned to Tennessee.

When I finished Avionics 'A' School, some of us were sent to the west coast, others to the east coast. So I began what could have become a Navy career at the Norfolk Naval Air Station, in an anti-submarine warfare squadron. They asked if I'd fly; I said sure so I was assigned to Flight Crew 9. VP-24 had P2-V Neptunes at the time, and my station in the plane was in the nose, where the gunner – bombardier was when the plane was a medium bomber. I had the best seat in the house! More than 180 degree vision above and below, port and starboard! I operated sub detection equipment, was the flight photographer, and forward observer.

We began training to change from P2's to P3-B Orions, so in late summer or early fall of '67 we got the new planes and were moved from Norfolk to Pax River NAS in Maryland. We were deployed to Iceland in March of '68 for six months of operational duty, mostly in the North Atlantic.

We returned from Iceland to Pax River in September of '68, and somewhere along in there I began reading about the war, the reasons for it, and some of the questions about those reasons. Heck, I enlisted to go to Vietnam. The Navy had their own plans for what, when and where they wanted me and others, so whatever I thought I wanted didn't count. The age-old problem of kids who go to recruiters and are told all kinds of things about where we would go and the glories of serving there!

By the time we were deployed to Iceland again, in March '69, I had turned from an essentially apolitical Republican kid from Nebraska and Ohio to an anti-war activist who had been to a couple big demonstrations in DC with tear gas and riot police, and I subscribed to some underground GI newsletters and newspapers. I remember going to those demonstrations with a plastic bag and a damp cloth in case I got caught in the tear gas – I knew what it was like from my training in Tennessee.

Through the first half of my four-year enlistment I thought I could make a career of naval aviation, what with flying all over, visiting places in the U.S., the Caribbean and Europe. I spent a lot of time at NAS Key West, NAS Roosevelt Roads in Puerto Rico, and visits to Oslo, Copenhagen, Rota, Edinburgh, London, Thule, the North Pole and even Waco, Texas!

But my thoughts of a Navy career changed after I realized the Admirals and Generals and the President were lying to us. A couple of my high school buddies and neighbors were casualties in Vietnam before I enlisted, and I found out that the leaders of America, they lied! It really pissed me off, so I began writing an anti-Vietnam War newsletter while I was deployed, running it off on a hand-cranked mimeograph machine and distributing it on base, all in the wee hours. I was an anti-war activist in uniform, who woulda thunk it! I never considered refusing to do my job. They would have just thrown me in the brig, out-of-sight, out-of-mind. So I ranted, held barracks bull sessions, I was the "squadron radical."

Another guy and I were flown back stateside, in a C-141, ahead of the rest of the squadron so we could be processed out early when Nixon began reductions in authorized force. I got out on 6 November '69 instead of 6 January '70, two months early. I came to Baltimore to be with the young woman who became my wife before long. We were arrested on Christmas Eve for painting military recruiting signs, those big metal ones, near Baltimore's Memorial Stadium, the home of the Colts and Orioles. Get this: Army   Navy   Marines   Air Force   Coast Guard   National Guard

P   E   A   C   E

It was just before Nixon's "secret plan for ending the war," the Christmas bombing that mobilized people all over the country and led to the Kent State shootings on 4 May 1970, followed by Jackson State a week or so later and uprisings at hundreds of campuses across the country.

I've visited you many times. I've looked and walked, touched and despaired, and there are those who now would try to whitewash the history of the war you are here to help us, MAKE us, remember. I've been blessed to have had leaders in the veterans and labor movements whom I respect and appreciate. They include Fred Mason, Jr., a long-time friend and now President of the Maryland/DC AFL-CIO. He was one of six original co-conveners of U.S. Labor Against War, USLAW.

Another is Dave Cline, a former President of Veterans For Peace, an Army vet who, like me, turned against the war while still in uniform. He was seriously wounded there, whereas I spent my overseas time on the opposite side of the planet. I always appreciated his stories about his time in Vietnam, and his work afterwards, against war, and FOR workers as a leader in his union in the postal service. Dave is gone now, since September 2007, but I remember him playing his guitar and singing "Touch A Name On The Wall." As I did when I wrote last year,

Jim Baldridge
USN 6 January 66 – 6 November 69
ATN2 (E5), VP-24, Flight Crew 9

We wonder

We wonder why academia hasn't protested the Global War On Terror, like asking, "what the hell is a global war on terror"? Then we recall how academia protested the war on Vietnam.

I remember 1970 in Brunswick (that's a town in Maine) in the strike season after the incursion into Cambodia by the President who removed US troops from Vietnam. The mall in Brunswick was full of displays about the war and none of them seemed to me, a fifteen-year-old, to have anything to say.

Then my brother gave me "A Bright Shining Lie" in the '90's — the same brother with whom I drifted into the strike season, etc. — and I read that Ike had been told by the CIA that if the 1954-conference-mandated referendum took place, the communists would take 80% of the votes, if only because they controlled the territory. Then I checked sources and found that Ike had told the world about this decision — oh, the referendum didn't get held — in Mandate for Change, a memoir published in 1963. So everybody in Washington and academia knew in 1963 that Kennedy et. al. were fighting against the mass of Vietnamese public opinion. Hence it was a war on Vietnam.

Why? How? I might suggest that there is a WASP racist imperialist genocidal power structure in place in the US as it has been for centuries (The Imperial Cruise by James Bradley will put you in the mood).

Can't we blame all this on the Israel lobby? I searched for the name "Bernstein" on Harvard Medical School's website and got, as I recall, 16 different people. I realize now that's like touting the influence of the Israel lobby in Congress. ("The Israel lobby has never been stronger in Congress." George Mitchell to a colloquium at USM-Portland four or five years ago.)

A small minority, even willing to disproportionately invest itself in politics, cannot change nor even shift the weight of opinion evidently at work in such acts as the invasions of Afghanistan and Iraq (and Syria, Yemen, Somalia, Libya) and go on back to Panama, Grenada, Lebanon, Nicaragua, keep on going to Congo (killing Lumumba and possibly Dag Hammarskjold, see the interview with the Norwegian deputy commander of

NATO who was a UN-seconded colonel Northern Rhodesia and saw Hammarskjold's body with a "round hole in its forehead"), Guatemala, Iran.

How do you hide such a monstrous edifice ("establishment")?

Pope John Paul II accused the US of having a culture of death, and I would specify that a bit: it's a fundamentally violent culture, and lying is the main vehicle and means of violence: it is the poor person's strategic weaponry, the rich person's terrorism, it is the essence of racism, and it is what WASP children are suckled on.

Why didn't we learn anything from the war on Vietnam? Because the experiment isn't finished yet.

Christopher C. Rushlau

Thank you for taking my letter to the wall.

Dear names on the wall,

You will always be more than names on a wall to me.

I wish you had all come home, that the war had never happened and we could go back into time to fix it. I was a child when my father served in Vietnam and I have wanted to end war ever since. Most every day since seeing the picture of Kim Phuc running after being napalmed I have prayed and tried to use my life to end war but now I am almost 53. I am getting old and I have had no successes.

It seems sometimes we are only getting closer to even more war, to nuclear war and destroying our planet, but then I have this stubborn hope in my heart: You have not died in vain and maybe I can feel your spirits are there helping us to try to end war and injustice.

My letter to your names on the wall is my prayer for help. Please help. I know you have and you will, but I am getting old now and with climate change, I am not sure we can make it if we spend all our resources on more nuclear weapons and war instead of meeting human needs to get through.

Love always, I carry you all in my heart,

Linda Marie Richards

Memorial Day, 2016

Thank you for reading my letter.

I especially remember Larry Welch

I especially remember Larry Welch, a friend from high school days in Jacksonville, Illinois. Larry was a star on the JHS football team. Although I don't have many details, Larry died in Vietnam. Like so many serving in Southeast Asia, his life was cut short.

He will always be remembered.

My wife and I have visited the Wall in Washington, DC. The experience was overwhelming for us, as it surely must be for you.

I was a Navy veteran who served two tours in the Vietnam War. Retired for a few years I spend much of my time volunteering.

One interest resulted in joining a local chapter of Veterans for Peace. Here is a quick summary of what VFP is about:

"Our collective experience tells us wars are easy to start and hard to stop and that those hurt are often the innocent. As veterans, we draw on our personal experiences and perspectives to raise public awareness of the true costs and consequences of militarism and war – and to seek peaceful, effective alternatives."

In peace,

Jim Woods

To the Guys on the Wall

There you are
All you guys
Who didn't survive
A roll call of so many names
In rows upon rows
Like eyes front faces on parade
Reconstituted ranks
Reassembled from the chaos of
Battlefields
Airplane crashes
Helicopter crashes
Mortar attacks
Rocket attacks
Friendly fire
Field hospitals
Returned to duty
To wall up another corner
Of the capital
So it shan't collapse
Of its military follies

–Jan Barry

To Don MacLaughlin

To Don MacLaughlin — my friend commemorated on panel 4E, line 51

You would remember, Don, I visited you on the slightly overcast morning of June 10th, 1995. Along with many other of our fellow Naval Academy graduates, family members and friends, I had come to formally pay respects to you and our 12 other fallen classmates, victims of the grossest of our nation's many military misadventures. In that solemn ceremony conducted on the lawn of the Ellipse, within sight of the black granite panels on which your name and the names of over 58,000 other American men and eight women are etched, a close friend of each fallen classmate spoke. You would have thought that each of you was a more-than-mortal soul as your singular virtues were extolled with heartfelt sincerity. As one among many who was honored to know your friendship, I was proud to make the case that you were the best of the best. The memory of that day sticks with me, not because I presented your case well — that was easy — but because I expressed on that day sentiment I'd come to embrace, sentiment that then was generally unshared and unappreciated and, worse, rejected by most in the audience.

In speaking of you I said, "Since I learned of Don's death in 1966, I have struggled to put meaning to his loss, just as I know his family, his parents, his brother and sisters, and wife, Gail, all struggled. And I am certain that the families and loved ones of the thousands of other young people memorialized here also have searched for meaning, just as I am certain that the 1-2 million Vietnamese who died also had wives and sons and daughters, brothers and sisters, and parents who mourned their premature demise. Those losses were just as assuredly monumental and overwhelming and they, too, have struggled to make some sense of the insanity and the inanity of it all. Now I have found some solace in the recognition that these losses have served to move me away from militarism and resolutely toward pacifism. And, while I know it's unlikely many of you would go that far I do believe it's quite possible we all have been moved toward negotiation and reason as a means of conflict resolution and away from war."

I went on to quote the former Senator, J. William Fulbright, on that day in 1995. "We must dare to think 'unthinkable' thoughts. We must learn to welcome and not to fear the voices of dissent. We must dare to think about 'unthinkable things' because when things become unthinkable, thinking stops, and action becomes mindless."

Fulbright's was a lonely voice of dissent as he called for withdrawal from the conflict in Vietnam; his perspective rooted in common sense and a respect for the brotherhood of man and his conclusion that the true enemy was war itself.

I came away from that day at the wall in 1995 proud for having expressed my deeply-felt sentiment with regards to the American criminality and futility of the Vietnam war and all of our militarism over the intervening years, but feeling depressed and alone as the reaction to my words had been generally chilly, and in the case of one former classmate downright hostile. He had said, "Today wasn't the place and time to acknowledge Vietnam's casualties." I was speechless. In retrospect I have concluded that my dissent in my classmate's opinion was an "unthinkable thing."

Now, 21 years later, I feel vindicated and validated, but nonetheless, disheartened when I consider the history since. U.S. military interventions in foreign lands are undertaken with an every day regularity that barely provokes Congressional scrutiny and, generally, escapes media comment or public attention. The author Andrew Bacevich documents that we have bombed 14 Islamic countries. Drone attacks, simply targeted, extrajudicial assassinations or murders, and the miscarriage of, nay — the absolute disregard for — justice at Guantanamo stand as policies of a country that refuses to hold itself accountable. This refusal is, I believe, a legacy of the Vietnam War. It is behavior that has been facilitated by the disregard, if not the absolute distortion, of the lessons of Vietnam.

This brings me to the Veterans for Peace (VFP) Full Disclosure campaign, a response to the Pentagon's more generously funded commemoration of the war. The 2008 National Defense Authorization Act authorized the Secretary of

Defense to launch a program, commemorating the 50th anniversary of the war that would extend from Memorial Day of 2012 through Veterans Day of 2025, the stated purpose, among other things, to "thank and honor veterans of the Vietnam War." Nice and meaningful enough, but nowhere there will you find acknowledgment of the truths of that war as are widely known today. Nowhere will you find defendable rationale for the war for there is none. And the failure to disclose those truths has served to feed the cannons for all the wars that have followed.

At the VFP website vietnamfulldisclosure.org the goal is "to speak truth to power and keep alive the antiwar perspective on the American war in Vietnam. It represents a clear alternative to the Pentagon's current efforts to sanitize and mythologize the Vietnam war and to thereby legitimize further unnecessary and destructive wars."

I believe that from the other side of the divide over which you, our twelve classmates, and the more than 58,000 others have so prematurely and so pointlessly been taken, you would commend us for our work. May it ultimately not be in vain.

Rest in peace, my friend.

Dud Hendrick, Deer Isle, Maine

In Memory of my husband

May 2016

In Memory of my husband:

Michael D. Chwan – Panel 2E – Line 99
Captain, USAF, October 26, 1938 – September 30, 1965
Interred at Arlington April 16, 1985

In 1965, fifty-one years ago, I kissed my pilot husband good-bye, feeling confident that we would see each other in 90 days, the time of his assignment to a base in Ubon, Thailand.

That 90 days stretched to 19 ½ years before a handful of remains were finally returned to American soil for burial and closure in 1985.

Six months after his plane was shot down over North Vietnam, our daughter Michele was born and grew into young womanhood without the love, guidance and care of her missing father.

Our patriotic military personnel who serve their government sincerely believe that they are acting in the highest tradition of helping an ally fight for freedom and the right of self-determination in various countries all over the world wherever they are ordered to go.

As a military widow, I can tell you that the price of service in these wars that are not for our country's benefit is paid in grim coin.

In my opinion the loss of our best, brightest and most promising young people is a travesty and a drain on our American society.

The only ones who benefit are the arms and materiel manufacturers. I pray that someday our government leaders will finally come to realize and understand that in war there are no winners…

Battered, battle-weary soldiers and their bereft family members are then left to pick up the pieces, heal the emotional and physical wounds and strive to carry on when promised services and care are sometimes sub-par or non-existent.

209

This Wall of names is sacred ground. Seeing 58,000+ names is sobering and tragic – and a reminder that all these American citizens died not for glory or any good reason except for a false idea that democracy for an ally could be gained through our going to war for them.

Still the South Vietnamese could not sustain after all our efforts, expense and losses and fell anyway after so many deaths on all sides: North, South, Laotian, American and Russian.

When will we ever learn? When we ever learn...............

With gratitude for those who served, came back and now stand with others working for peace with their hopes and intention for a world without war.

Dana Chwan, Santa Fe, New Mexico Author, The Reluctant Sorority: The Life, Loves and Loss of Three Vietnam War Widows

Dear Friends of Consciousness,

So, it has come down to this, has it? We can either celebrate one side of the Civil War of the U.S. . . . or the other?

Cherish battle flags, honor, oh yes, Honor the dead on one side, or perhaps both sides of war. A War Heritage Month?

Just what the doctor ordered . . . relieve stress by honoring the deadliest conflict the U.S. has ever known.

Shall we continue this rivalry, when a simple understanding of our common need, our universal Humanity is obvious?

I submit to you, this war appreciation is absurd. We honor the contributions of all people who have furthered Humanity with millions of genuine contributions of knowledge, compassion, integrity, and, yes sacrifice. But to honor war . . . is an abomination of truth and kindness. With empathy and respect, I'd call for Peace. Honor Peace!

Peace Is Void Is Love Is Action.

Gov. Whomever: work for peace, spend for peace, diminish anything that silences peace; you must perpetuate peace, recognize peace builders, spend time for peace, communicate peace, meditate for peace, move for peace.

But any who monger for war or hate or fear deserve no monuments, deserve no special recognition, require no superb enhancement. War catches up our best intentions and lays them out as travesty! War flags, symbology so beautiful and colorful and inspiring, lead us only to the cold, solemn earth and final rest, despite our best efforts.

Let us advocate for seeing each other, eyes into eyes, to perceive our deepest truths, our most painful recollections, our sincerest passion for the well-being of all persons. Surrender to the highest calling a human being can attain.

Our work is love and love is action! No Dreams without Dreams Of Peace. Any separation must now be seen as illusion. Any tactic of division must now be seen as the darkest treachery. Let us say, "Honor Peace!"

Let each of us become a Personal Practice of Peace.

There are no dreams without the seeking of Peace. Our longing, our future, our best feelings and thoughts are Of Peace.

There can be no satisfaction in denying peace to others, our fellow Dreamers of Peace. There can be no future for our closest friends and loves without constructions, parameters, paradigms of peace. We have before us the need to mediate for peace, to simply allow peace to happen, before our very eyes, daily practice for the growing of peace.

Who can deny peace with a clear conscience? Who can celebrate any noble virtue or accomplishment without Peace!

Who, in their own Soul, can claim any meaningful existence, throughout eternity, without contributions to Peace?

In our every waking moment we wish to Experience Peace Together, to walk a path that brings all to peace, sweet peace.

Listen to the quiet and careful breeze of peace play the bamboo flute in the tavern pavilion of our hearts, and act accordingly.

Our work is awesome, it is forever, it is as clear as a sunrise horizon, and instantaneous, like the clicking of a clock.

Bullies shrink and disintegrate in the blink of an eye when presented with the seed of Peace. The beauty, the strength, the clarity, and the quickness of Peace infiltrate our bodies at the cellular level and Ecstatically Nurture Peace, undeniable and sensuous peace.

Peace dances in the face of demagogues! Pours tea in the laps of tyrants!

We inculcate peace into our offspring, from each generation to the next. We Imagine peace for the souls of our future, for All of Time.

Overwhelming Peace, Shimmering Peace, Nestling Peace, Embracing and Harmonious and Luxurious Peace.

Accepting Peace, So Be Peace.

h h higgins, 3/15/16

Stop the madness, please

Stop the madness, please. The only way I can think of to lessen the impact of loss of lives, is to reinstate a draft and have a MICROSCOPE and the press on every child of every parent in high government positions so that it will be much harder to wheel and deal their own kids out of service. Greed and lust for status/power are so powerfully corrosive drives; however, I won't hold my breath that even the death of a loved child will deter the war mongers and all the pawns supporting their efforts. God help us all! What can we do????

P. Selby

In memory of PFC Russell Cornish

This note is sent in memory of PFC Russell Cornish, who died on patrol in Vietnam and whose name is inscribed on The Wall: Dear Russ, You were more a friend of my brother than I , but I still miss you and think of you.

I feel sad that you did not return to your home in Maplewood, New Jersey on Prospect Street and resume a normal life.

I feel angry that misguided civilian and military leaders colluded to send you and millions of other young men and women to Vietnam for what noble purpose? You were a victim of cold war paranoia and fear.

Vietnam was a poor, underdeveloped, rural nation with no interest or capability of threatening the United States homeland.

I bid you goodbye again and hope that you rest in peace.

Your friend,
George Taylor,
Maplewood, New Jersey

Dear Lucky:

There's never a day that I don't think of you, never a day that I don't feel thankful for you, never a day that I don't try to make my life count as a way of paying you back and making your life matter.

Clear left,
Larry Shook

PFC PAUL JAMES GORMAN USMC

PFC PAUL JAMES GORMAN USMC
7/26/48- 7/30/68
WATERTOWN MA
KIA VIET NAM 7/30/68
DMZ KHE SANH
QUANG TRI PROVINCE
BLT 2/4 9THMAB FMFPAC

With Love & Peace from your Sister and Family who have been working for Peace since then.

Bonnie Gorman RN,
Quincy MA

As a Navy nurse, I worked for two years in the Vietnam Air Evacuation Hospital network (1967-69).

In July 1968, my brother Paul, a young Marine, was killed in action along the DMZ in Vietnam. Our mother then had a massive heart attack and eventually died. As a result of our personal losses and involvement with many wounded and dying soldiers and their families, I joined Vietnam Veterans Against the War (VVAW) and other peace groups working to end the Vietnam war and prevent future wars.

I continue to work for Peace and Justice with: Gold Star & Military Families Speak Out (GSFSO/MFSO), Veterans for Peace, Smedley Chapter (VFP), Gold Star Families for Peace (GSFP), and Massachusetts Peace Action Board and Legislative Committee

Dear Friend in the Wall,

I sincerely hope that the day comes soon when no more young people are forced, or convinced, to go to war for the benefit of the American military-industrial complex, as we were in Vietnam.

Those of us who were lucky enough to live through the war are the ones responsible to find the will and the effort to make clear to our country the way that the system profits from constant war, and to bring that war to an end.

Sincerely,

Reid Byers
USN 1969-73, USS Coral Sea, Yankee Station

My father was 28 years old

My father was 28 years old when he was deployed to Vietnam. As a new F-4C Phantom Pilot, he was unsure of what was to come. He had all the training he needed but entering a live combat environment is something that you can't always prepare for. I admired his courage and his patriotism, as well as his bravery and willingness to sacrifice his life to defend our country.

Forty-eight years later, my father is a 76 year old war veteran and significantly different than the man who went to Vietnam. He never went into great details about his deployment but I remember him telling me that the true heroes were the men who died over there, not the men who were able to come back. He also mentioned how his return to the States wasn't as easy nor was it favorable. The effects of the Vietnam War are felt even decades later. Multiple Vietnam Veterans have developed diseases related to Agent Orange exposure, which was used to remove foliage that provided cover for the enemy. If the military was aware of the damaging effects that herbicides have, I doubt it would have been used during the war.

To the men and women whose names are engraved on this wall — you have done a great service for your country. You will never be forgotten and your memory has been passed down to future generations. I've heard many stories about my father's wingmen who ended up on the wall and had the opportunity to etch their names on a sheet of wax paper. The wax paper ended up in my 8th grade Washington DC Album project and I'll never forget that moment of being at the Wall with my dad. Just know that you'll never be forgotten and your service in the Vietnam War will be remembered by the future generations, including myself.

Sincerely,

Alexandra Lippincott
Georgetown University | Class of 2014

My dear PFC.....

For years, I knew your name, just as I remember your face, now. I still remember Joe Wallace, too, and I looked for his name on the Wall, the first time I went. I knew your name would be there because I watched you die. Joe looked a lot worse than you, but he kept breathing, and we managed to get him to the beach. He must have made it. He's not on the Wall.

While we made a fuss over Joe, who was bleeding from dozens of shrapnel wounds, you died quietly on the deck of that Mike boat, the one you were so proud to have known as the Black Boat. Here you were, our first boat with an all-black crew, doing the most mundane of war chores: hauling surgical waste to be dumped in the middle of the Mekong River. It was probably a kid younger than you, launching the only rocket he had before you even cleared the basin. And none of us ever bothered to put on our pots and flak jackets until we reached the river.

Captain Wilde and I talked about your boat, about pros and cons for a black identity. With his blonde hair and brilliant blue eyes, he could have passed for a model Nazi, but I was the one who was xenophobic, even if it was in a somewhat enlightened way, befitting my status as an officer and a white-privileged gentleman. As platoon leader, I had no run-ins with you, although you had a reputation as a trouble-maker. Joe and I, on the other hand, didn't like each other. I thought I was fair with him, to the point that I could have charged him with insubordination. He was careful not to yell at me, but he gave me some pretty pointed stares before I let him leave my boat. He had a little too much exposure to black power for an insecure white lieutenant. Anyway, the captain and I decided the Black Boat would do more for esprit d'corps than for polarization. After you were killed, we just shook our heads, feeling more unlucky than guilty.

I was never tempted to leave a message at the Black Wall, but after all these years of pondering the bigotry and immaturity of my role in the rape of Vietnam, I decided to write to you. I don't expect to reach you in heaven or in hell or to ease your cosmic mind. Souls of the dead are far beyond my reach, and I pity the thousands who write to the long-dead to tell them things they should have heard before they were misled to Southeast Asia. I believe in God, but not in the one warriors have created to justify their lust for killing and looting, and not one who picks winners and losers when rockets are fired and the air is filled with shards of boat steel. My God is not to be blamed for your premature death, or for the U.S. killing so many Vietnamese, our non-enemies in that non-war. I'm writing this only in the hope that some mortal will read it, someday. Read it and have his or her suspicions confirmed: War is bad. Peace is good. We never fight as a last resort, nor does any other nation which constantly prepares for war. We are addicted to war and oblivious to the infinite possibilities for peace.

I don't ask for your forgiveness. It's not your job. I've been forgiven for not even thinking of giving mouth-to-mouth resuscitation when we found you'd quit breathing. That young sergeant from California tried. Many times I wondered if I would have done that if you'd been white, or if he grew up in a mixed neighborhood, so unlike my segregated youth in Georgia. I didn't hate you. I didn't fear you. But you were "the other."

I wonder if Joe is an old man out there, somewhere. If I should find him, I'll ask him for forgiveness. I didn't want him to suffer, but I didn't want to admit he was as good as I. I was not an equal-opportunity officer. And I'd love to show him how far I've come since I was a hired killer of Asians, expecting black men to respect me because I was superior by rank and color. I'd like to show him pictures of my children and grandchildren, African American, every one. Perhaps he would show me pictures too, and shake my hand, if a hug would be too much to ask. We would agree that war is stupid and we were both lucky to get out of Vietnam alive. And we'd talk about you, that terrible moment on the Black Boat, how race issues have been better and worse and fouled by war and fear and self-righteousness, and how wars ensure that we'll always have plenty of "the other" to blame for the lack of human progress.

I don't understand how anyone who's been in combat can claim to have no regrets. I regret my part in putting you in harm's way. You were not the first man I lost to hostile fire, but you were the last, and I regret I didn't learn something about war in general and our war, in particular, in between. I should have gone home and helped to end the war.

Finally, thank you for being stuck in my mind and helping bring me to the work of peace.

Rusty Nelson
Former lieutenant, 1097th Combat Boat Company, RVN
Presently, President, Spokane Veterans for Peace #035

Thanks, Doug Rawlings

On Memorial Day, 5/30/2016

To the People on the Wall –

It's difficult to think of you there and not here with us, the living. How many died in that foolish war which no president had the guts to stop. So much was destroyed. I work with the Veterans for Peace gang in New York City, trying to teach some peaceful ways and trying to get the Congress to begin to repair the huge damages we perpetuated on the country of Vietnam... especially the sites where Agent Orange was sprayed and the children with birth defects are still being born. And of course the parents of children who have suffered so greatly from our endless destruction and more.

The U.S. has a habit of overreaching and that is what we did for ten or so years in Vietnam. Nothing gained except what should be a warning about the difficulty and danger of imposing our politics on others – especially when the battlefields are halfway around the world. I'm not sure we've learned it yet.

Much has been lost – your courage and your bodies. That is a tremendous loss for all of us.

Please know that we won't forget you and your service. The wall is there for good. Likewise our memories and our gratitude for your service. I wish we had used you better than we did.

With much love and respect,

Jill Godmilow.

I served as a Marine in Vietnam

Hi Doug;

My name is Patrick Muscarella. My email to you is in response to a request put out by Veterans For Peace regarding stories to be shared at the Vietnam Wall Memorial this coming Memorial Weekend.

I served as a Marine in Vietnam from just before the Tet offensive of 1969 until March of 1970. I was honorably discharged in Sept. of 1971, having served out a four year commitment with the Marine Corps. Almost immediately upon release from the military I began classes in L.A. and joined forces with Vietnam Veterans Against The War on campus at UCLA.

I am not much of a writer but, as best as I can convey it, this is a small window into my experience as a Vietnam War survivor.

I was 20 years old when I enlisted in the Marine Corps in October of 1967. I volunteered for jump school and ended up in Vietnam assigned to F-4 Phantom squadrons maintaining pilot flight gear, parachutes, and ejection seats in fighter aircraft. On two occasions I came within inches of serious injury or death and have now lived a long life and have many reflections that still haunt me.

I had personal contact with many of my fellow Marines who perished, some of them pilots who never came home to their families. At that young age it was so easy to fall prey to the lies of war, as day after day, aircraft, one after the other, launched from the airfield where I was stationed with great thunder, delivering lethal payloads of ordnance (much of it napalm) on human beings.

I've spent many hours since that time hearing a voice in the back of my head that asks, "what was I thinking that whole time"… surely I knew people were dying under those bombs and loads of napalm… I did have questions, there did exist an uneasy feeling that I was a cog in the wheel of something evil. I'd overheard stories from returning pilots bragging about catching "them" out in the open and turning them all into "crispy critters",... burning human beings alive with napalm. Along with the illegal carpet bombing of Cambodia and Laos the conflict in Vietnam never needed to happen. Somehow we never learned anything from that experience.

I took up with photography for the first time then. I have a sizable collection of original glossy images from my time there, many of them faces of other servicemen and of civilian villagers, many of them of innocent children. Those images still haunt me. They remind me of a time when I stood by silently as other's on both sides needlessly lost their lives. I simply don't know how to untangle the knots and reconcile with those memories, memories of death and all the unnecessary suffering that belongs to that war. Like so many I had fallen prey to the delusional thinking of others, to the war makers and to the war profiteers. Most of them, if not all, had never personally witnessed a moment of the horror they helped unleash on millions of innocent people.

The burden for me now, all these years later, is in knowing that the deception of delusional thinkers in government is still in place, manufacturing the myths that attract many of our best and brightest into the military. And like flies drawn to a bug zapper they will go willingly, high on someone else's lies about the necessity of killing. Their innocence, their potential for contributing something life giving, to harmony in the world, lost... their right to happiness stolen forever.

Until we come to a full understanding that the insatiable appetite for profit on the part of the war industry, the many billions and trillions, will continue to drive war policy, directly or indirectly, our youth and the youth of the entire global community will remain vulnerable to the lies and deceit that fuel conflict in the world.

For those of us who have seen the irreconcilable outcome of reckless interventions since Vietnam, the senseless murder that has taken place all over the globe for the sake of controlling territory and resources, the price is too high. The threat of retaliation by those affected and offended grows exponentially by the day. We owe it to our children and their children to wake up and insist that we've seen enough. It's time to pull together for the sake of our planet and our youth and expose the lies for what they are and for what they have always been.

It will almost certainly require mass disobedience and nation wide civil unrest in the streets of America to get the attention of those in power. It's probably all we have left. For now we can support a movement to get corporate money out of the political process, it's a start in the right direction. But it will take more than one person like Bernie Sanders to accomplish real change and wrest power back to the will of reasonable people. It will require all of us informing one another and standing in solidarity together. Along with a movement, we need national recognition of our failed policies and a reevaluation of our priorities to include a long term survival plan for all living things on earth. Enough with all the illegal, immoral, unnecessary wars.

My heart goes out to all the souls who made the ultimate sacrifice, who have been cheated of a full life of happiness. May you all rest in peace.

Former US Marine, Vietnam veteran
Patrick Muscarella

Spec Giacomo "Jocko" Liberatore

Spec Giacomo "Jocko" Liberatore
PDF1PDF2
Birth: Feb. 13, 1950, USA Death: Oct. 25, 2009,
USA Specialist Five US Army, Ammunition Specialist
131st Avn. Co., Hue Phu-Bai, RVN Dec '68-Dec '69 Burial:
Calverton National Cemetery
Suffolk County New York, USA
Plot: Sec. 34 Plot 4493
Record added: Dec 26, 2010
Find A Grave Memorial# 63338442
"Skunk Vietnam Story 1969"

Giacomo and I met about in 2008, and we liked each other instantly. My friend Steve Cordelli introduced us and was apprehensive because he said we were both like a force of nature, and didn't know how that would turn out… it turned out just fine…I met a wonderful person and friend that day.

Our dear friend Giacomo Liberatore: native Brooklyn born — An only son passed away form heart ailments at the age of 59. When stationed in Vietnam Jocko (Army) Flew in OV2 planes that held weapons for the troops & functioned as a supply unit…His job was to set up the base with a storage facility to hold all weapons/supplies for our troops – When needed he would build bunkers or use a suitable hut for storage…

In the 1980's Steve and Giacomo were down in Florida for spring training, as they would do every year –Steve noticed that Giacomo had a cute skunk tattoo (not masculine) on his Left shoulder — he asked what's up with that. At the time it was too difficult for Giacomo to speak about it … so he didn't… Steve didn't press him on it because he could see that it had some deeper meaning …Thinking it unusual for this big strong friend, who always joked around.

It took a few years before Giacomo could share the story of the Skunk tattoo. It turned out that while stationed in Vietnam…he was at his base…and one day there was lots of frantic activity…A Marine helicopter pilot flew in to express that

225

there was a big battle going on on the island, and they had to get to the wounded. Giacomo, immediately wanted to assist.

However, this was a Marine helicopter ...he asked if he could go with them... He was given permission to board...While on the helicopter, he met a young black man in his mid twenties (a door gunner) ... The fella introduced himself as Skunk ...When they got to this big vicious "major" battle...Prior to landing the helicopter... Skunk said: I'll stay in the door and COVER you, while you rescue those who are injured... please do this quickly...

While Giacomo ran out – there was an explosion and he was knocked down... when he was getting up the enemy was coming ... He was dazed by this event... then a second Explosion occurred... (He could feel an actual person jump on him.. it knock him down... Actually it was Skunk who did this to protect him, Skunk saved his life....a Granada or a Mortar exploded again....This fella Skunk, who saved Giocomo's life was now dead on top of him. While trying to access the situation...

The guys in the helicopter were screaming we've got to go... we've got to go... he tried to pick up Skunk, but they wouldn't let him...they said someone else would get this person on the next run... still in shock...he jumped on the helicopter...and was brought back to the camp. While in Vietnam and in the states, he tried to get Skunk's real name and rank... He couldn't find out who he was...this bothered him, so he put the Skunk tattoo on his left shoulder to keep him near to his heart and to always remember the unforgettable sacrifice this fellow veteran made on that day...

After his return to the states he remained in the Military. and was Stationed in US – somewhere in New Mexico or Arizona... Giacomo was awarded the Purple Heart, which he felt that his fellow-veteran brother Skunk should have received.

Giacomo shared a very difficult story with Steve about a person and time that he experienced in Vietnam, which remained with him all the days of his life.

We miss you Giacomo! Peace to you & Skunk

Love
Lee & Steve

For Joseph Hardy

Vietnam 1969

Tired and dirty from sleeping on sandbags at the LP, we returned to base camp in the deuce and a half. We were in a hurry to get some hot breakfast at the mess hall before the chow line closed. Still in our hooch putting up our gear we heard a small explosion. Didn't sound large enough for a mortar but some jumped for the bunker door. No siren to warn of incoming – what the hell. Let's get some chow. Outside there is a small commotion as a FNG has been taken to the hospital. He had been told to clear weeds near the perimeter wire and had stepped on an anti-personnel mine. He may have been lucky and only lost part of his foot. We don't know; per usual he was quickly removed and nobody heard any more about it. But his boot remained. His fuckin boot with the heel blown off the back.

Joe, you were my good buddy, so why didn't you get out of the field when they needed an Officer's Club bookkeeper? I took it when you wouldn't. Did you really need that Combat Infantry badge? You know if I hadn't taken that job I probably would have been with you. I can hear you now, "Come on, it'll be a fuckin blast. They want me to destroy some of the old ordinance at the ammo dump. BOOM!!!"

Boom alright, there wasn't enough left of you, Joe, or the other three guys to send home in a jar.

The cherry on this cake, later the CO and chaplain tell the troops in the chapel that these men died as heroes. That the VC planted a booby trap and that their death was heroic. Made me want to puke. I tried to get some of the guys to help me blow the steeple off the chapel, but couldn't get any serious help and lacked the balls to do it myself.

Shit, Joe, you didn't even leave me a fuckin boot.

Jack Ogden
VN 69-70
Veteran for Peace

I Dream of Dirty Faces

by Daniel Shea,
Viet Nam Veteran,
5/13/2016

I dream of dirty faces
boys unwashed, baptized under fire
Engraved Zippo cigarette lighters
Smoke mingled with burning diesel shit

Lean bodies hung in rags
Sweat, spills, beer, spit, crap
Military jungle fashion for young
men at war playing soldiers, for real

Accessories, helmets & weapons
notched in Kills & Peace Signs
M60 Machine Gun on my shoulder
Bandolier across my chest
45 calibre pistol on my hip

Oh boy I'm going to die
names carved in a black granite
mirrored wall, for families
to reflect on their loss

They need instead
to reflect on the whitewashed
Lie, that sent children to risk
their lives in Viet Nam

A country that was crying
to be free, independent,
liberated from colonial powers
their goal, ours to rule with puppets

Dirty faces of young men
like me, invade my dreams
names forgotten, carved in stone
their futures washed away in time

To Whom it May Concern…(all of us!)

May 12, 2016

To Whom it May Concern…(all of us!)

The wars now seem continuous and yet for the most part far away. What to do? How to be? The literal "overkill" of OUR military resources forces one to wonder why. Who is afraid and what fears are being used to justify such obscene misuse of our strength. Causes are intertwined and the situation can seem intractable.

It is by looking without filters at what happened in the past and what is going on now that can cause change. The efforts of VFP to tell the truth of their experience and bear witness in the face of the glorification of war give me hope.

There is a better way…or perhaps I should say there are better ways…to organize our culture. I was inspired by Michael Moore's latest film to really see this. Sometimes we need to get out of our own polluted environment to see other ways.

And so, another memorial day when we mourn what has been lost…all the unrealized potential that lies behind the names on the wall in Washington. We can only hope that, through the efforts of those who remain, the future can be made livable for our children and grandchildren and all who follow us on this beautiful gift of a planet.

Sincerely,

Carol Scribner
Topsham, Maine

As I grew up

As I grew up in the waning shadow of my namesake, my dad's twin brother, who died in Belgium during WW2, I was captivated by the extreme measures that were adopted to end the fascist scourge. I collected war comics, then throughout my youth I went to the library to check out books on war. For my 16th birthday what I wanted most and got was a large coffee table book, A Pictorial History Of World War 2. I had collections of books on fighter pilots, I built plastic models of WW2 war planes, I went to or watched on TV every war movie ever made, some many times over. Then one day at the library I checked out a small book called, This Must Never Happen Again. It chronicled with script and photos the holocausts of Armenia and World War 2. It was so shocking to my soul that I put it under my mattress and returned it to the Library a day later. I was ashamed to even know about such things.

However when I was drafted in January of 1967, I didn't turn away. Instead I went with the program and eventually was shipped off to "the Nam" in early 1968. I rationalized it by thinking that I had to go in order to really know it was right. I found out all too soon, and spent my 9 months doing my best to avoid the "service" I was sent to perform.

Since then I have spent my life getting my head together so I could educate others of the futility of war. I have also endeavored to be an example of a human dedicated to living a life based on Peace, Love, and Justice. In this way I have honored my dad's twin brother and many others who know that working for peace is the only way to create it.

Tomas Heikkala

Here is a poem I wrote a few years ago:

What the Fuck is Spree de Core?

Wow man,
I haven't had a shower in
A week… maybe two…
Wacha doing…..
Sandbaggin yer bunkers some more?
Took some speed last night…
Only a half a vile…
The others took a whole one. I feel like shit today.
You goin out to the boonies
Tomorrow?
We are too.
I hate humping the rice patties.

Heard Sgt. Perez got blown away
By a ARVN gunboat…
He's little, yeah…
Musta thought he was a gook…..

How short are you now?
47 days? Wow….
I still got 206.
I'm goin over to the
Bloods bunker tonight
And listen to soul music
And smoke some gan sai…
Wanna go? It's cool.

Nah…I don't miss Recon.
Last time I was with them
We humped all night
In the jungle near Trang Bom.
We all got leeches
The next day,
And Herbie couldn't find us

From his Huey.
Herbie, man…All he wants
Is a body count.
Remember boot camp, man?
What the fuck is
Spree de Core?

Tomas Heikkala

Dear Reader,

I am writing this with several objectives in mind.

One is to remember my friend and baseball team member Carey Hess. Carey was killed early in the war. I remember how broken his family was. I wonder what effect Carey would have had on our world today. He may have invented some marvelous thing that would have been of great use still today. He may have written or composed something that would be historical. Or his children or grandchildren might have done so. We can only wonder.

I also think about what the many people who have been killed in our wars, especially since the 60s, would have accomplished. So many are dead and do not have the opportunity to follow their heart's dreams. Especially the children in the countries we invaded. Perhaps one or many of those children might have striven and been successful in bringing more peace to our world.

And for myself. I joined ROTC to stay out of the draft for a war that so strongly affected our country and world. I was fortunate to be stateside during my service, but sometimes pause to consider how my life may have played out without my 'volunteering' for the Air Force. It certainly would have been different. I don't begrudge the way life went because it is in the past and I have 4 wonderful children that elevate my life to this day. I do though wonder if I might have invented or composed something marvelous with a different life path.

If I remember correctly, the oath of military service states that the US government will not send its individual soldiers into harm's way unless there is the utmost necessity. Which is certainly a judgment call by our elected officials. It is very obvious to me that we have lost many many more of our military personnel by invading other countries than we would have lost by not invading them. And we would have satisfied that clause in our oath.

I ask that you not let your sense of patriotism overarch a realistic, unencumbered perspective of how the United States conducts its business. Peace and Healing,

Herb Williams

In memory of my high school friend

In memory of my high school friend Orville Curtis Rogers
I was in the band with Orville Curtis Rogers in high school in Dallas. He was a first lieutenant when he died trying to save seven fellow Marines. Who would have ever thought that he would give his life for our country in Vietnam, and that I, myself, would be there for four years before he got there and would be one of the lucky ones who came back?

I did not know Curtis well, but he played coronet, and I played clarinet. All of the guys in the band had to be in the ROTC until our senior year so you would be in the marching band. We all loved marching at the Woodrow Wilson High School football games.

I am proud of what he became and what he did and grateful that I knew him. When you can put a person to a name on the memorial, you really get the full impact of the lives lost.

Curtis Hoffman
Dallas TX

A Post Vietnam Memorial Day

The guns were fired,
The wreath was laid,
A widow cried,
A speech was made.

Some poor bastard,
Laid out in a tomb
They said he died for his country,
But he died too soon.

If they'd have told him what
He was really fighting for
He'd have stayed at home,
He'd have locked his door.

He'd have raised his kids
And made love to his wife.
He'd have helped his neighbors.
He'd have had a good life.

Instead he died for old men
Growin' mouldy on the shelf.
He died fightin' communism
Which died by itself.
He died for Halliburton,
He died for Lockheed.
He died for power
He died for greed.
And when this veterans
Time has passed
They can bury me face down
So Bush can kiss my ass.

Richard Chamberlain

Shortly after college graduation

Shortly after college graduation in 1968, I joined the U.S. Army to preempt my draft notice. I was going to go to Officers' Candidate School. While in Advanced Infantry Training I came to the realization that I could not become a "leader" for a cause I did not believe in. I served out my 2 years, including a year in Vietnam with the First Cavalry (Airmobile), working for nearly 11 months in a Fire Direction Center of a 155-mm artillery unit on temporary remote bases.

Our unit was dropped into the Cambodia Invasion in June of 1970 and spent some days there as a participant in the shooting of artillery rounds. We were then returned back across the border into Vietnam but continued shooting ordnance back into Cambodia in support of U.S. troops still there.

After returning home to Washington State in November, I came to believe that the American public and I had been lied to. President Nixon, I discovered, had assured the public that all U.S. troops had been withdrawn from Cambodia by a certain date, perhaps it was June 30.

My artillery unit had fired rounds back across the border after that date in support of U.S. soldiers still in Cambodia. I was angry. Very angry. I knew that Vietnam veterans were having some difficulty transitioning back into the American culture. There was no public support of what we had participated in. In fact, it was often the opposite, to the point that many returning veterans were being ridiculed and disparaged by the general citizenry. The result was an increase in the level of anger among vets. Some went up into "the hills," living the solitary life of a hermit, to overcome their anger and shame. Some tried to find solace in bottles of alcohol; others escaped through drugs. Still others began participating in acts of violence against the government, some with crude homemade bombs and the like, against family and friends. I joined the Peace Corps.

Within 6 months of my return from Vietnam I was on an airplane that landed in Tehran, Iran. I spent 3 memorably rewarding years teaching English at a boarding school in Shiraz to children from migratory tribes, tribes with no written language.

I will always appreciate my service in Vietnam, but only because it was the impetus for spending 3 years in Iran, a place that is in my heart and part of my daily existence 42 years after my return. But I will also always feel the pain that my veteran brothers suffered, and continue to suffer, trying to deal with the verifying experiential knowledge that many initially learned prior to going: "War is not healthy for children and other living things." Where have all the flowers gone?

Peace,

Jim Endicott

Helen Keller Revisited

Now it's time to go to sleep
And dream of a different world.
No more war, no more killing,
Just peace and love and a girl.
But still tomorrow will come too soon,
For I know that I will find
People that cheat and steal and hate
And treat each other unkind.
Now it's time to rise once more
And smile not today
For I must kill to end all death.
There must be some other way.
For still tomorrow will come too soon
For still I know that I will find
People not knowing of brotherly love,
Why is man so blind?

Those Army days in Vietnam

Thirteen Echo Forty

I get up every morning at an hour that shouldn't exist.
I stand there at attention while The Man goes down the list.
Then I wait and wait and wait and wait in line to get my chow
Of leather pancakes and muddy coffee, not knowing why or how!
I grab my books and sticks and charts and hurry to catch the bus,
For I know if I am late to class The Man will raise a fuss.
I jump on the bus at noontime and hurry back in line
For food that is not like mother's:
Meat that was soaked in brine?
I hurry back to class again
For four more hours of the same.
My mind begins to wonder.
Who is the one to blame?
The day finally ends, the day begins,
Whichever the case may be?
I put on my jeans and go downtown
I guess that I am free!?!?!?

By Jim Endicott
Artillery Fire Direction Training
Fort Sill, Oklahoma 1969

As I come up on the 46th anniversary

Letter to the Wall — 2016

As I come up on the 46th anniversary of my direct involvement in the Viet Nam War, my first involvement of telling your mother that you had been killed Johnny has not lessened in intensity. I still feel every blow to the chest that she gave me. Unfortunately, those blows still say the same thing to me. Waste, waste, waste. Latter wars have only further shown me how violence only begets more violence.

I am under no illusion that I may change things in my lifetime, but I do take from all of your deaths an inspiration to have the moral courage to not give into fear. St. Augustine said it well when he said that hope had two beautiful daughters whose names are Anger and Courage. "Anger at the way things are, and Courage to see that they do not remain as they are."

I easily get the anger part of hope from not only those of you that have your names on the Wall, but even more so from the many who should have their names on the wall — the suicides, the agent orange caused deaths, but mostly the millions of Vietnamese killed in the war.

The courage part is harder to get, but you all do encourage that beautiful daughter also. As Joseph Conrad wrote much later than St. Augustine, "You know that in cowardice is every evil — especially that cruelty so characteristic of our civilization.... We are born initiated, and succeeding generations clutch the inheritance of fear and brutality without a thought, without a doubt, without compunction."

I take from the Wall the companionship of both of the daughters that St. Augustine wrote about to do my best to keep the enduring flame of hope alive.

Paul Appell

Viet Nam 70-71

240

Dear Jacqueline,

Writing to you again, out of love, out of compulsion, out of habit, it really doesn't matter. I have to express these things to someone and you're it.

I'm going back to walk through that hell again and still trying to figure out why. Maybe I can't handle civilian life, maybe I don't want to, maybe I'm brainwashed. There is no sense of duty, sacrifice, and certainly none of defeat.

The fact is that it is still going on and the only way to stop thinking about it is to go back over to stop tearing my mind up. I'm looking for a statement that answers WHY? About all I can come up with is: The sonofabitch isn't over with yet.

Some have finer talents. One of mine is being decent infantry (grunt) Corpsman.

To the platoon you are the man only concerned with their welfare. And once you go out under fire, once you put your ass on the line for them, for the rest of the time you work and die together... more than God, more than country... nothing means more than "doc" hauling ass, scared as hell out to patch someone up.

That's the kind of work, I don't know why, I want. Sometimes I'm scared shitlessly. I don't want to die yet. No martyr. I'm also afraid of the bleak and frustrating and probably neurotic existence left if I don't do this thing. I've been through enough of that shit already.

Robert A. "Doc" Lindstrom HM2/USN
H Company, Second Platoon, 2nd Battalion 9th Marines
Third Marine Division
Vietnam 65-66
11th Marines (Artillery) and First Medical Battalion
Vietnam 70-71
USS Kitty Hawk 1971-72

To whom it may concern,

I'm Percy Hilo; An air force veteran from November 18th, 1966-May 5th, 1970 – #af11670967. I served my basic training at Amarillo Air Force Base in Amarillo, Texas, then went to Shepard in Wichita Falls, Texas, and then served a 3 years overseas tour at Hickam in Honolulu, Hawaii from May 29th, 67 to May 5th, 70.

I found the military to be extremely oppressive, absolutely insensitive and cruel to its own and with no compassion or interest in the fate of any other peoples the world over! I never went to Vietnam and never wanted to go! Once I awoke to what was being done in my name and of the complete lack of feeling towards the Vietnamese people as well as the inhumane treatment and feeling of fear placed upon our own soldiers I went through many changes in my belief system. One of the most important was my letting go of the horrible belief in "My country, right or wrong" and replacing it with a genuine empathy and compassion for all people's everywhere. This new belief is the foundation of what I've become in the 46 years since my discharge.

A few years back I became a member of Veterans For Peace (which I'd been since 1969 when there was no formal organization for it) and have continued to build a lifestyle that includes feelings for all living things and the belief that all God's children can learn to love and appreciate each other and work out all differences! It hasn't yet fully manifested but I feel that it's possible at some time in the future that I won't live to see. Many blessings on all of our good work.

Peace to all and Namaste,

Percy Hilo

Dear Jim Waulk and Bill Wood,

Both of you fellows hailed from the land of rural Ohio. A person can draw a straight line on a map between the two townships that you both came from. Both of you were husbands and one of you was a father-to-be. That wife miscarried when she learned of her husband's death. I even talked with that woman on the phone. This has been so long ago. All of this has been so long ago.

The atrocities continue, gentlemen. The country that you were born in to and died for is a lie. The lie started when those white men sat in council to form the United States of America. United we are not, and divided we are.

Tomorrow is Mother's Day, gentlemen. Another lie perpetuated by commerce. For the dollar to rule. As a Veterans For Peace member(Life) I will be giving out the original Mother's Day Proclamation, Julie Ward Howe(1819-1910) with a carnation. This will be handed to women only. If your Mothers are alive they miss you terribly. My Mother is alive(91) and she loves me dearly, as I love her.

As young men we did not understand or know how oppressive and hateful this country(USA) is. For we were born as white men; not men of color.

I do hope you both are at peace in your final rest. We survivors of combat though are another story. Suicide, alcohol, drugs, meanness to other people, broken marriages, broken hearts, locked up, locked down, and not facing the moral truth of their actions.

I am so lucky to be able to write this letter to you both. I am in my own home, in the kitchen, at the table finishing my own home cooked meal. Jim W. I was able to visit with your in-laws in rural Ohio. I had lunch with them in their farm house and then they drove me out to your grave site. Near their home. You're laid to rest in a peaceful place with others. I sat with you.

I have been to the traveling "Wall" three different times to pay my respects to you and Bill. Maybe some day I will get to DC and actually lay my hands on your names.

Because of the violence and tragedies that I was a witness to and participated in for 10 months, I put my weapon down. I was done emotionally. This was my first political action. I would not carry a weapon, nor take life for the sake of Empire.

I cry tears when I relive your deaths. Two nights before on the Firebase we had toked together; and in an instant you were gone. Ed D. (CA) is gone. His kidneys finally stopped. Paul F. (NY) and Ron W. (NY) think of you and Bill W. We talk on occasion and they are both doing good. Both are married.

I am drinking a good micro brew and listening to Lucinda Williams. Good tough southern woman.

Tomorrow I will wear my "Muslims Are Not Our Enemy" t-shirt for the 3rd day. Me and my VFP brother Ralph H. today on the square were photographed with a Muslim man between us. His wife took the picture. This was a great moment for all of us. Some simple encouragement. Not to be angry. I know so many kind people. People holding hands. People hugging. People kissing.

I, Jim W and Bill W, am 69 as I scratch this writing. I have many good and some bad experiences since I stepped out of the military machine. I am happy, along with sad, but I am present. I am still participating in the cycle of life.

I have a younger brother and sister. They both have families. I am single and Pop to a grown son who I am very proud of. I have no grandchildren.

The organization Veterans For Peace is very active trying to put an end to warfare. The United States of America military machine is huge and bloated. The young men and women serving during the occupation of Viet Nam helped stop that war. The young people who are serving now in illegal conflicts will stop the machine. The military will break down from within.

Veterans For Peace has its own Peace Navy now. The Golden Rule sail boat is back in the water and sailing for nuclear disarmament by all Nation/States. I am happily participating with this project.

Hopefully I will be writing again next year. Good for me and you both. You are not forgotten.

Love,

Rw Cage
VFP (Life)

James Harold Waulk Jr.   William Wayne Wood
    Ohio-KI2/20/1970   Ohio-KI2/20/1970

I was called upon to serve

I was called upon to serve during the Korean War which, in retrospect, I think of as two years of my life substantially wasted.

But, the experience did succeed in at least temporarily warping my mind. For, during the Vietnam War, I was initially shocked and disgusted by the large number of draft dodgers and resisters.

Indeed, it wasn't till America's apparently endless campaign to destroy Iraq, Afghanistan, Libya, and Syria that I realized — in Maj. Gen. Smedley Butler's famous words — war is a racket.

It should be obvious that this so-called War on Terror is a gold mine for the military-industrial-security complex and the One Percent who are its stockholders.

Today, thoughtful writers like Dr. Paul Craig Roberts suspect USA may be laying the groundwork for a Third and final World War (for the purpose of obliterating North Korea, China, Iran, and Russia). It's alleged that there are those in high places within the Pentagon who believe America can fight and win a nuclear war. To which I would say only that, if W.W. III comes, the survival of the "Establishment" ought not be considered a priority.

Please: DON'T thank me for my service.

Smith, Frederick S., Pfc.
U.S. 51043206
Proud member of Veterans for Peace, Inc.

I did my time in Vietnam

I did my time in Vietnam from 9/67 to 9/68. Tet was my time in combat. I was supposed to be a Process Photographer with the 66th Engineer Company, Topographic, but the VC decided otherwise. Obviously, I made it home.

A friend of mine did not, however. His name is listed on this great, black Wall. Some of us made it home, and some of us did not. Who is luckier? The America we fought for didn't care. Not even the army we were in cared. We can only care for each other, and for the dead we left behind. It would be nice if this all meant that the same mistakes will not be made again. Like in Iraq and Afghanistan and where is the next one?

Let us all hope for and pray for an end to all the violence and hate.

Thomas F. Bayard, RA11857325, SP-5
66th ENGR CO TOPO, of the 20th ENGR GP.RVN, 9/67 – 9/68

~

Years after I got back from Vietnam

Years after I got back from Vietnam while I was in Seattle I visited a replica of the Vietnam Memorial Wall. Of all the dozens of things left in loss and sadness there, only one will forever remain in my memory. It was a letter of apology from a young girl to her father, a father whose name was on that wall, a father she had never known. "I am so sorry that I was so angry with you daddy, but it was just that I wanted a daddy so much – like the other kids." As I read this simple sentence, it seemed to capture all the grief and anguish of that war, and of all wars.

Tom Charles, VFP Chapter #35, Spokane, WA

Dear Names on the Wall

May 6, 2016
Seaside, Oregon

Dear Names on the Wall,

The following is a eulogy for a real hero to honor the ultimate sacrifice you made as young men and women in our name:

A Eulogy for Rev. Daniel Berrigan

Frail, but always nonviolently defiant for peace with social justice, you died the other day, letting loose your vibrant spirit from its well-worn body. To the very end, you never wavered in your dedication and commitment to peace, to end all war, to oppose the destructive capacities of governments, of armies, of missiles, of heavily armed men and women fighting mostly for venal politicians' quest for power.

Heroically, you often placed your body on the line, being arrested numerous times, serving time in city, county, and federal prisons, for daring to speak truthfully and compassionately against the horrors of modern war, burning draft documents, hammering missile heads, symbolically turning them into plowshares and pruning forks. You even went underground for several years while continuing to speak out for peace.

I am so grateful I had the privilege to know you, to communicate with you, to be in your most holy presence. The first time was at the retreat you lead in 1987 with Thich Nhat Hahn, when I was still so ravaged, shamed and guilty about my participation in the terrible and long war in Vietnam, for which I gleefully volunteered in accordance with my southern heritage of duty, honor, country. You and Thich Nhat Hahn helped heal me by suggesting whenever I hear a Huey to be grateful I survived instead of being racked by keening guilt.

A couple of years later, I had a simple lunch with you and the UN ambassador from communist Vietnam, a former enemy whom I was most grateful to call my comrade in seeking peace and reconciliation for the millions of Vietnamese peoples so brutalized by and still suffering from the war we both fought in on opposing sides. To this day, I accept that I fought on the wrong side, an illegal invader of a country that did the US no harm.

I was most pleased to attend your 78th birthday celebration, where I met a close friend of yours, Kurt Vonnegut, someone whom I've always admired. When I told him I was a Vietnam veteran platoon leader, he took my hand in both of his, looked up at me with such compassion, and apologized for what my country had done to me. Recalling that moment, I again sob healing tears of gratitude.

Were I in New York today, I would march with many others from E. 3rd Street to W. 16th Street to honor you and to attend the memorial mass. Know in the unutterable mystery of being, I am with you in deep connection as your spirit spreads its powerful beneficence throughout the wide and ineffable Kosmos.

Spread your healing, peaceful energy in the memory of all who needlessly died in this unjust, illegal, unnecessary war. Thank you deeply !~!~!

In Memoriam for all of you,

Thomas Brinson, ILT, US Army
II Corps, Vietnam,
April 67-April 68

An Operating Room Nurse Speaks To The Wall

by Susan O'Neill,
RVN 1969-70

My face in your slick black mirror
lurks undefined
over graved letters that bear no link
    to men I knew for moments or hours
    to men over whose inert bodies I passed threads
        nylon / gut / steel
too fragile to bind restive souls into their broken casks
    to men over whose secret red meat
my gloved fingers probed
before it fell still.

You deal in names
I deal in nameless shades
    that slipped anesthetized shells
    that left me
        numb / dumb /stunned
my hand too weak to grave labels in my brain.

You are past
    history /herstory / ourstory
58,286 hungry ghosts
    among millions here
    among billions there
cyphers that though graved
my memory can not touch
pragmatic count of time-blind grief.

Oh black mirror:
    Call your phantom legions to formation
    call them to march howling waving flagged transparent gore
    call them to spill their precious wasted
        blood / bones / meat
on grand oak desks
their sweet lost dreams on manicured hands
of The Powers That Were, That Be, That Will Be

call them to grave on foreheads of kings and presidents and
dictators and generals in funeral black
    the vast permanent cost of transitory wars
    call them to trumpet their names
          for all who have eyes and ears and hearts and mouths
          for all who have wisdom and fire and love and outrage
    call them to stand ruined and proud
    relentless and brave before the stone
call them to fix us with their flamed unwavering eyes
 until we feel the price that
         they / we / all
have paid
and cry:
    enough, enough.
    Enough.

I didn't go

I didn't go. Fortunately my name is not on this wall. I suspect some of the guys I trained with at Ft Polk, LA in August of 1970 are among the thousands of names here. I didn't go. I volunteered to go in 1971 while stationed at Ft. Wainwright, AK but my request was denied. I didn't go.

I was 18 years old at the time and totally ignorant about the foreign affairs of the day. I understand today the male brain is not fully formed until about the age of 25. Insurance companies understand this and charge higher rates of those under 25 because of the poor decision making, particularly not understanding future consequences of actions.

Upon my entry into the Army at 17 I was trained to kill. I still have this jingle etched in my mind "I wanna be an airborne ranger, I wanna live a life of danger, I wanna go to Vietnam, I wanna kill the Viet Cong, kill, kill, kill." I didn't go, I didn't kill.

My brother, a Marine Alpha 19 1968 Tet offensive was there.. He's not on the wall but wounded by friendly fire. Psychologically wounded, 100% disability PTSD. Over the years drank himself into dementia, he never really recovered from his Vietnam experience. How long of a wall would it be if those like him were included?

Today, I leave this letter at the wall as a 62 year old husband, father and grandfather because I Didn't GO.

Charles Hearington

I was an organizer

I was an organizer and longtime participant in demonstrations against this horrible war. and was on many committees opposing the draft, etc.

We spent 12 or more years, billions of dollars, almost 60,000 US lives and probably over million Vietnamese lives for what was clearly an irresponsible and probably illegal war. But we learned our lesson only for a few years, and are now again invading other countries as an element of US foreign policy.

When and how can we learn??

Gerson Lesser, M.D.

I joined the Army reserve

I joined the Army reserve in October 1966 just after getting married and a month before my 21st birthday being 1A in the draft didn't know what else to do. Wasn't aware of being a conscientious objector or even where Canada was, even way back then I wasn't a war person. My dad wasn't in the military ever, so no influence from family.

Did basic and AIT in the winter of 1967 at Ft. Leonard wood a miserable spot in Missouri went to summer camp for two weeks 67 68 69. By that time my beliefs in war and the Governments trip in Vietnam had come to a head and no longer wanted any involvement with it. The marriage was coming to a end also it was time for something new went West young man to California.

Did nothing about the Army just stopped going to meetings, got involved with Peace and protest activities like so many folks. Got paper work from the Army was activated and to report to Ft. Jackson S.C. which I did at 26 yrs of age in the spring of 1971 with my hippie look and long hair told them I want nothing to do with the Army or the war machine. I refused to do anything at the reception unit so got put in the stockade spent three months kept putting in for a chapter10 discharge.

After three times doing it I knew it was time to move on went to a court martial they wanted me to go to Germany for 20 months to finish my two year obligation, I said OK got out of the stockade that day and left the base awol they call it. I call it freedom.

Finally I was dropped from the Army along with many others in 1975 by Gerald Ford. Have no vet rights which is fine with me. I feel honored and humbled by my association with Vets for Peace folks

Peace

Frank E. Donnelly

A Letter of Resistance

In early December of 1967 at the Lutheran Church of St. John the Evangelist in Brooklyn, New York, the Rev. Richard John Neuhaus presided at a service of conscience and hope. At that service more than 200 young men walked to the altar to deposit their draft cards in the offering plates, declaring their disaffiliation with the Selective Service system and their determination to resist being conscripted to fight in the war in Vietnam. I was one of those men.

After my second year as a divinity student at Princeton Theological Seminary, I engaged in a rite of passage following in the footsteps of many other young people. After purchasing a cheap ticket to Luxembourg, I hitchhiked my way through Europe and the British Isles, also traveling across North Africa. As the 6-Day War ended, I was on the beach in Tunisia preparing to leave for Italy. It was a beautiful day, the Mediterranean was warm and inviting, and I was thinking about my long-time friend, George Fry, who had been drafted into the Army and was somewhere in Vietnam. He'd left his young wife behind and dutifully answered the call, and I was sitting in the sun, aware that I was safe yet feeling very conflicted.

On my travels in Europe, especially in France, I'd taken rides with many people who were against the war. France had had its own unfortunate experience in Vietnam, and the people I spoke with couldn't understand why we were there. And I found that parroting the reasons usually given....the domino theory of the spread of communism being the most popular....were not compelling. This exposure to world public opinion which had not reached me at home, weighed heavily on me and upon my return I began in earnest to study the history of our involvement in this conflict.

My third year of divinity school landed me in New York City where I was doing an internship in an experimental program sponsored by General Theological Seminary. It was an exploration of the mass media and how it works to create public opinion and it required us all to find a job in some form of media. After weeks of applications and interviews and lots of frustration,

I was offered a position with the American Heritage Publishing Company working on the first edition of the American Heritage Dictionary.

This turned out to be a great job as I met many wonderful people who were very open and accepting of this seminarian who just arrived. Coming from a small farming town in western New York, I'd never lived in a city among so many different people and it was very stimulating for me. And it was here that my education took me deep into exposure to the antiwar movement. I attended demonstrations, teach-ins, lectures, and had many conversations with fellow students.

All of this was chronicled in a documentary film that focused on the work of the internship group of which I was a member. The director of the film, Bill Jersey, who had won prizes for documentaries, like A Time For Burning, said that the National Council of Churches had contracted him to do a film on new forms of ministry in the church, and he met with our group and decided to follow our work for the next 9 months or so. And he said that it works best to single out one person and show the work of the group through that person's eyes, and I was the one he chose.

That's why this film crew was also present at the church that day in December of 1967 when I turned in my draft card and went public with my decision not to cooperate with the Selective Service system. As a seminarian, I was entitled to the 4D deferment which was for clergy and divinity students. There was no way I could be drafted. But holding that deferment, I reasoned, would make my words of opposition to the war hollow and meaningless because I was taking no risk. Giving up that deferment would make me as vulnerable as any other guy my age.

The fallout from this act of resistance and non-cooperation was both positive and negative as the film was shown in many churches. In my hometown I became a polarizing figure. My dad had died suddenly 2 years before and my mother lived alone in the home where I grew up with a brother and sister. She was also the Postmaster in town; a position she held for nearly 35 years. And now her son, had done this deed which made him a traitor in the eyes of many. It was very hard on her.

There's one scene in the film where we're standing alone in the greenhouse.....she also raised African violets....and we were talking about what I'd done and why. I wanted her to understand why I took this step of faith, and she said, "you get to go back to the city, but I have to stay here." And I said "I know you have to stay here, why do you say that?" And her reply was, "This is where the people are." Being a public person in that small conservative town, with a son who had done this radical thing, was not what she wanted. And "Where The People Are," became the name of that film.

That was 48 years ago when I was 24. My mom lived to be 92 dying on Mother's Day in 2008. In the intervening years it became clear to many people that the Vietnam War was a terrible mistake. Many thousands of people died on all sides, including my friend, George. The suffering of the Vietnamese people, the spraying of Agent Orange, the wounding, both physical and psychological of those who served there, is testimony to the barbarism and futility of war as a means of solving problems. And we still haven't learned. The war machine keeps on churning creating horror wherever it goes. And now we have a volunteer army. If we still relied on conscription, I believe the American people would rise up to stop these misadventures, but since the armed forces offer jobs and training with pay and benefits, the public at large has been bought off.

Wake up, America! These are your sons and daughters, and what are they fighting for? For you? To keep us safe? I don't think so! What do you think?

Brian Lyke
May 5, 2016
Carmel Valley, CA

I am a terrible golfer

I am a terrible golfer. I know that now. But before I learned it I thought one day to go practice and hit a bucket of balls. Our village had thoughtfully constructed a driving range on the old town dump. As I drove up in the afternoon I noted that there was only one other car there, it must be for the attendant, the guy who gets to drive around in that cart with a cage on it so he doesn't get hit. Typically he is retired and just killing time, like me. Then I noticed that he had veteran's license plates on his car, just like my truck, so we started in talking. It turns out we were both in the same place in Vietnam, in Chu Lai. He was the only person I have ever met that was there. Once we realized that the very first words he said were, "It's a shame about that nurse." Forty-five years after it happened and it was right in the front of his mind, waiting to be said. "It's a shame about that nurse."

On June 8th, 1969 1LT Sharon Ann Lane from Zanesville, Ohio was on duty in the ward that treated wounded Vietnamese soldiers when a Viet Cong rocket struck between two wards, killing two and wounding twenty-seven. She died instantly. 1LT Lane was the only female to die from direct enemy fire in the entire war.

Forty-five years later two guys who never met her took a sudden moment of silence remembering her loss. She was not forgotten by us. I'm writing this in the hope that her memory will live on with others and her sacrifice and the sacrifices of others will not fade with time.

— Paul Donahue

To those on the wall

I wanted to give you an update. First everyone of you and our experience in Vietnam is never far from my mind or my heart. I can look at my grand children and know that I am fortunate. I can talk to my children as adults and I am grateful. I can also remember that you can not, never could; you were robbed of the joys I enjoyed over the past almost 50 years now.

I go to VFP meetings and VVA meetings and I believe that you would be glad to know that we are graying with commitment, graying with energy, graying with grace. Many of us do anything and everything we can to promote peace from blocking Creech Airforce Base to marching at the School of Americas, to sailing the Golden Rule, to sitting in silent vigil outside of an NRA convention. We also try to get into the high schools to counter the efforts of the recruiters. But I have to tell you things are not good.

Twenty-two veterans take their own lives every day. Many of them are our generation but many of them are young veterans. Young veterans who were sold a bill of goods like we were. Many of whom believed that they were on an honorable mission only to find out that, like us, they were pawns in the scheme of the rich. However, these youngsters are part of an all volunteer army. That's right — no more draft. That means that the public is deathly silent when they come home dead and injured. That means that when they look for assistance often the response is "well, you volunteered."

Something else troubling, militarism is now the chief export of the US and we are internationally viewed as the biggest threat to world peace. Seriously, Gallup did an international poll in 2014 and the US was seen by 24% of the people as the biggest threat to peace. Second place I think went to China or Pakistan at 8%.

And then there are drones, but that might be another letter.

I truly believed that our generation would be the last to suffer this fate. I thought that as we grew older that we would stand up and forbid our politicians to send us into another debacle, but we didn't. We allowed it to happen again and again and again from

259

incursions into Central American to endless war in Afghanistan and Iraq. And we lead the world in the sale of arms to other countries. So we are perpetuating not only our own wars but those of other countries.

I hate to say this because I do not want to disturb you anymore than dying in Vietnam already has but sometimes I feel that all the soldiers and sailors and airmen who died for this country may have died for nothing. I know I said all from the Revolution on. We are only 240 years old but we have lost many aspects of our democracy and have become the world's bully. Those who died fighting the Nazis a mere 75 years ago would not recognize our country. The 750,000 who died in the Civil War would be so disappointed to see that we are no longer a country of the people, by the people, and for the people, and the people don't seem to care. The Founders, who realized that in order for this country to succeed would require an engaged populace and never a peace time army, are probably rolling over in their graves and saying to each other: "Well, we tried!"

There is a glimmer of hope in the youth right now who seem to be getting engaged behind an old conscientious objector by the name of Bernie Sanders. I know many of you probably don't think much about a CO but when you hear his story it is compelling. He is truly a man of commitment and he has helped those of us who survived more than anyone else in the Congress. But his efforts only provide a glimmer of hope, as the moneyed and militarized powers are fighting back hard.

So if you can, as the collective spirit that you are, visit us here in the country you died for so many years ago and fill our hearts with compassion for each other and compassion for the others throughout the world. We are not sustainable as we are and we need your help.

God Bless each of you; you are remembered and loved.

Jim Wohlgemuth
RD2 from the Westchester Cty Lst 1167
And Point Defiance LSD 31

For my childhood friend David Thomas

Dearest David,

Marcia told me you were killed in Vietnam. She said you had planned to go back and start an orphanage. I wasn't clear about whether you were in the Army or had gone as a missionary. Either way I know how loved you would have been! I wrote a poem about you back in the '80's. You and your field organ. How I have missed your shyness all these years. I never saw you after your family left Cali but the image of you climbing the tree with your skinny legs and big grin is as vivid now as that day in 1949.
Love always,

Christine

> Hyacinth watches
> first one leg then the other,
> smiling approval
> ~~ctCa

~~~

I was drafted in 65

I was drafted in 65, but didn't go to Vietnam. But some of my friends did, and some left their lives there. Now, and even then, it seems so senseless. I would hope that mistake would be a constant reminder of America's arrogance. But we continue to invade and get stuck in other countries. So maybe the names on this wall died in vain?

George Coopey

Message to Thomas A. Williams

L/Cpl, USMC, CAP 3-1-4
Born September 21, 1950,
Died February 18, 1970
Panel 13 W, Line 30;
Vietnam Veterans Memorial

Dear Tom:

This is Mike Peterson. I contacted your sister in Wilkes-Barre around 2000, but lost touch. Among other things I said that you did not suffer; that your death was quick. In all honesty, I didn't know your death was all that quick; somewhere (I believe it was our skipper, I forget the name) I learned that the medics on the chopper said that you had expired en route to the medevac hospital.

I did not know you all that well, and that's not right; but now it's too late. I did dedicate my book, The Combined Action Platoons: The U.S. Marines' other war in Vietnam to you; but I'd rather you be alive than I ever wrote that book, if this makes any sense.

I thought that we had fought in America's last Bad War; silly me! With the on-going wars in Afghanistan and Iraq promising to be "endless wars," I hold dim hopes for us to be at peace anytime soon; or even grow up as a society. I do hate war. As William Tecumsah Sherman said: "War is all hell." I am a member of Veterans For Peace, and will be for as long as I live.

Just checkin' in

Michael Ernst Peterson

Hello my friend.

If not for WW-2 my older sister and I would not have been born, which was the result of my Welsh mother having met an American GI, who was stationed at a nearby airbase in Wales, UK during the war.

I grew up in Wales without the help of my father who abandoned us all very soon after the war was over.

Since then my views have remained the same about war.

I condemn all wars without hesitation, and yet I have great pity and empathy for the soldier, who is used then soon disposed of, after the war is over.

A few years ago I took my father-in-law, a veteran of the Pacific Theater, to visit the Vietnam Memorial, where a close relative of his deceased wife was carved into one of the stones. It was an Honor Flight and my father-in-law felt a healing that he had never known before.

He was 92, and he cried as his finger ran over a hallowed name once so fondly remembered by his late wife.

I came to America in 1966 having learned the history of post WW-2 Vietnam in school and I knew that America was deeply involving itself with a needless, and avoidable, tragedy.

I had come in search of my father, and soon after I arrived in the USA the Selective Service wanted me to join the Vietnam War.

I explained my education and refused to participate in the carnage. I wanted to cry for America not to kill someone I never met for it, or to be killed in some far off place for no sensible reason at all. I have opposed every war since.

Before President H W Bush made his greatest mistake, I begged him not to send a military force to eject Saddam Hussein but to use our far more effective financial powers instead.

I reminded the then president that our country was violent enough without presenting the thought that violence is always the best way to solve a problem.

Tourists from Germany were being shot in Florida in random acts while another war was being fashioned, I asked could there be an end to this madness?

My letter went unheeded. War resulted and it led to the most recent catastrophic exchanges of violence and began a religious war that now spreads like an unconstrained and virulent virus.

After stealing the election of 2000, his son compounded the misery of war and for insane, and unfounded reasons, he justified making things far worse.

We are now in a constant-war mode eagerly fed by the makers of arms and ammunition to every side. They must be making a fortune.

We send off a missile costing $200,000, to kill a human being that is holding a $20.00 AK47. They might be standing on a street corner or hiding in a building, and we call it a fantastic victory.

Let us not count the cost of the devastation we reap and sow, of the minds and limbs lost, and never to be the same, ever again on every side of this bloody carnage.

When will we have the sense to put an end to war?

We fight an enemy, then the enemy becomes our friend, why not skip the stupid war that precedes the in-between?

Senseless, bloody wars, hospitals and schools never built, hungry children never fed, because the cost of war is always so expensive.

Let us all please put an end to this madness now, before this madness puts an end to us all.

Roger W. Imes,

Spokane, WA.

MAY ALL THESE SOULS

MAY ALL THESE SOULS BE 'OF BLESSED MEMORY'
ETERNALLY _/|_

Arnie Welber
Veteran

From an Air Force widow

From an Air Force widow to all the people whose names are on this memorial:

My husband was in final training in an RF101 aircraft, having already received his orders to the Viet Nam war theater. This model plane was getting old, and parts were being pirated from other planes to keep them in the sky. One day a malfunction of some sort happened with the plane, and my husband crashed. That was on March 17, 1966.

Had he not crashed that day, it is my conviction that the way things were going, he would have been shot out of the sky somewhere over Southeast Asia, as was one of his closest friends. So, he died answering the same call that you did, but his name is not on your memorial.

I want for you to know that I still love and miss my husband, and I know that your families also have not forgotten you. If they are like me, not a day goes by that you are not thought of and missed. Time does not really heal our losses, we just go on as you would have liked us to. We go to the memorial, and we weep. The tears are always just a blink away wherever we are.

I want you to know also, that I try as best as I can to work for peace, so that other people such as you will not die, and so that families all over the world can live in peace and security. This is the very least that I can do for you.

Thank you.

Myrna Fox
Widow of Capt. William R. Wilson

I grew up in Maine

I grew up in Maine. Chris was my best friend for many years. They moved to another town in Maine, but we stayed in contact. Sometime while I was in the Air Force we lost contact. I started to look for him a few years ago. It took a while, but I found him.

Michael Colfer
Bellingham WA
Chapter 111

Chris

Can it be sixty years ago?
My God, the time's just gone.
We were close as brothers then.
We played at war
In Gannet's Wood,
On the ledges, and down the draw.
And still when we were teenage boys
And I just got my car
Chris stole my new girlfriend.
[What was her name? I don't recall.]
It doesn't matter now.
He was my brother, after all.
When I enlisted
He just said
That I was crazy, I'd end up dead.
He wouldn't come.
I left, instead.
And he stayed home to play.
In my third year in Germany
I heard they'd drafted him.
Oh shit, I said. You should have
Come with me, my brother

He'd laugh, I knew, and toss his head
And tell me he'd had all the girls
While I was alone in bed.

How can it be so many years?
I'm silver gray these days.
And he's still young in memory
His freckled nose and forelock's fall
Are all that's left of him today.
Chris's name is on the Wall.

My military duty was as a navy officer

My military duty was as a navy officer with DASA (Defense Atomic Support Agency) maintaining our nuclear capability. I visited Nagasaki to appreciate the insanity of war. I have also visited the war museums of Hanoi and became acquainted with the war crimes we committed in Vietnam. WAR IS NEVER THE ANSWER, although I honor the memory of those who served.

Walter Gundel

To Robert Sinclair

To Robert Sinclair, name on the Wall, and the only African-American male classmate of mine from high school. I'm so sorry you never made it back home. I did. But as a Vietnam Era Navy veteran, I did my job so others could do theirs. So I'm an accomplice to the murder of some three million Vietnamese, Cambodians, and Laotians, mostly women and children.

Like others serving then, I thought my service was justified if my beloved country could be again at peace. For every veteran, the sense of betrayal comes with the next war, or the one after that. It has something to do with so many veterans young and old committing suicide. Veterans For Peace has saved me to be sober and make amends.

Truth has been the first casualty in Vietnam and our every other war since. War is a lie, and we've become addicted to it. I have an email from Colonel Gregory Daddis, then-faculty department head at West Point. He agreed with my theory, that the defense industry won't let peace break out and stick them with a trillion dollars in unsold inventory on their shelves.

I'm on Facebook today with almost a hundred former members of 2nd Battalion, 7th Regiment, First Marine Division, which has had 14 to 25 suicides among active and former members, since tours in Iraq and Afghanistan. The unit is now again deploying to fight ISIS. How many more will bring their war home and die from it here?

The "2/7" Marines are probably the canary in the coal mine. Endless, winless wars will destroy our military on the installment plan, and who will defend us then? We veterans left alive are less than 10% of the population. We need our civilians to read the truth about war from us, and help us end war before it ends us.

Roland Van Deusen,

Clayton NY

Dear Mr. Rawlings,

I was recently loaned a copy of a 1994 book by Jonathan Shay, M.D., Ph.D titled, Achilles in Vietnam.

Amazingly well thought out and presented.

I can hardly believe the Bush/Cheney Administration claims that PTSD was not well understood when they put so many more of our military into it unnecessarily. Even if we really did need to go into the Middle East – much of the 21st Century PTSD could have been prevented by understanding the role that leadership (via the betrayal of "what's right") plays in its development and persistence.

Thank you for what you are doing for Memorial Day – with the letters.

I will be displaying the RRug in Portland, OR.

Sincerely,

Rodger Asai
Remembrance Rug

One kid's response to Nam.

To Doug Rawlings,

Veterans For Peace, Maine, USA May 4, 2016.

Dear Doug and Families of Nam,

The sadness of human growth is a deep part of my reflection during the Nam years, even as now. From the military during Korea, I switched career paths from CIA and diplomacy/Georgetown or AU to Andover Theological School to better pursue my early childhood dream of fostering peace. By Nam I was able to be alert enough that our own three sons and many from our Church took heed of what the Quakers in Boston were teaching about negative-registering for the draft. One of my youth group leaders became a CO.

Throughout my ministry I accepted shorter pastorates due to my views on race and war and the environment, as I, with excellent scholarship and education guiding me, often pointed to what was called "the social gospel." That is, our job is to grow up to peace and DO IT. Parishioners would refuse to receive me or "talk it over." It often meant one more move for our dear family, and I must admit to being pretty much a "stuck in the mud, home happy, trail happy, greenery happy, good water happy" New Englander, despite my family history of "South Africa," "Lebanon," "the Levant," "Chicago," "San Francisco," "Plymouth migrants" et al. Even so, I was not intelligent enough or learned enough to be more influential against what IKE had termed the "military industrial complex" and now is known as the "military industrial congressional complex" and probably should be known as the "military industrial war profiteers congressional pentagon public ignorance complex."

I have sought every way possible within the socio-economic reactionary frames of the churches to oppose war. What I have done as the many before me, as the one Congressman who voted against WWII, the American Field Service of WWI, and the many such as Saint Francis of Assisi and Brother Martin et al, is not enough. That is what gives me grief right now as I consider those who have lived valiantly and died or been maimed as human fodder before the corporate war machine.

As one in my ninth decade, I pray that Louise and I may have the strength to change the paradigm, change the empowering human story as from destructive competition to creative competition and obvious cooperation, change the story that empowers people from depreciation toward appreciation of our planet and its life. Even as I felt pledged as a young child, through being close to my Church and faith and other faith groups as well as my dear family who had all served in the military and who lived lives in opposition to warfare, I continue to pledge to be and do whatever I can to be effective in what I term from my religious background and leaning as God's call to every human being to grow this world beyond war and the destructiveness of violent response.

My tears remain for you as families as they do for my own slowness to respond and often ineptness in response. They are good tears and from them I feel each day a bit more empowered to speak and act for peace, which we all needs must do. May God bless you even as I feel empowered, forgiven and blessed forward and backward both, toward God's goal of a dynamic, loving, caring, responsive world choosing not the easy way of conflict and war and ignorance and avoidance and denial, but doing the hard work and knowing the blessed creative and active rest of peace.

Our love, David P. Ransom,
Waterville, Vermont 05492

War Is Slavery

It was January of 2003, late at night, and I was home alone. I turned on the TV. The movie "Platoon" was on. I had never watched any violent shows nor read anything about war or Viet Nam since I left there in March of 1971. Now, all these years later, I figured it was time and I could handle it. The scene was a U.S. patrol entering a village. I saw the kids with their big dark eyes, skinny bodies and ragged clothes – and it all came back, like a lightening bolt. The sights, the sounds, the smells. I was stunned. I turned off the TV and sat in the darkened room.

The next day the internet became my soul-mate. Unstructured for the first few months, I consumed a world of information. At 57 years of age with an MBA, it seemed like I should have known these things. But I was almost totally ignorant. Information on war, peace, politics, world affairs, religion, organizations, books, magazines, videos, DVDs, radio and TV shows – and the list grew with each passing day. I needed structure. I finally formulated two questions: why war? and why do we so proudly send our children to kill other children?

These two questions burned my brain. Howard Zinn helped with his book on US history – "The Peoples History of the United States." Marine Major General Smedley Butler helped with his booklet on war – "War is a Racket." Many other authors and people and programs moved me along the path.

I concluded that the main causes of war are money and markets. There is always plenty of flag waving and bluster about the "evil ones," but every war I've studied, once you begin peeling back the layers, has the same core.

Why do we send our kids to kill? Because that's how we raise them. Sometimes subtle, sometimes overt, but there is an ever present message that violence is the solution to conflict. Go into any park in any town and you'll probably see a military statue or a cannon. Veterans' memorials are everywhere. Parades are led by weapons-carrying veterans and the military. The military carries the flag into sporting events. Military ads are ubiquitous. POW-MIA flags fly from Post Offices and other buildings. Highways are named after wars, war veterans, and generals. Battleships are named after Presidents. We have civil war re-enactments. Our language is violent – " I could just kill my kids," "bullet points," and sports announcers inject "kill," "beat," "destroyed" into their descriptions. The more overt influences are easy to notice once you become aware – video games, weapon toys, paintball parks. They are there. Everyday. All of these, the subtle and the overt, lower the barrier to hurting others.

I've tried to summarize my findings into short, snappy slogans to get people to think. I used to say, "war is failure." But war is only failure for one side. For the other side, war is the best business in the world. High profits, little competition, products rapidly used, price is seldom questioned. Weapons are the number one export product of the USA. Hundreds of thousands of people are employed in the death and destruction industry. Thousands also spend their lives teaching at war colleges and military schools and in JROTC and Cadet programs. Other thousands plan wars and "covert actions." Mercenary companies and contractors are ubiquitous. They are involved in every U.S. conflict and sometimes outnumber the military.

Thus I needed a new slogan, a new summary of my research. I found it in an unusual location. As I walked through the Underground Railroad Museum in Cincinnati I began to feel what slavery was/is. It felt vaguely familiar. The oppression, the hatred, the total dominance, the violence, the tearing apart of families are part of slavery, but there is also the "other side." On the other side are the money and the righteous – the people who were not only comfortable with slavery, but promoted it. The preachers, the politicians, the teachers, the business people, the pillars of society said slavery was not only necessary, it was the only way the country could survive. The slaves weren't people. They weren't human. It was OK to torture them and shoot them and hang them. It was OK to use dogs on them and beat them. They didn't have a brain. The Golden Rule didn't apply to them. I realized that slaves have much in common with those we label as the "enemy," or "terrorists."

Slavery will never be forgotten on the one side. The scars are deep, bone deep, generations deep. Like war. On the other side the masters and their families and the foremen and slave traders and the bankers and the pillars of society and all those who supported and profited from slavery didn't have bad memories. They didn't have losses. There was nothing for them to forget.

As I thought about slavery over the next months I began to realize that slavery and war are very similar. The one side (the civilians and the lower ranks of the military on both sides) suffers. The other side says war is the only way the country can survive. War is slavery. I'm an abolitionist.

THE BOX
Arny Stieber
(Army, infantry in the U.S. war against the people of Viet Nam)

With their backs board straight,
and their hands to their heads,
the draped box passes by.

With their uniforms crisp,
and their eyes steely fixed,
the draped box passes by.

Gone are the "who-yahs" and the high fives
and the beers, and the babes and the bitchin'.
As the draped box passes by.

"Kill the bastards – THEY killed ours."
"THEY're all bad."
"We go there to help them. For freedom! Democracy!"
"We serve our country!"
"It's NOT about money or markets or oil!
We're defending our freedom and our soil!"
"There's no other way! Sometimes we must!
Send in the few . . . the proud . . . . . the . . ."
the young? . . . . the pawns?
The Draped box passes by.

"THEY can't speak our language.
THEY don't know our customs.
THEY are HEINIES, and JAPS, and CHINKS,

and GOOKS, and HAJJIS, and RAG HEADS.
(and before that . . . THEY were SAVAGES)
They're evil. They're terrorists!"
They are "THEM." They are "THOSE." They are "THEY."
So it's OK – – – – to kill them.
There's no other way,
That's what the box makers say.

We have courts – but not for "THEM."
We don't torture people – but "THEY" are not.
We are CIVIL – with our approved assassination lists,
We are HUMANE with our surgical drone strikes.
"THEY" are not.

We have our flag. We sing our songs.
We love our country. "U-S-A U-S-A
We're # 1. We're # 1!"
"THEY" are not.
Don't bother your beautiful brain.
Don't think . . . . avoid the pain.
As the draped box passes by.

Who makes the box in which soldiers lay?
This well crafted box for the remains to stay.
Is it more than a box to carry the dead?
Is the box mental and fixed in our head,
By those who profit from wars and destruction
Because they know we'll follow instruction?

Some of the box makers are out in the light,
They're proud of the fact they cause us to fight.
But most of the makers work in the stealth,
Applying their trade and amassing huge wealth.

From Presidents to talking heads and others less known –
– – Create fear . . . , make a box . . . , keep the masses alone – – .
"We know what we're doing, we'll save the day,"
"Stay in the box and just do as . . . WE say."

The boxes are made as they always have been,
By those with the power to develop the spin.
Their words are repeated – –
Down is up . . . up is down
Killing is good . . . they are not
Down is up . . . up is down
Soon the box closes . . . without a sound.

Violence and power are global pollution.
Dialogue and education are the solution.
Talk to those you know . . . and to the "THEY."
(very slowly) Read and share . . . . and show the way . . . . . .

With their backs board straight,
and their hands to their heads . . . . . .
With their uniforms crisp,
and their eyes steely fixed . . . . . ,
Gone are the "who-yahs" and the high fives,
What's left are the whys . . . . ,
As the draped box passes by.
To my brothers and sisters remembered here:

My heart breaks

My heart breaks whenever I remember that awful war, the American War, that took you from us. I was not in Vietnam as I served my enlistment in the US Army before the tragedy in Southeast Asia began in earnest in 1964. I am very fortunate that due to circumstances of age and economics I was already a veteran and was not called to serve, but, strange as it may seem, especially when I am actively protesting US military adventurism, I feel guilty about not having been there with you.

I visited the wall in 1992 with my family and I still remember clearly how my breath was taken away when I first came upon that beautiful, black edifice, so majestic in its simplicity. It seemed so fitting for what it represents. I was deeply moved as I approached and I remember weeping quietly as I mourned you and the countless others who were sacrificed to our country's hubris and warped view of the world.

Sadly we have not learned much in the decades since that terrible action, but I can only hope that maybe, even before I depart this earth, we finally do learn the lessons of Vietnam and all the conflicts since, and realize that peace, not war, is our only option if we are to be a successful species. If we can get there, then finally you and all who gave their lives before and since, can finally really rest in peace.

You live in my heart, always,

David Larsen
US Army, 1960-1963

Dear Bobby,

Dear Bobby,

Well, big brother, I know you will forgive me for calling you Bobby. I'm sure you would prefer Bob or "Arnie" but Bobby is how I remember you. I sent "The Elephant Smiled" to our close friend Bonnie in Texas last week. She loved it. Actually, through the miracle of genealogy, we are blood. Cousins, just like Lew from Alpha North is our 8th cousin. Tomorrow a copy of "The Elephant Smiled" goes to your best friend, Harold. I can see you riding with him in his new red corvette. Who would ever have thought 50 years ago that a book would be dedicated to you and the other 6 who died at Alpha North? Who would have thought that I would find so many of your fellow Marines who fought the battle that took your life and that we would all get together for reunions ? I'm so grateful to Scott for bringing the team from the University of Florida at Gainesville to our first reunion in 2012. That allowed the Marines to share their stories of the battle for Alpha North. Much of what happened is forever archived at the University and also The Library of Congress. You know that I have the rest written down to be shared with our family. I have also included the narrative I wrote about Alpha North for our 50 year commemorative reunion in DC this year. It is directly under this letter to you. It may or may not be added to this letter that I am writing to you. I do hope it will be though.

I'm still looking for John William Bell. Sadly, I learned of the deaths of Ron Smeberg, Nickie Owens, David Alberson and Grant Baldwin. Guess you knew about them long before me. You know how my entire life I was haunted by these names and my intense need to know about them and all that happened the night you were killed. With the exception of Bell, I learned the fates of your friends. You also know why I went into the Veteran's Administration to work as a psychiatric registered nurse. Chills came over me in the early 80s because I had a vision of things to come and it was then I knew there was something big coming, just did not realize how big or how long it would take to materialize.

I'm confident that you enjoyed the picture of Jay and George at the "Wall." When we laid the wreath, I didn't cry. I do plenty of that when I'm by myself. Whenever I feel sad or hesitant to do something, I think of you and the courage you had during your short time in Vietnam. I think of the many stories of your bravery shared by your buddies. I can't say that any of those stories surprised me. From the time we were kids, I knew your courage would serve you well when life challenged you. Even at the end, you gave your life for your friends, not for support of the war. While functioning as a "grunt" shortly after arriving for Operation Double Eagle, I remember the letter you sent us when you said, " I don't understand why the U.S. gets involved in wars they do not belong in." You were right then Bobby, and you are right now. The whole world finally understands that war was a mistake.

I think you, mom and dad were finally able to reunite our sister and me. What a surprise! You knew about her once you crossed over but there had to come a time when Sandy and I were meant to know that each of us existed as full biological sisters. I know you watch over her and her entire family and of course me too. I have felt you around me so many times. So..... Bobby.......eternal peace and love my dear big brother. Can't wait to see you again when I join you in spirit.

Forever your little sister,

Bonnie

Alpha North

In the spring of 1966, Battery A, 1st Bn, 11th Marines remained attached to the 1st Bn, 12th Marines, designated as Alpha North. The 105 artillery battery was located 30 kilometers northwest of Da Nang. During the early morning hours of April 18, under cover of a dark moon, "an estimated main force" of North Vietnamese sappers attacked the position. The intent of the enemy was to destroy the six 105 howitzers and kill as many

Marines as possible. The revenge mission was retribution for the heavy casualties inflicted upon the Viet Cong by Alpha North during Operation Harvest Moon. Hanoi Hannah taunted on the radio that the Marines would feel the vengeance of North Vietnam. For months the enemy combatants trained on a battery mock-up which they built in the nearby hills, only discovered by an investigative patrol after the attack.

The outposts and gun line were hit hard as the sappers penetrated the position through a drainage ditch and heavy foliage. Five Marines were killed and 28 were wounded as gun two was destroyed and gun one was crippled. Official documents vary on how many attackers were killed. Never completely determined, two estimates were between 15 and 40 dead. The actual count may have been higher. It was the practice of the enemy to drag away their dead and wounded as they rapidly withdrew from a battle ground. The North Vietnamese greatly underestimated the fighting ability of the fierce young Marines they encountered as they attacked the guns and outposts of Alpha North. There would be no second opportunity for them to seek revenge and decimate the battery.

The five Marines killed at Alpha North on April 18, 1966 were PFC Robert Dwain "Arnie" Arnold, LCpl Danny Arnold Bolin, LCpl Frederick "Fred" Homeyer, PFC Ralph Richard "Junior" Lind and PFC William Terry "Jake" Main.

Eighteen year old PFC Robert Dwain Arnold nicknamed "Arnie" felt fortunate that his asthma did not prevent him from serving in the Corps. He was an outdoorsman and avid reader, with a strong focus on military history. He dreamed of a future life in journalism, possibly as an outdoor writer. Good friend Jay Booher met him on Okinawa. Their friendship lasted through Operation Double Eagle 1 & 2, Bravo 1/12 and finally Alpha North. Jay would honor his fellow cannoneers, Arnie and Fred Homeyer with a memorial stone in his home state of Oregon. Another Marine who remembered Arnie fondly was Ace Cardenas. Born on the same month and day, Ace good-naturedly would tease his new friend about his baby face and generally young looks. On April 18th, as the battle raged, George Wirtz found Arnie where he fell, guarding and comforting him until his last breath.

L/Cpl Danny Arnold Bolin 19, loved sports. He participated in high school football, basketball and track. In July, 1965 he married his high school sweetheart, Rhonda. Of the 5 KIAs from Alpha North, Danny was with the battery the longest. Well liked and respected by all members of the group, he would help out on gun # 1. He enjoyed his battery armorer MOS but also wanted to learn the job of cannoneer. Gun 1 crew chief Ray Glynn took this opportunity to allow Danny two hours a day on the 105 howitzer as gunner/assistant gunner as long as he would pull outpost watch whenever possible. The battery was short of help and Danny played a significant role in relieving his tired fellow crewmen. The outpost forward of gun # 1 was his assignment on April 18th with Martin Vigil, Jake Main and one other Marine. He was killed instantly as the enemy moved on the outpost.

L/Cpl Frederick "Fred" Homeyer 21, was affectionately known as "Freddie" by his mom, close friend and fellow Marine, Al Maglietto. He was on his second tour in Vietnam when he lost his life. In his teen years, fishing and high school sports were his interests. Assigned to gun # 2, there is a picture of Fred at Alpha North taken by Jay Booher. Ray Glynn remembered Fred being assigned to gun # 1 for a short while. Always interested in current events, he would repeatedly ask for "scoopies" from Ray. At the time, the same question over and over annoyed Ray but now he states, "how I would love to hear him ask me that again." He died instantly near gun # 2 as the area was in heavy explosions. His last words to friend Al Maglietto as Al dropped him off at Pendleton in '66 were "Semper Fi Teufel Hunden." Two months later he was gone.

Nineteen year old PFC William Terry "Jake" Main had a very close relationship with his sister, Marilyn. Niece, Lori Fennewald, described her uncle as a "jokester who was charming, smart and loyal." Assigned to gun # 1, Ray Glynn remembered the young Marine as a good worker with the ability of using humor to defuse an argument. Scott Camil stated that Jake was his first friend in the battery, forming an instant bond with him when he learned they were both from Florida. As stated previously, Jake was on watch with his three Marine buddies on the outpost forward of gun # 1 as the enemy creeped in. When the battle ended and as the sun rose, Scott felt the loss of his new friend. He looked at his face for the last time and said a quiet, sorrowful good-bye. Upon his return to the states, Scott reached out to the Main family.

Nicknamed "Junior" by his family and friends, PFC Ralph Richard Lind, 20, arrived in Vietnam in November of 1965. Before transferring to artillery, he had been in a mortar battery. Back in the states, Ralph enjoyed fishing with his dad and had recently proposed to his steady girlfriend from high school, Linda. He was described by his family as "witty, kind, just the nicest guy you ever met." During the attack on Alpha North, Ralph was fatally wounded as he ran from his tent to assist his fellow Marines. Corpsman "Doc" Hodgson attended his wounds until the chopper arrived for medical transport. Ralph's sister-in-law, Diane Lind, has a family poem that was written for Ralph's parents. Three pages long, three lines from the poem were shared: "Yesterdays-Tomorrows, dedicated to mom and dad: Dad looked at mom, then mom looked at dad. They laughed and they loved and guess what they had? 'Junior' now a memory of years that are past but the love for him will always last."

In addition to the 5 Marines killed on April 18th, two forward observers from Alpha North lost their lives in an amtrac accident on November 22, 1965. They were nineteen year olds, PFC Michael August Beringer and PFC John Drew Campbell. Their disabled amtrac was being towed on the Cau Do river near the Nam O bridge when the tow line broke and the amphibious vehicle drifted helplessly in the dangerous current, finally sinking into the turbulent water. Three men were observed swimming in the strong current. A rescue team was sent but arrived too late to save them. The bodies of Mike Beringer and John Campbell were found by Vietnamese fishermen and carried to shore the next day. The other 7 deceased Marines were found in December, 6 were inside the sunken amtrac.

John Campbell was a powerful, gifted swimmer. Many theorized that John was able to swim out of the amtrac, possibly assisting Mike and Richard Wick as he exited, but the deadly, swift current and tumultuous swells could not be overcome.

Several Alpha North Marines remember John and Mike very well. Jerry Fankhouser went with John on liberty many times, describing him as being a very giving person with a great sense of humor. John continues to enter his dreams at night. When Wayne Martin heard the tragic news of the deaths of Mike and John from his 1st sergeant, he felt certain either of them, given the opportunity, would have tried to save the other. Jack Huelskamp was on the same forward observer team with the drowned Marines. Quotes from Jack, "Yes, I knew them well. Formed our FO team at Camp Pendleton just prior to embarking for Vietnam. Had liberty calls in Hong Kong, the Philippines and Australia. Chipped paint on the USS Lenawee for days at a time with the guys. Spent some star-filled nights sharing thoughts about our futures and such. John was a Christian. Mike was always smiling, very easy going." Denny Forsyth occasionally swam with John at the base pool. He shared that "John practiced diving and swam like a fish." He remembered that Mike's nickname was "Wadena" since he was from the Wadena, Minnesota area. Hayward Paul also has great memories of the two Marines. As a new F0, he served with the guys in 1965 during Operation Silver Lance.

Mike came from a large family and John a smaller one, being adopted by a loving couple who taught him important values. Alyce Campbell Crownover Keesee, married daughter of the Campbell's was very pleased to welcome her little brother to the family. Gail Anderson and Christine Riebold heard many remarkable stories about their cousin. As shared previously, Gail said he was kind, generous, athletic, and very popular. His strong beliefs kept him focused, allowing him to help several individuals in his short time on this earth.

The 7 Alpha North Marines who died in Vietnam will never be forgotten. "Long Time Passing" as we think back 50 years. Some speak of finding CLOSURE as we honor members of our fallen family.

Maybe it is more fitting to say that we found some PEACE as we discovered and shared the truth of what happened at Alpha North.

THANK YOU FOR YOUR SERVICE

— Jay Wenk

Gregory, nicknamed Raj,
from Bangor, Maine,
a vet of Iraq,
hooked up a vacuum cleaner hose
to his car's exhaust.

These are today's dead veterans.
There were others yesterday.

Living alone in a fifth floor walkup
on East 111th Street in New York,
Antoine raised and flew pigeons
from his rooftop chicken wire and slatted frame cage.
As he plunged into the backyard,
he took out several clotheslines.

There was Irv, Helen, George, Harold
Rennie and Harry.
Harold was gay, was called Roxy
among his friends, and he used a knife.

Frenchy never made it to the Post Office.
That's where he told his wife he was going.
He drove head-on into the side of
a concrete bridge abutment
on Route 66 in Arizona, at 120 MPH.
It was a clear, bright morning.

A Lieutenant Carbonaro took his '45 along
on a hunting trip upstate in North Dakota.

The medic who used to shoot up prisoners with
morphine, Carlos, saved up enough for himself.
He injected it while on leave, in Germany.

Angel, a guard at
our prison camp in the desert,
was a huge, smiling man, very friendly.
After discharge, he got a job as a warder
in a State prison near Biloxi.
He hung himself in his secondhand RV,
parked in a shady cottonwood grove.

There was Rudy, James and Eduardo,
living in ghetto flops in several different cities.
They combined booze and pills.

Reuben's father was an Air Force officer,
so Reuben was born into it.
Everyone called him "Hey, Rube".
When off duty from guiding armed Drones,
he loved to go up with the Paratroops.
On a flight yesterday,
he pushed his way past the jump master.

There was Bennie, Vera, Eli and Chris.
Chris was trained to defuse mines. Last evening,
on patrol, he jumped on one in plain sight.
The taxi driver who took Vera to
Chicago's railroad yards reported that
she was drunk.

During the night, Juan, in Nevada, and
Eugene, in Colorado, both walked out
into their respective deserts,
stripped, in spite of bitter cold,
lay down, cut their wrists, and died,
looking up at the full moon.

There'll be 22 more tomorrow.

My only direct knowledge of the war

Dear Doug:

My only direct knowledge of the war comes from growing up among its veterans – such as yourself. So, I cannot provide the kind of personal account that many of the people writing these letters will offer. I have, however, become an academic specialist in international relations, and I teach a class in a British university titled The US in Vietnam. This class attracts students from throughout the university and throughout the world. The fact that so many young people in 2016 recognise that this cataclysm which took place two generations ago should be learned from and commemorated is, to me at least, as small reason for hope.

Tom Kane

Memorial Day 2016,

To our Brothers and Sisters on the Wall,

I am a Vietnam-era Veteran, USN 1961-15; served active duty on-board a very old submarine, the USS Grouper AGSS-214, from October 1963-65. I had joined the Navy as an obligation to my country, which I truly loved and believed in, and had great camaraderie with shipmates.

In late 1964, following the "Tonkin Gulf Incident," which was fabricated to provide the basis for escalation of U.S. involvement in open warfare against North Vietnam, there was a request for volunteers to serve there. Many of us young sailors tried to volunteer, as we believed the lies that our Navy comrades had been attacked for no reason, and wanted to support them. We were told that submariners were not being accepted for service in Vietnam at that time, due to our extensive specialized training. However, I remained concerned about the escalation of the conflict in Vietnam, and learned all I could about developments there.

After leaving active duty service in October 1965, I returned to a pursuit of college studies at night, and continued interest in developments in Vietnam, reading everything I could find about the escalating war, in which many friends and comrades had now become involved. Upon learning the truth about the lies that led to the war, I became active in the peace movement, and joined antiwar demonstrations and organizations, including Vietnam Veterans Against the War (VVAW).

I have been active in the Veterans Peace Movement since that time, currently as an officer in my local chapter of Veterans For Peace, doing as much as I can to educate the public about the true costs of war, as a necessary counter to the wars which are so often started by lies. Many of us Veterans continue to serve the cause of peace.

The unnecessary illegal American War in Vietnam was a shameful time in our nation's history, resulting in three million Vietnamese deaths, over half of whom were civilians. The war has left a great feeling of shame for my country's behavior, which continues to this day. I often find it necessary to explain to my 6 grandchildren why I can never "salute" the American flag or sing the "Star Spangled Banner" at the numerous school events that we attend.

No More War!

Robert Keilbach

In these United States

May 3, 2016

Dear Reader:

In these United States our government and many citizens seem to believe that our intervention in the politics of other countries is best for the world. And yet, the history of many U.S. interventions is, at best, a difficult one to read and understand.

As various as those interventions have been, there is one factor that links each one to the others; our citizens have been sacrificed to whatever the cause may have been. Do we know or understand what that cause was?

My memories of Vietnam begin at the time that I heard of "military advisors" being sent into that country. I was young, not yet in secondary school, but I wanted to know more. My Dad was a veteran of World War II and I wondered what I was about to witness.

I learned. I witnessed and I still witness today the deaths, mental and physical damages of what became the Vietnam war. Some of my high school buddies were just memories before I even had a chance to graduate; many of my friends today carry scars from their time there.

I could not be drafted because of my physical disability and yet many who were drafted came home with disabilities that were worse than mine and some couldn't come home at all.

Steve Hoad

I didn't go to the Vietnam War

I didn't go to the Vietnam War. But the Vietnam War came to me. I was drafted but refused to go. Instead, I went to Canada. I lived there for only a year or so due to a fluke postponement of the draft call, which meant, in those lottery years, that I got off the hook without a warrant being issued for my arrest.

But the war changed my life. It brought me to the stark realization that we all had been lied to in our schools and churches about what country we were living in. We were not the good guys defending freedom around the world. We were the aggressors wreaking massive death and destruction, with an imperial vengeance.

I could see the casualties every night on TV and in the disruption happening in our streets. I could feel the pain of those on both sides in Vietnam and suffered an intense moral crisis that came with my conviction that I could not be any part of this war. This was a big awakening for a working class kid whose father worked for the army for 30 years and who actually had been offered an appointment to the Naval Academy from his U.S. Senator. I went from being a contender to being an outlaw.

I dropped out of college in my senior year because I could no longer concentrate on the studies that were leading me to join the ranks of the powerful. I spent some time in a monastery in New Mexico trying to understand my own spiritual truth. Then I sent my draft cards back to the draft board and hitchhiked with my backpack to Montreal, then to Toronto, a refugee of sorts, looking for asylum.

It was 1971. I was 22, alone, poor, and homeless in a foreign country, struggling to come to terms with the reality that I could be in exile from my country for the rest of my life. And with even more clarity, being outside the U.S., I could see the evil of my country's ways. And not just in the war itself, but in the racism, classism, and militarism that was so endemic to our culture. It was a deep disillusionment.

When it turned out that I was out of the draft, I returned to the U.S., but with a different view of myself and my identity vis-à-vis my country. Although I still bore the privilege of being white and male, I was now alienated from my "homeland." In my head and heart, I was now a resister to the dominant mainstream culture. I spent years smoking dope and avoiding any upward social or economic mobility.

Throughout the rest of my life, I have continued to feel like a man opposed to his own country. On the one hand, it has motivated me to join with others in the struggle for peace and justice. And on the other hand, the sense of alienation remains and I carry an abiding sense of sadness about the way things are.

In my later years, I have found common ground with many veterans from the Vietnam War who belong to the organization Veterans for Peace (VFP). These are men and women who carry the heavy burden of having been in war and who have learned the hard way that there is no such thing as a good war. They have unseen scars from their experiences. I also have scars from that war, though not comparable.

Once a VFP man asked me what branch of the armed forces I had been in and I told him, somewhat sheepishly, that I had not been in the armed forces, that I was not in fact a veteran. He smiled and assured me that we all were veterans of the war, all damaged in one way or the other. I could feel the truth of that and felt grateful for the understanding from a fellow refugee.

Ken Jones
Swannanoa, NC
May 2, 2016

Semper Fi

"Semper Fi", Always Faithful

George Lee, Jr.

2nd Letter to the Wall

The Wall is hard for me. I am not a military veteran: I was an opponent of the war for which those memorialized sacrificed their lives. I cannot think about the wall without remembering those millions of Southeast Asian deaths not memorialized. Some of those memorialized in the wall did horrible things in the war. I also understand that these victims of the war served out of honorable motivations of patriotism, who confronted an enemy of whom they had no real sense. Enemy soldiers were also patriots.

The Wall is America's official memory of the war. It is not celebratory and its somber tone implies that war may not be as glorious as other parts of the culture suggest. So I hope that the Wall might serve as a good possible starting point for an honest commemoration since it allows for new generations to connect to what is now receding into historical memory. The great historian Hobsbaum writes somewhere about the movement from the memory of those still living into the recesses beyond it; from family lore and journalism to history. We are on that cusp.

So how can we build on what the Wall evokes. The proponents of the war promoted it as a noble fight for freedom, appealing to traditional American notions of idealism. It became a war in defense of a corrupt puppet government, led to a military strategy of "kill anything that moves"; and ended up sacrificing 58,000+ Americans and perhaps 3 million Southeast Asians; cost billions in national treasure, and deeply dividing the nation. As a 60s youth, I experienced that same transition. The obvious lesson (for me) was to not repeat this kind of monumental mistake.

For the militarists and the imperialists, this was disparaged as the "Vietnam syndrome" to be overcome as soon as possible. And they have succeeded. War has been normalized, torture legitimized, even celebrated, and peoples in other nations demonized. The military option is more and more the default option on all sides to resolve conflict and civilians are now routinely targeted or collateralized.

So for Americans at large, and especially our rulers, the opportunity for sober learning offered by the American experience in Southeast Asia has been consigned to the dustbin of history in favor of a so-called realism that so far has only spread the chaos and deepened the conflicts. The narrow logic of war has triumphed as each inhumane debacle leads to increasing polarization, bad blood and the seeming necessity of further escalation. What can upset this poisonous apple cart, which runs in dizzying circles digging us deeper into our ruts?

It remains for us the living to do our best to expand the circles of honest memory to truly honor the victims — which include the survivors who still bear the war's consequences. This is not so much about who was right back then (or now); but to move beyond the follies and disasters of imperial war to imagine peace, what Viet Thanh Nguyen calls "a realism of the impossible." Let's begin at the Wall and move on out from there.

Howie M.

In 1968 I was a junior in college,

May 1, 2016

In 1968, I was a junior in college. I was opposed to the US war in Vietnam and I was equally opposed to the II-S Deferment which allowed college students to avoid the draft. If a country's young people need to kill and die to preserve and protect the country and its Constitution, why should the privileged be exempt? Isn't that privilege both the opposite of democracy and the insidious curse which undermines it?

And the US war in Vietnam was wrong for so many reasons — a continuation of French colonialism, an intrusion into a country's civil war, fundamentally racist, a wilful misreading of regional history, and based on lies told to the American people to promote it. The war was illegal and a moral abomination. It was a war of choice. It was a war of empire. It was a war in which the soldiers and civilians on both sides were objectified and diminished to be expended in a US geo-political shell game.

I felt I had to fully engage the moral crisis of this time — either I go to war or do everything in my power to stop it and help bring an end to the killing of Americans, Vietnamese, Cambodians & Laotians. I turned in my draft card with the expectation that I would be sent to jail. I was re-classified 1-A, and when I refused to sign the loyalty oath at my physical, I was classified 1-A delinquent. For reasons never made clear to me, I was never prosecuted. My assumption was that if enough sons and daughters of the middle and upper-middle classes went to prison to protest the war, enormous pressure would be brought to bear to end the war.

When I experience The Wall now, my feelings are complex and overwhelming.

First there is the great sadness. All that suffering. Guilt. Shame. Heroism. Degradation. Anger. And the continuing legacy of Agent Orange plaguing the Vietnamese. I feel the same anger that I do about the Iraq War: A crime was committed. The Wall is the perpetual evidence of that crime. But the truth is never acknowledged; the US never holds itself accountable for this crime.

I was never opposed to US soldiers. They, like the Vietnamese, were victims of bankrupt policy. I was opposed to the people who sent them to do and suffer such physical and moral injury. Part of the shame I feel is that I did not do enough to end the war. Daniel Ellsberg and the Berrigan brothers are reminders of what more could have been done. Because of that personal failure, The Wall represents a part of me that died, too.

As long as the truth about the Vietnam War is not officially acknowledged, we can say in the words of T. S. Eliot, "We had the experience, but missed the meaning." Without the meaning, our souls embrace an essential hypocrisy. Our schools fail to teach the young the truth. The Wall, at the least, continues to offer the possibility of redemption.

Robert Shetterly

Brooksville, Maine

Last night

Last night I met a vibrant, funny, determined young man. As I watched his movie, listened to him answer questions and helped with his book signing I was at once awed by his courageous story of survival and healing .....and so overwhelmed by the atrocities of war! In 2012 Sergeant Travis Mills put his backpack on a land mine in Afghanistan and today is a quad amputee who has started a foundation to open a respite, resort camp in Maine for disabled vets and their families.

My friend teaches Travis and Kristen's 5 year old!

She hosted a sold out event and raised about $5,000 for the foundation. Travis's message of hope and healing and family resonated so deeply with me, but I so just wanted him to tell us war just sucks and we as a nation and people can do better. We just don't need any more names of dead soldiers on walls and Travis talked about how he was so lucky to survive because many of his friends are not at home with families and loved ones. He feels blessed and is so articulate, but I wanted to hug him and tell him or ask him why he felt a young, healthy man had to go to war,..what was the purpose? He loved the feeling of belonging to a unit and leading his men and being involved! So why can't we have an army of water and all the armies in the world fight the battle of fresh water until every person on earth has fresh water. Then just fill in the blanks...army of food, housing, disease.

Margy Burns Knight
Winthrop, Maine

I enlisted in the US Air Force

May 1,2016

I enlisted in the US Air Force in 1968 three months before graduating from high school. This was prior to the draft lottery. I was not planning on going to college so I knew I would be drafted shortly after graduation.

Following basic training and ten months of tech school in Texas I received orders for Wheeler Air Base, Oahu, Hawaii, a 36 months assignment. While serving in Hawaii I became involved in the GI anti-Vietnam War movement. In 1971 I attended an anti – Vietnam War demonstration at the front gates of Schoffield Barracks, Army Base, Wahiawa, Oahu. Within weeks following the demonstration my 36 months assignment was curtailed and I received orders for Thule Air Base, Greenland.

My participation in the GI Anti-Vietnam War movement and participation in a demonstration against the War are what I am most proud of in my 3 years, 11 months and 11 days in the military.

Michael F. Turek, US Air Force 1968-7

I, Sheridan Peterson

I, Sheridan Peterson, a World War II Marine Corps vet, spent 7 years in Vietnam as a civilian throughout the war. As a refugee adviser for USAID/CORDS in the Mekong Delta at Phu Vinh, Vinh Binh and at Cao Lanh at the Sea of Reeds, I saw America at its worst. I went to Vietnam with the express purpose of writing a literary documentary of the war and wrote a 600 page manuscript. No reputable publisher wants to peruse it.

Among so much else, I witnessed genocide frequently – napalm and white phosphorus drops on peaceful villagers, burning them to cinders. Carpet bombings, ordinary troops mutilating corpses and proudly passing the photos about. The horrors of the Phoenix Program, torture, dropping prisoners from helicopters. Hanging out at the Cheiu Hoi camps I saw the war through the eyes of the Viet Cong and NVA.

I am 90 and won't be around much longer. I have Agent Orange poisoning and the VA refuses to compensate me because I was a civilian under the command of colonel, Province Senior Adviser.

I am anxious to see this manuscript widely distributed before I die. It may simply disappear.

I wrote a letter to the Wall

I wrote a letter to the Wall last year, and here is another. I hope to continue this until I am no longer able and as long as that wall exists as a reminder of the needless death and destruction wrought by the American War in Viet Nam.

Acts of heroism, compassion and bravery under fire, regardless of the side, are worthy of respect but the war itself from the U.S. side, a war of domination and empire waged on a people struggling to be free from exploitive colonial power, was not. Those who died or were wounded and the many, on all sides, who still suffer from that war, and all wars, what relief is there for them?

Perhaps the only relief will come, if ever, when this country, the U.S., which has been an example to the world in many ways – some good, most of them not, stops waging war, both military and economic, on the rest of the world. But we, the living, have little time to wait for that to happen. In our short time left, let us put all our efforts into the quest for a peaceful world.

Maybe then, when the world is free of war, those whose names are inscribed here at the wall and the many, many others, who are not, can finally rest in peace.

Tarak Kauff
U.S. Army Airborne 1959-62
Veterans For Peace
Board of Directors

May the millions of human beings

May the millions of human beings who suffered death, disability, pain, imprisonment or the pain of separation as a result of the US War in Vietnam inspire us to work harder and think more clearly for peace and justice. May their suffering help us to root out the causes of war, the greatest scourge of humanity.

While we cannot undo their suffering, we can stop the suffering in today's wars, and prevent the wars of tomorrow. For Vietnam we can only help heal the remaining wounds of past wars, but for Syria, now the bloodiest war on the planet, we can do better to end the conflict and bring peace and justice to that beleaguered nation. For all the current armed conflicts on earth and for all the hatred and xenophobia in Asia, Africa, Europe and the Americas, may the remembrance of past suffering help us to find peaceful and just solutions to present conflicts.

Andrew S. Berman
US Army 1971-73

LETTER TO THE WALL

To all my sisters and brothers named on this Wall

To all who came back wounded in body and soul

To my son who returned from another American WAR

To everyone of the world affected by endless WAR

To Richard B. Clements, Panel 42W Line 54, of this Wall

May you all be at peace, find peace, rest in peace

I first visited here at the Wall in 2005. I looked up Richard B. Clements as I am Richard B. Clement (without the s). As a Vietnam Era Veteran this could have been me. Fortunately for me I only saw this war from a distance and did not join my brother in name on the Wall.

My first remembrance of Vietnam Vets came in the early 70's when I was a wide eyed 11B infantry private stationed in Germany. Two Sergeants came into our Ordnance Company, fresh out of Vietnam. In dress uniforms. Overseas Service Bars/Combat Stripes on the right arm. Service Stripes on the left arm. Sergeant Stripes on both arms. Blue Infantry cord and tabs. CIB. Medals. A sight to behold for a young man coming from a small rural town in Maine!

As it was and is for many Nam Vets, this story does not end well. One Sergeant hoped to be a policeman when he got discharged. He was so laid back and mellow that he was essentially disengaged from reality. He did not get promoted. The other Sergeant immediately started drinking heavily and lost one stripe after another and soon "made" private. In a couple of short months he was shipped out of our Company. Assuredly both these men had PTSD which took years for the VA to recognize for the illness it is. It is my hope that these two men found ways to cope and overcome their war experiences and to find comfort and peace in their lives.

When I visited this hallowed Wall my eldest son was with me. From this sacred ground we walked to the "Iraq Veterans Wall." A temporary Wall with names of war dead from yet another war had been set up. My son is an Iraq War Veteran.

My son found the name of a friend, a fellow Mainer, who had been killed in a mortar attack while they were stationed together in Taji, Iraq. The pain on my son's face remembering a comrade killed in action was as heartbreaking as the pain on my face looking on. At least here I could hold him. As a parent, the year he was in the war zone of Iraq was the total year from HELL. The infrequent phone calls. The infrequent emails. The constant barrage of the war from the media. The constant dread of a government vehicle coming up the drive.

To all my brothers and sisters who survived, WELCOME HOME. I hope you have found peace and comfort in your lives. To those who did not return, please know that many will never forget you and you live on in our thoughts and memories.

To all who have read this simple letter, know that war is unconscionable. From the Veterans' perspective, from the fathers' perspective, from the humanitarian perspective. May we find a way to end all wars before they end all of us.

In sadness but also in hope,

Peace

Richard
30 May 2016

I have posted these Coast Guard recruit names

Vietnam Veterans Memorial
National Park Service
National Capitol Parks – Central
900 Ohio Drive, S.W.
Washington, D.C. 20242

I have posted these Coast Guard recruit names on the Memorial on my visits to Washington, previously. Though they did not make their sacrifices in Vietnam, they and their families have losses similar to those who did. Countless other sacrifices should be recognized in the cost of wars.

Prior generations of my family fought with pride; my paternal grandfather, Philip Morgan, during World War I and my father, Peter S. Morgan, in the U.S. Army Infantry 1943 – 1946. With the Selective Service due to arrive at my doorstep, I chose to enlist in a humanitarian service rather than support the questionable objectives (later acknowledged by Robert S. McNamara's In Retrospect: The Tragedy and Lessons of Vietnam) in Southeast Asia.

My wife and I who raised two sons a generation later, know too well of the value of a continued family legacy. (Shameful that the United States invaded Iraq during their eligibility, ignoring Dick Cheney's 1994 warning of a quagmire.)

Peter S. Morgan, Jr. /
active duty USCG 1969 – 1973

My life has been touched

LETTER TO THE WALL

My life has been touched by the suffering of Vietnam veterans since I was a teenager. My first lover was a Vietnam veteran who eventually killed himself. I began to fall in love with my husband when I heard him tell a military age young man why he had risked his own health to avoid the draft during the Vietnam war: he knew that his government was lying to him.

My friends in the current antiwar movement often are veterans of Vietnam who have sustained the moral injuries of combat and who struggle with depression and despair. Many family members of students I've taught have suffered from PTSD, substance abuse, cancer and other health effects of being Vietnam vets. This continues to put stress on families down through the generations.

Lisa Savage

I did my basic training at Fort Lewis

I did my basic training at Fort Lewis in Washington State; my Advanced Infantry Training at Fort Polk, Louisiana (affectionately referred to as the armpit of the Army) and my Armored Personnel Carrier Driver training at Fort Knox, Kentucky. I turned 21 while flying home from Fort Knox for a week's leave before flying to the Republic of Viet Nam.

I was assigned to the 4th Infantry Division 2/8 Mechanized Infantry. I went into the bush on December 8, 1967. After a few days in some base camp I was sent by chopper to my unit. I climbed up onto my APC, looked at the track next to mine and sitting there was one of my best friends from childhood. He had moved from Seattle to Aberdeen when we were about 13-14. He had been with the 9th Division and had recently been assigned to the 4th. Max went home a couple months later.

Between December 17-26 we spent our time on foot sweeping an area North of Pleiku in the Central Highlands. I first came under fire December 27. The track came off the APC I was driving and while I was outside trying to fix it we came under sniper fire and grenade attack.

Between then and Jan. 2, 1968 we were in a Fire Support Base. January 3 we got a report from a Montagnard that he had helped bury 2 NVA in a nearby village. Being one of the new guys I got to dig up this grave.

> we move out of the tree line
> spread out surround the huts
> the village headman says
> two wounded men died
> and were buried
> several days before
> a green black shimmer
> rises (after three days;
>   the sun)
> the skin
> taut with gangrenous gas
> bursts

with the weight of a landing fly
spewing
pus to dust

we dig
small men's bones
in a small hole
a soup of khaki straps and steel buckles
stirred and sifted
for intelligence

On February 1, 1968 we were on patrol and got word that a
chopper was under fire half a kilometer away. We moved in and
cut an LZ with our tracks. An aero-rifle platoon landed and we all
opened fire with M-16s and .50 calibers. In the middle of this I
drove through some high grass and threw a track. When I got out
of the APC to fix the track I found that I had run over a man
hiding in the grass. In fact, he had become caught in my track and
was the reason for throwing the track. I had to pull his headless
body out of the thrown track before I could straighten in out and
replace the track.

The first man I killed was small and
hidden in the tall grass.

Being a killer forever changes you.
Even if you learn to be kind and considerate and civilized
that part of you is always
hiding down inside
awaiting a chance.

A normal person does not want to kill and
will avoid it at all costs.
The military won't allow you to remain normal.
It doesn't matter if you think
you are smart enough
not to get caught up in their lies.
They will change you

Don't be sucked into the biggest myth and lie
that dying for your country is somehow heroic.

Really be all that you can be.

Later after this fire fight I was patrolling on foot and found a Vietnamese man who must have had 15 bullet holes in his body struggling to move away. I felt that he had no chance to live so I put him out of his misery with several rounds through the head. We found that we had killed 110 that day and captured 140. Unfortunately there were women and kids among the dead. To this day I don't know if they were an enemy or just unfortunates in the wrong place.

An Army of One

Do you hear the dead complaining?
Killing is easy –
it don't mean shit.

What's that look for?

You think I should be touched by
the death of mother/brother/son/daughter/uncle/father/child?

The only touch I feel is
the half ounce of pressure on the trigger –
then
I get to be
all I can be.

We stayed in the area until Feb. 4 when the Army sent out bulldozers to bury all the bodies. Soon thereafter I was smoking 2 packs per day of cigarettes and daily marijuana. Once we went into Pleiku and bought opium from the Governor of the Province.

We came under periodic fire and I came close to dying so many times I finally concluded that I was invincible. Once a B-40 rocket came under my chin so close I could feel the wind. Once we were walking in 2 lines through some elephant grass following some commo wire. I was walking point on one line. A Vietnamese man stood up about 10 feet away and sprayed us with full automatic and the guys on both sides of me got shot.

I shot an NVA officer in the face and took his belt with a red star and rifled his pockets for his 300 piastres. When we would drive our APCs near indigenous personnel (Vietnamese citizens) we would throw C-ration cans at the kids begging at the side of the road cheering when a kid was hit.

nights he still comes to me
eyes clear

black and white
unlike his body
yellow and red

this spectre
of a rising tide of godless communism
turning
amidst the tangled pile
of bodies

the 300 piastres
and the red-starred belt
I took from his body

We had a first sergeant who was a total asshole (not recognizing at the time that we all were total assholes). We used to take C-4 explosive and take the tops off flares and pop them off so that they would explode in the air. Some one handed the First Sergeant one that was doctored a little so when he popped it it exploded in his hand blowing off several fingers.

this militaristic corporate statist
religion alive in our midst
barely hides the bronze face of Moloch
Canaanite sun god risen again amongst us
this god whose face is ours

whose name is consumption
whose tongue is greed
demands the sacrifice of our children
in blood and madness
name them warriors these boy soldiers
and our daughters now
to kill or be killed
a death hunger never satisfied

dance with the flute and cymbal
sing the patriotic anthems
loud martial songs
to drown the voices
and screams of the dying

This same guy remains in my prime image of the Army in Viet Nam. After about 10 months when I was sure I wouldn't get killed I decided to extend my tour to get an early out. At that time we were drafted for 24 months. If you had less than 5 months left when you got back to the world you got out of the army. I hated the Army more than I hated the possibility of something bad happening during the extra time I'd spend in Viet Nam.

We stopped a checkpoint to re-supply (i.e. buy beer and weed) and I signed the papers. We went out on a patrol near Plei Mrong and were attacked. The first and third APCs in line hit mines and the 2nd and 4th were hit by rockets. I was in the 5th APC.

I could see smoke coming from the one in front of me so I went around back to take a look. All the while we were under intense fire. It looked like a small fire near the battery so I stepped back to grab a breath before trying to put the fire out.

In the instant I stepped back another guy stepped between me and the door of the track and a grenade inside went off. He had a flack vest on and wasn't hurt and I just got some minor leg shrapnel. The explosion threw me back a ways and when I looked up I saw the First Sergeant with an M-16 in one hand and a case of beer under the other arm running away from us. This is my full impression of the U.S. military.

I will teach you how
to perform a war
a clean operation
to remove that dangerous tissue
which can no longer be controlled
we first name it cancer
we curse it for an inhuman bastard
nothing legitimate to be found
the pathologic question
must be asked and answered
weighing whether a pound of flesh will be enough
shared definitions in hand
we sharpen our knives
sanitary
chrome and steel
bright lights
remove any shadow
of doubts
patriotic anesthesia dulls the senses
common and other
to the loud cutting
ripping and
bleeding to come
once hidden viscera bloody red
broken bone white
and hypoxic blue tissue
stare out at us
unexpected collateral damage
can be dressed
with sterile white gauze
although the bloated smell
sometimes remains

afterwards
we will remove our gloves
and wash our hands

I went to Viet Nam an average twenty year old. I was totally
ignorant of American history and American foreign policy

intentions. I was a leader in my high school and involved in many issues. Since then, I recently realized, I have had no close friends. I find it difficult to get close to people. It sounds strange but part of my consciousness is still in Viet Nam waiting for that bullet. When I walk along trails I am constantly watching for any disturbances in the dirt which might signal land mines. I always, when driving or walking, look for good ambush sites.

driving I remember to note
sites which would be good for an ambush
walking I watch the ground for
dirt which may have been disturbed
in the laying of mines
nearly forty years later
I still expect the bullet
to hit that spot
just below my left scapula
that always itches
like a target

nearly forty years later
I remember when we were boy warriors
thrown together far from home
(gun smoke thick as fog
hot brass litter
the lamb-like smell of napalm
burnt indigenous personnel
pile of bodies
slowly moving limbs in rigor
greenthick vietnamese jungle vines
sticky red clay mud in monsoon reason)

if he wasn't part of that
piece of me that couldn't come home
maybe I could
remember my friend's face
nearly forty years later

I have found in recent years especially I have nightmares and wake commonly soaking wet. That NVA officer that I shot in the face is a common visitor. I am a professional and self-controlled and have never gone seeking any professional help related to this. I'm not convinced that it would make any difference.

after we are the ones to survive
after the chill
after the heat
after we have killed but
before we have thoughts of being loved
we sing a manly song
martial and stirring
not low and blue we sing
when and because
we are distanced from the front
a reminder to remember
to forget what we want forgotten
we sing our loud song of silence
we sing again
and again
until it is done
until it is gone

Being drafted and sent to kill or be killed made me a different person than I would have been. I spent the first 3-4 years after I returned using marijuana, hashish and alcohol almost daily in an attempt to self-medicate. I then saw the futility of that and have been generally drug free since then.

When my son was old enough to start asking questions about the draft, I resumed my work with peace and justice groups. I have mainly been involved with Fellowship of Reconciliation. I was involved as a founding member of both Western Washington VFP chapter #92 and more recently VFP-Rachel Corrie Chapter #109.

Memorial Day

a black granite wall to rest against
each name an act calling for re-write
58,195 times rendered unto Caesar
58,195 rendered like fat on a hot stove

Larry Kershner

Dear brothers and sisters:

Memorial Day is on us again. Last year, I joined others to deliver our letters to The Wall in our first effort to let you know that you are not forgotten. All of us, no matter what our relationship to this war, anguish over your loss. Yet as I read over my letter from last year, I catch a strong whiff of survivor's guilt — you know, why are you on The Wall and not me? One move one way or the other, and I may have joined you. So be it. I have lived a full life since those 411 days I was in Vietnam (July 1969 to August 1970). And I have been blessed with two children. That's what I'd like to talk about this year.

One of the great sadnesses of your physical absence from this world is that you were robbed of sharing your unique life with your own children. I can tell you that having my own children puts the lives of the Vietnamese children I encountered into sharp relief. Looking into the eyes of my own children brimming over with wonder and joy made me think of how our presence often closed off those experiences from the eyes of those village kids. I live with that regret to this day. But watching my own children grow and flourish has offered me some solace as a counter-weight. I wish you could have had the same opportunity.

Here are two poems I have written for/to my own kids. The first I wrote for my daughter as she was turning three; the second I wrote for my son on his thirteenth birthday. They look to the future, which I will continue to do on your behalf, my friends. That is what our children offer us. Rest in peace.

Your brother,

Doug Rawlings

JEN TURNING THREE

The birch splits
its bark
the snake its skin
the child leaps
into the woman
she always has been

Nothing is new
nothing is changing
the birch is the bark
the snake the skin
the child the woman

The seed, flowering,
dies back into the earth
as the child, growing,
turns forward toward
her new birth

GIVING SILENCE
For My Son Josh turning thirteen

If 'namvets were ancient shamans
now would be the moment
we'd choose
to give you shelter
from the coming storm
But we are merely
survivors of suburbs and cities
not forest nor mountain
Modern men
offering you our silences
our words
to guide you going out on your own

Yet we have known for years now
that the silences of our fathers will not do
And we have known that words alone
cannot bleed you free
of your raging doubts

So listen up
to what we have found
between silences and words:

Open up your fists

Watch women move

Scorn uniforms

Don't march

Dance

Doug Rawlings

319

For those memorialized on The Wall:

Thank you for your courage, and I am sorry you had to make a supreme sacrifice of your life for our government's misguided adventure in Vietnam. I hope those in government will remember that people's lives are on the line when we have conflicts with other nations. There are other ways to resolve these conflicts, so I will do what I can to prevent any future sacrifices similar to what you have gone through. I know your efforts have not been forgotten.

Larry Dansinger

You were our fathers

You were our fathers in the town that I grew up in without fathers. Those that survived and came home were ghosts that passed through our doors in the night. We missed you, our fathers. To some you were sons, and brothers and lovers, but to us you were fathers. In the town I grew up in with no fathers.

Katrazyna Randall

Here are my thoughts.

As Memorial Day rolls around again, my thoughts are drawn to military families. I think of one of my uncles who lost his son. Uncle Emil's last name was Kreutz and his son died in Vietnam, so my visits to the wall always draw me to his name which is the same as mine.

But in addition to private memories and family members, I mourn on Memorial Day for our country and its perpetual state of war, about which we were warned by president Eisenhower to beware the military industrial complex which at that time was a glimmer of the monstrosity that it has now become. I am grateful to President Obama and John Kerry for their excellent efforts at negotiation, especially with Iran. At the same time, I fear that the drone warfare campaign is creating more terrorism and more spirit of reprisal by attacks on citizens every day. Thus the whole world moves toward global warfare, and since the United States has as its primary product weapons and more weapons, the conclusion can be nothing but devastation.

We need to turn to negotiations and peace as our national product and honor life not death and destruction.

Eileen Kreutz
Industry, Maine

I stood before you alone

To The Vietnam Veterans Memorial Wall, And More Importantly, To Those Who Visit It:

I stood before you alone on a warm, sunny August day, and fought to keep my tears to myself. I wished desperately that my father could be there too, but he was 3000 miles away, and we didn't talk much anymore anyway. I was awed by the simplicity of your portrayal of such heavy sorrow. I was awed by how much sadness you stirred in me. There are no names on that wall that I recognize. I didn't lose a loved one to this war, my father came home physically intact from his year in Vietnam. If he hadn't, if his name were inscribed on your surface, I would not have been alive to stand before you, to touch your smooth granite and read the names of people I didn't know, people I could never know.

My emotion that day was partly a reflection of my father's feelings about you. Even though he never had the opportunity to visit you, it meant a lot to him knowing you had been built to honor those who died in the war he too had served in. The only time we ever talked about his service in Vietnam was when he shed a tear over an essay I wrote about you in sixth grade. It was such a powerful moment, and it felt a bit as though I stood before you in his honor.

But my feeling as I touched your cold, shiny surface that day was also a sadness of loss. My understanding of this war, and all wars, had come a long way since I wrote that essay in sixth grade. I feel the things that are lost to war very strongly. They are a weight on our society much greater than that of your granite slabs.

The loss of so many American lives is beyond tragic. But there are so many sad things about this war, so many more things than the loss you represent. An estimated 1,313,000 deaths occurred as a result of war in North and South Vietnam, Laos, and Cambodia in the years between 1955 and 1975, and only a little over 58,000 of those are inscribed on your surface. At least 587,000 of those were civilians. Men, women, children. Every single one is a tragedy.

And people continued to die after 1975; they are still dying as a result of this war. We left behind a legacy of unexploded ordnance, waiting for innocent people to stumble upon them. We left behind a legacy of people poisoned by Agent Orange. We left behind a legacy of refugees and instability in many of these countries resulting in more death, more destruction. Those names are not on your surface.

And those who came home to America? They were left alone to face what they had done, what they had seen, what they had experienced, what they had suffered. How many, unable to deal with their horrors, took their own lives? How many also suffered from the toxic effects of Agent Orange? Where are their names on your surface?

Your moving simplicity leaves out so much, as if to excuse our ignorance in this nation of the devastating effects our wars have on generations of Americans, and on generations of people around the world, and on the world itself. As if war, and soldiers dying, is as clean as your shiny wall and the simple white crosses of Arlington Cemetery.

I wish the American people would see a reflection of all that loss in your surface, so we might all rise up together and bring an end to the wars and devastation our nation is waging around the globe. I wish we would honor the many who have died for the few who profit from war by refusing to fight. I wish you said that on your surface, especially to the young men and women thinking of enlisting who happen to pass you by.

Katie Aguiler

On Memorial Day

On Memorial Day, May 30th, we will be delivering letters to the Vietnam Veterans Memorial (The Wall) with heartfelt messages to those young men and women whose names are on The Wall. Please join us.

My Letter: To those lost on the 67-68 Cruise of the USS Kitty Hawk CV63 (Operation Rolling Thunder) you will never be forgotten!

CV Holgate

MESSAGE TO THE WALL

Dear Wall,

Your polished surface deceives.
You appear serene, yet you are bursting with anguish and lost potential.
You are a wall of great sadness.
You remember the young, whose lives were engulfed in the flames of war.
They wanted to live and love, but the cruel war stopped them.
They had lives before the lies of their leaders took them to war.
Their mistake was to trust.
And they never returned to their loved ones.
Wall, their names are carved into you.
Their hearts flutter around you.
These young who died are sentinels, warning of danger,
Reminding us that war is a fool's game,
A game in which everyone loses,
Except for the arms merchants.
Wall, you reflect war's human price.
Let the old and gray pay the price, if they must.
But youth, be wary of war.

David Krieger, President
Nuclear Age Peace Foundation
April 2016

From: Margaret Gallagher

Wales, UK

April 2016.

For the Vietnam War commemoration.

I hope you don't mind some input from an Aussie.

I am an Australian woman and former Rehabilitation Counsellor. Used to work for the Department of Veterans' Affairs in Sydney – 20-odd years ago – doing assessments for veterans' pension tribunals.

Many of the men of my generation fought alongside US troops in Vietnam. Some were regular army – but an awful lot were conscripts – kids barely out of school.

Growing up in Australia after WW2 was probably quite similar to growing up in the USA – there were a lot of jobs around and most of us had relatively untroubled childhoods – even if there was not much money around. So, for these young men, having to go and fight in Vietnam was an enormous shock – particularly as WW2 had been so romanticised in the movies that we grew up watching. The things they saw and experienced – and had to participate in – and the fact that you were never safe, even on R&R, meant that, apart from physical wounds – and the Agent Orange damage – very many of those boys came home with undiagnosed and untreated emotional and mental health issues.

20-odd years later I was doing 'work assessments' for these ex-servicemen, as a result of them having made an appeal to the tribunal for a veteran's pension, because they stated they were disabled and unable to work – but it was not physical – so the system automatically assumed they were faking and did not believe them. The tribunal was the last resort after having been rejected twice already.

I was part of the assessment process put in place before the tribunal to provide reports that would provide the evidence on which they could base their decision to deny or accept the claim. All but one of the men I assessed were Vietnam veterans. The other one was a WW2 veteran who had been an officer during the Vietnam war. He had to take these school-kids and prepare them for the insanity and horror that faced them – and lead them into the fray.

Every last one of these men was an emotional wreck – many of them for the entire time since they had got home – while some had tried to hold it together but, over the years, had fallen apart. Lost jobs, lost families, self-medication with drink and/or drugs, and, in some cases, lost everything. The worst affected I never got to see. I heard about them, though, more than once. There were a significant number of them back then – living rough in the jungle, up north. Armed to the teeth – waiting for the Indonesians to invade. Went into the army as school-kids – came out with their lives totally trashed.

Everyone I saw, without exception, had PTSD. You could spot it a mile off – and it certainly is not something you can fake. All their emotions were on the surface and they were hyper-alert – both fragile and angry at the same time. It was absolutely heart-breaking. And reading their files and hearing their stories was shocking – the way they had been treated – as if they were making it up. Especially those who had 'Agent Orange' stamped on their file.

Some guys were up to their 3rd or 4th wife, some still had their first love – who had hung on in there, despite the anger, aggression, drinking, job losses – the works – that happen as you can't hold it in anymore and all the pain and anger explodes out into your life – devastating it – and everyone around you. And they both blamed and hated themselves – for something that was not their fault – and for which they had no help or support – apart from family, if they could cope. I've had grown men – sometimes big 6 ft blokes – sit crying in my office – just because someone was finally listening to them and taking them seriously. I had to go see one man at his home – because it was the only place he felt safe. And his wife had to ride shotgun because he was so angry that she was worried he might lose his temper at me – just because I came from 'the Department'. Can't say as I blame him, either.

And as for the officer. He held it all in until he retired – self-medicating in the acceptable way, with booze. He was old enough to be my dad. He sat in my office and cried – and talked about the guilt he felt at sending all those young men to that awful war to be killed and maimed and broken. He loved those boys as if they were his own kids – and he felt totally responsible for what happened to them. None of his peers could understand what happened to him when he retired. They all thought he was putting it on – because he kept the front up while he was still enlisted. But it was the structure that allowed him to do that – and helped him to block it out. Once that was gone, he fell to pieces. And he was all alone in trying to cope, because of the disbelief – and the stigma.

I was regularly offered security outside my office because these poor men had to run the gamut of everyone in the rehab team during their assessment visit: doctor, occupational therapist, physiotherapist – and finally me, the rehab counsellor. And my boss – the rehab doctor – had the bedside manner and empathy of a drill instructor – it was all my way or the highway with him. He was actually a good man – but no idea of compassion or empathy at all. Mental illness was not part of his universe – he had no clue – and he was bossy.

So by the time these poor men had seen him, and all the rest, they were exhausted (some had travelled hundreds of miles) – and ready to throttle someone. Not least because all this came after the drama of having got the summons to come for the assessment. They all received a formal and quite threatening letter a week or two beforehand – telling them to come in and be assessed. So, from the day they received the letter, they had been bouncing off the walls with stress – not sleeping, and generally being angry and frightened they would be judged and not believed – and thus lose this last chance for help. I begged to be allowed to write letters – to make them more human and explanatory – but the bureaucracy did not allow it.

I always refused security when it was offered – and I never needed it. How would it have made them feel to come see someone with a guard at the door? The whole system made them feel as if they were not considered fellow humans, just fakers and liars looking for a buck – and something like that would have just made it worse.

I did no formal assessments. I just got them to tell me what their everyday life was like. All of it. And my 'formal' report told their stories – of life and work and family – warts and all – and I made them human in the eyes of the suited folks on the tribunal whose middle-class lives bore no resemblance to what these men had to live with every day.

Nobody I saw was 'just a number' at the tribunal. And, because I was a 'professional', notice was taken of what I said – and they got the money they needed and deserved. And therein lies a major problem – oftentimes only 'professionals' seem to get listened to – and a lot of them are like my old boss.. Some of these poor men were not able to hold down a job – yet they had been fighting for years to get their pension – all because nobody would take them seriously – because it wasn't physical. Still makes me steam.

I think of those men often and hope they eventually managed to get some effective help. EMDR was just starting to get noticed in Australia at the time. The Vietnam Vets' Association were doing good work – but the local psychiatrists were a total waste of oxygen. There were only about 2 in all of Sydney that were human and empathic – but even so, all they knew to do was throw drugs at the problem. Which was like a band-aid over a severed artery. There were a lot of suicides.

I suspect that it was the same – or worse – in the USA for your returned young men after Vietnam. Hearts and minds broken, along with bodies oftentimes. And little or no support or help. In Oz, the best work that was happening then, as now, was being done by the organisations set up by and for the veterans themselves and those who cared about them. I am guessing it will be the same there too. Empathy and compassion are more readily available from those who have walked the same path – and support is more likely to be accepted from them as well. Shared experience takes down a lot of barriers.

I hope very much that grassroots support like yours is growing and bringing the new generations of service men and women into your fold. We older generations surely have a responsibility to share the love and support – and the lessons we've learned along the way.

All the very best to you.

A Second Response to the War in Vietnam

18 March 2016

John Rosenwald

A Second Response to the War in Vietnam

In Farmington, Maine, we stand for a half-hour every Friday noon in front of the town post office to show our support for peaceful solutions to political conflicts. Some of us are Quakers, some atheists, some veterans, some radicals, some traditionalists, some native Mainers, many "from away" as one says in this state.

All of us, however, have touched and been touched by the notion that our government has often chosen to use war as a means of trying to reconcile disagreements between nations, tribes, ethnic groups, and geographical regions. And we reject that notion.

One of the first instances in my life where I began to reject the notion of war occurred in the early 1970s in a small restaurant in Worcester, Massachusetts. My wife and I had little money, ate out very rarely, and didn't frequent this place. But that evening, as we sat in semi-darkness, we began to talk to a man at the next table. Or perhaps he began to talk with us.

He had just returned from Vietnam. If he had been wounded, it was not physically obvious: no bandages, no slings, no casts. But the wounds were clearly present. He spoke with us for perhaps an hour, talking of his grief, his fears, his anger, his fundamental rejection of what he had done, what he had been forced to do.

We didn't know him. We never saw him again. But I have carried with me now for more than forty years the intensity of his suffering, the recognition that we as a nation, that we as citizens, that I as an individual, have no right to make human beings endure what he had endured. I write this letter in tribute to him, for educating me about the world of what we sometimes call warriors. I write in tribute to those veterans who have come together in the organization called Veterans for Peace, believing deeply that all of us must take our stances against the violence that is war, and the violence that accompanies war wherever it occurs.

As I stand vigil in front of the Farmington Post Office each Friday, I see the face of that soldier. I owe him a deep debt. I take comfort in the presence of members of Veterans for Peace and in the companionship that all of us — despite our different visions of the world — bring to our desire for an end of war, of all wars. Those of us who stand, those of us who have created letters to be placed at the Vietnam Memorial again this May, must continue to speak and to write on behalf of those whose names and faces are etched in our memories and on that wall.

Letter to the Wall

This letter is addressed to my friend and comrade Gary Jones who was from and lived in Oregon. We sailed on the U.S. Coast Guard Cutter Barataria from Portland, Maine to Pearl Harbor in a small convoy of like ships. The ships were from New York, Florida, Long Beach, and San Francisco. We were officially Coast Guard Squadron Three and served under the U.S. Navy during this time of war in 1967. Our ultimate destination was the South China Sea and Vietnam.

To the Wall:

I'm writing with respect to Gary Jones as per above. I realize that you are a magnificent piece of Black Granite that contains nearly 58,000 brothers' and sisters' names. I visited one time and found it extremely difficult to touch you. I believe I have a picture of that kicking around somewhere in my collection of trash and treasures.

I believe that to those of us who served - our loss of fellow military lives makes us remember all those years ago. We became closer than outsiders can understand. I've tried to explain it but I always fall short and perhaps that makes our loss special because it can't be explained? However, my brother I will not forget that you and I were shipmates and saw some good times but mostly bad. I can only say that if any family member goes to the wall for solace, Gary is part of this wall. We came home in one physical piece but we were never the same after our WAR Experience. I wrote a poem to try to capture this:

WAR Brothers

I don't know how to explain this/
I can only try/
A Vietnam comrade/
Just recently died/

I have no blood brother/
He was much more than that/
We shared our lives/
During war that's a fact/

We weren't heroes/
We just did our jobs/
Gave everything we had/
Our pride can't be robbed/

Looking back now/
Is not easy to do/
Our flames burned brightly/
Now another is through/

Life's funny that way/
It begins and it ends/
War-brothers are loved/
We just can't pretend/

A part of my heart/
Was just torn away/
I miss him for sure/
For his soul I do pray/

He's not the first/
He won't be the last/
Our futures uncertain/
Some day we all pass/

Crossing over is tough/
Losing a war-brother I love/
We hope there's a place/
We pray it's high above/

I see him there now/
I can't help but to cry/

War-brothers don't fade away/
We just flat out die/

By G R Kamke

Gerry Kamke
Litchfield Maine

A 'LETTER' ON MEMORIAL DAY 2016

ANOTHER MEMORIAL DAY...
CALL IT FIFTY MORE YEARS OR SO
ON DOWN THE ROAD FROM VIỆT NAM

DOUG HAS SUGGESTED A LETTER
HE SAYS, 'A LETTER TO THE WALL'
OR, MORE PRECISELY, I SUPPOSE
SOME WORDS TODAY TO THOSE OF YOU
WHO LIVE ON BUT IN MEMORY
AND SOMEWHERE HERE INSIDE THE WALL
IN ALL THESE STARK ENGRAVED GRAY NAMES
SHARP CUT DEEP UNTIL FOREVER
INTO THIS COLD BLACK GRANITE STONE
IT'S JUST 'A LETTER', HE SAYS, BUT
IT SHOULD BE SOMETHING 'FROM THE HEART'

IF I COULD, I'D WRITE MYSTIC WORDS
THAT WOULD ROLL BACK TIME ITSELF
TO FIFTY SOMETHING YEARS AGO
ERASING SO-CALLED 'MESSAGES'
SENT BY THOSE FOOLS TO VIỆT NAM
BY WAY OF ALL OF YOUR BODIES
AND, IN THE END, YOUR VERY LIVES
IN THE EXPLICIT HARSH REPLIES
YOUR ALL TOO NEEDLESS DEATHS BROUGHT HOME,
AS WORD CAME BACK FROM OVER THERE
FOREVER PAST UNDERSTANDING

BUT, FOR ME, HERE, WORDS ONLY FAIL
BEYOND THE SAYING ONE MORE TIME
THAT I STILL WISH THE ALL OF IT
HAD NOT EVER EVEN HAPPENED
AND THAT YOU WOULD HAVE ALL BEEN SPARED
THE WANTON, WASTED, SENSELESS DEATHS
THAT CUT SO SHORT THE OLDER ONES
YOU WOULD HAVE, LIVING, NOW BECOME...

MAYBE AS TODAY'S MESSENGERS
WHO COULD'VE TAUGHT US ONCE FOR ALL
TO JUST STOP DOING IT AGAIN

SO, I GUESS THAT'S IT… THERE IT IS…
NOT REALLY MUCH OF A LETTER
BUT, AS I SAID AND SAY AGAIN,
WORDS SIMPLY FAIL ME HERE… ALTHOUGH,
THIS BRIEF MISSIVE TO YOU BROTHERS,
IS SINCERELY STRAIGHT FROM THE HEART

Ex-Sp5 John Buquoi
3rd RRU, Tân Sơn Nhất
and
'Detachment 'J', 'Trại Bắc'
(Northern Station),
Phú Bài, Republic of Việt Nam
1963-1965

Author, 'snapshots from the edge of a war'

Captain Herbert F. Hardy Jr.

1/27/2016

Captain Herbert F. Hardy Jr.
First Special Forces

I don't know how to start this letter because I never gave you a specific nickname, and it feels inappropriate to call you by your first name. Most of the time I just refer to you as "my grandfather."

I was told about this letter project today in one of my college classes, and I immediately wanted to write to you. I don't really know why. I know you won't answer me. Maybe it's because I feel like when I put these words down on paper you might be able to see them, and you might know that I'm writing to you and thinking about you. There are things you should know, but mostly I have a lot of questions.

You should know that Nanny, your wife Helen, stands up every Thanksgiving and thanks you for your sacrifice. Sometimes she cries. Everyone is always trying to hold in their tears anyway. Fifty-two years have passed since you died, but you haven't been forgotten. I grew up knowing about you, and learning about you. I've been told about all of the brave and unusual things that you did.

The gong that was given to Nanny in memory of you hangs up in our living room. It's been in the background of every prom and family picture. I guess that means that you've been in the pictures too, in a way. Your children have been interested in you. Especially Mom. She found William Edge, and she talked to him for a few years before he died. After the war he was a pastor somewhere out West. Isn't it crazy that time brought this man to you, and then when you saved him, you gave him time so that he could be brought to us?

We have pictures that you had from Vietnam and Cambodia. You riding an elephant, and holding an enormous snake. Did you ever imagine that the pictures you took would be the only way that your grandchildren would see you alive? I've read some letters you sent to Nanny. The monkey who lived with you, and how you shot off its tail.

I've asked her about the time she spent in Okinawa. Her body might be failing, but her brain still remembers. Did you ever think that someday memories and stories would be the only way that your children and grandchildren would know you? I think you would be proud of your family for carrying on your story. I know that they are proud of you. I'm proud of you.

Sometimes I find myself wondering what life would've been like if you hadn't died in Cambodia. Would Uncle Bob have spent all that time in prison? Would Uncle Steve be able to keep a job or a wife?

Would Uncle Andy still self-medicate? How would Aunt Kathy be different if she had ever had the chance to meet you? How would my mom be different if she wasn't constantly trying to piece together a father she can't remember?

Would I even be alive today if you had lived?

Would you have taught your grandsons to love the outdoors, fishing, and hunting like you did?

Would you have come to our football, field hockey, and soccer games?

Would you have sat me on your lap and read me stories?

Would you look like the picture that's been on my wall since I can remember?

Would you smell like aftershave or soap? What would your voice sound like when you told me that you loved me?

I wonder if you thought that it was worth it in the end. Did you whole-heartedly believe in your mission and purpose for being there? Did you regret being there in your last moments? Did you regret anything in your last moments?

I wonder what your last thoughts were. Did you think about your mom and dad? Your wife? Your four small children? Your unborn baby? Was there anything that you wanted to say? Was there anyone there to say it to? Could you have spoken, with the bullet in your neck? Did the person who killed you see your face? Did they even think for a second, before they pulled the trigger, about the hole they would be blasting through the lives of the people that you knew and loved? Could they have fathomed that your death would shatter a family for two generations? Did you ever think about that?

I know it wasn't your intention to end up on a wall. I don't think it was anyone's intention. My mom always says that there's a reason for everything. I think there are some things that you can't find reasons for.

Love,

Your granddaughter Linsay